The Ethical Will And Memoirs Of
Ruby Ray Karzen

Be Inspired! Enjoy!

Best,

Ruby Karzen

Mazo Publishers

B"H

Cherry On The Top
ISBN 978-1-936778-29-4

Copyright © 2014 Ruby Ray Karzen
1 Diskin Street / Jerusalem, Israel 96440

E-mail: mail@rubydesigns.net
www.rubydesigns.net

Cover Artist
Odeya Trebelsi

Published by
Mazo Publishers
Chaim Mazo, Publisher
PO Box 36084 / Jerusalem, Israel 91360

Email: mazopublishers@gmail.com
www.mazopublishers.com

Names in some of the stories have been changed for reasons of privacy.

Printed in Israel

The Rubin Clan ...

Tammy and Morris
  Elichai and Racheli
    Racheli and Nir
      Neriyah
        Nitzi
          Bentzi
            Avichayil

The Karzen "Klan" ...

Uri And Shelli
  Elimelech and Noa
    Odeya and Yehudah
      Michael
        Emunah
          Ayelet Hashachar

The Miniature Jewels ...

Kana Karzen
  Tzofia Karzen
    Dvir Karzen

Shaked Trebelsi
  Eytan Trebelsi

And Those Yet To Come!!!!!!

Contents

Author's Preface

CHERRY ON THE TOP reflects a philosophy of life that I try to live by. The basis of a worthwhile existence is a belief in the Almighty and all of life's activities flow from that act of *Emunah*. If we follow the rules to the best of our ability, our Ice Cream Sundae rises higher and higher with acts of goodness and charity, until it finally reaches the top. On the very highest point the cherry is placed – it represents the achievement of becoming a *Mentsh*. I hope that this missive will help you attain that goal.

This work covers a span of over one hundred fifty years. It brings to life the history of people who lived, loved and struggled with human concerns against the background of various cultures. We are the people who we are because of the decisions they made – both good and bad.

From the small towns of Poland to the America of the 30s through the 80s as well as the State of Israel, I have tried to tell the stories that fashioned their, and ultimately our world. Some of these places have vanished, such as the West Side of Chicago and the hundreds of smaller Jewish communities that dotted the landscape of America since its inception.

The original idea for this book was to write in a pleasurable style, an Ethical Will not only for my children, but also for the grandchildren and great-grandchildren. The fact that I have reached this age of Senior Citizen status and have the *Zechut* to be blessed with these treasures is a wonder that I ponder and thank the Lord daily. An additional fact is that not one of my four grandparents even reached the age of fifty, that my mother passed away at age thirty-two, and my father in his early fifties, gives my state of wonder credence. But, as I began to pen the qualities of the Will that I wished to convey, it appeared dry and lifeless – that would not do! So, an idea slowly formed that a history of the Ray / Gartner families would clearly picture and show concretely, the ideas in a narrative fashion that I wished to convey with laughter and a few tears along the way.

The preface to a book can take many forms. It can explain why the book was written – what the purpose was behind it. I believe that has been clarified. At times, it can be an addendum and enhance the ideas that are presented, which is what you will find in these first few pages and it is the place where the author expresses gratefulness to the individuals who aided in the creating of this work.

In chronological order, I have been a daughter, granddaughter, sister, niece, sister-in-law, wife, mother, grandmother and great-grandmother. I have enjoyed every aspect as they arrived. I have tried to keep an open mind and have learned something new every step of the way. I have never been afraid of new experiences and believe in the maxim of *"Doing The Same Thing Over And Over Again And Expecting Different Results"* is sheer folly. My history is one of change and challenge; as will be yours, as is the path of every person. The manner in which you handle the situations that are presented to you will determine the quality of your life.

Ruby Ray Karzen
(A Proud Ex-Ray)

Acknowledgments

HEARTFELT GRATITUDE TO *Saba*, husband, Jay, who has listened patiently and has made suggestions every step of the way, as well as relinquished control of the computer for the past two years! Without his encouragement, at my sometimes impatience in producing this manuscript, it would not have happened. So, to my best roommate … Thanks, an inadequate word, but it is truly meant from my heart.

To Rabbi Ben Shandalov, many thanks for corroborating my memories of the "Great Vest Side."

To the family and friends who have been the "Guinea Pigs" and have listened patiently without rolling their eyes upon hearing the same incident numerous times … You are all the best.

To the original family history storytellers, Aunt Zira, Uncles Manny and Joe Ray, all of blessed memory, many thanks for imparting this fascinating material, so that all of us, your descendants, will know from where they came and see more clearly the correct path to choose.

The Ethical Will and Memoirs of Ruby Ray Karzen

I MUST HAVE ASKED THIS QUESTION dozens of times upon hearing the telling of an incident in someone's personal experience. "Have you written down your life story?" The answers are invariably similar. Usually, the excuse is lack of time or the question is dismissed, "My life is nothing unique and my children wouldn't care." Unfortunately, most people never relate family histories and the accounts are lost in the mists of time.

After relating tidbits of my family history to numberless cousins, I decided to take my own advice, the result of which you are now reading. I've been thinking about this moment for years; how and where to begin.

This story covers almost seven decades and I hope to relate the stories of the people upon whose shoulders I metaphorically stand to have become the person I am today.

This is a narrative of historical events, descriptions of places and incidents, both true and anecdotal which are the framework on which this Ethical Will hinges.

Cherry On The Top is dedicated to my husband, children, grandchildren and great-grandchildren, as well as the entire Ray / Gartner family … past, present and future.

To distribute one's wealth is common practice. I hope to leave physical traces that I was part of your lives. However, more important is to transmit the important qualities that will enable you to transverse the planes of your life in a successful manner and be a person who will be a credit to his People and be a part of the *Tikun Olam* that the world desperately needs.

CHERRY ON THE TOP

Part One

From Poland To America
1840-1961

I AM HOLDING a yellowed, partly tattered certificate dated May 9, 1938. It was issued at Jewish Maternity Hospital in the City of New York to Isadore Ray and Minnie Gartner Ray, both born in Poland in 1907 and married on November 1, 1931. The fancy lace border of the certificate states that it was at 9:15 a.m. when I entered this world. It was a year that the noises of war in Europe were resounding louder and uglier. It became a conflict that turned the world upside down, changed the future of untold numbers of people and saw millions dead. It was named the Second World War and became known as the last "Good" war.

But, I'm getting ahead of myself … My story truly begins in the late 1800s in Eastern Europe, where at that time, Poland was home to tens of thousands of Jews. In Staszow, (pronounced Stashov) a fairly good-sized town, the Raja family was established as merchants, dealing in lumber and leather.

The Raja Family
The Raja family had lived in the city for 200 years, as far back as the 1600s. Sholem Ber, married to Rochel, were my great-great-great-grandparents. My great-great-grandparents were Getzel Ray, married to Hinda Leah, who was born in Nerviosgastes, Poland, a small village not far from Stashov. Only the sparse information listed here is known to the family. However, with the entrance on the scene of my great-grandfather, Reb Avrum

Moshe Raja (pronounced Raya) the modern story of our family begins.

From all accounts of the town at the time, Stashov was the main business and shopping area for the surrounding villages and farms. Many lush forests encircled the "Gmina Staszow," the County of Stashov, enabling the Jewish population to engage in dealing in the lumber business, as well as producing leather suitcases, the thriving enterprises at the time. There were also a number of Torah scholars sprinkled among the numerous family members. One such individual was Reb Avrum Moshe Raja, who was the director, leader and head of a *Kollel* in the city.

The family adhered to the ideology of the *Trisker Rebbe*, Rav Motele Kozmis, a spin-off of the Ger dynasty. Family lore has it that on *Rosh Hashanah*, Reb Avrum would travel and take his sons with him to spend the holy days with the *Rebbe*. Baruch Moshe, my grandfather, was one of the boys, who subsequently named one of his sons after the *Rebbe*, my Uncle Manny (Motele). Reb Avrum was a *melamed* in the truest sense of the word. Among his students were the children of the *Trisker Rebbe*. He spent his life educating Jews in the ways of the Torah.

Avrum and Tzutel Raya

My great-grandfather, Avrum Moshe (b.1872) was married to Tzutel. She was known as an activist and was well known in the community. They were blessed with three children – Baruch (b.1891), Rachel (b.1905) and Morris (b.1910).

While the family did not live with the level of poverty of Tevya of "Fiddler On The Roof" fame, it was ever present. The world at that time was divided into the very wealthy and the poor. The middle class was not yet a factor in the economy and life was harsh.

The Holocaust was still years in the future, but Jews were routinely oppressed, subtly and not so subtly, with European Jews caught in crusades, pogroms and all types of anti-Semitic behavior for hundreds of years. Nothing seemed to change and it appeared that better times would never come.

THERE IS A CHARMING STORY told about *Savta Raba* Tzutel. Each Friday, all the families would bring their pots of *cholent* to a nearby bakery where it would simmer all Friday evening and had to be fully cooked in order to be picked up after Shabbat morning services. Friday afternoon, as the community's pots would arrive at the baker's oven, *Savta Raba* Tzutel would arrange each pot to get the maximum heat and therefore be ready to eat for lunch! And so it was … It appears that the administrative streak so evident in the family to this day, began many years ago.

Baruch Moshe

Looking at a map of the area Stashov, you can well imagine the horse and buggy bringing Chaya Rasha Lass to Baruch Moshe Raja to be wed.

Baruch Moshe and Chaya Rasha (my grandparents) married and settled down to the life of a young couple. Life was hard and they struggled constantly. Poverty was an unwelcome companion.

Professionally, Baruch Moshe (Ben) was a teacher as well as a businessman, dealing with leather steamer trunks and suitcases, as many other Jews, who were also employed in this business, in this section of Poland.

He grew up in Stashov and learned in *Cheder*, but had no formal secular education, as was the norm for the times. His first language was Yiddish. Hebrew, of the sacred texts that he studied all of his life, was not for everyday use, but for prayer only. He was a *Ben Torah* first and foremost. He was a renowned Cantor and since the days of his youth chanted the High Holy Days services. Until the last year of his life, each *Yom Tov*, Rev. Ben (as he was affectionately known), along with his two youngest sons as part of a choir, created beautiful music which enhanced every service. This talent of possessing a beautiful, melodic voice, has been passed down through the generations. To this day, there are many Cantors and *Baalay Tefilah* among his male descendants. The women are also blessed with pleasing voices.

My grandparents were blessed with three children. Ruth, the eldest, Yisroel Tzvi (my father) and Getzel (the youngest.)

The Goldina Medina

The year of 1914 saw the start of the First World War. To build the needed armies, men and boys were plucked off the streets and in many cases never seen again. Jews changed their family names, cut off fingers, toes and physically harmed themselves to avoid conscription. The 25 years to be spent in the Russian or Polish army was a life sentence; few returned. However, since the 1800s, the spirit of emancipation fired imaginations and the European population began to immigrate to various parts of the world. America was the foremost destination – it was called *The Goldina Medina*.

Jews and other minorities streamed to America to find a better life – one of opportunity and improved economic conditions. There, the future beckoned as the brightest of lights, as opposed to the oppressive darkness that was the European continent for centuries.

Millions of immigrants to the United States arrived by ship. Ellis Island was the entry point. The first landmark that was encountered by the travelers crossing the Atlantic Ocean to America was the Statue of Liberty, the symbol of freedom and democracy. It was a gift from the people of France to the USA in 1886. It is situated on Liberty Island, which is a small stretch of land off the coast of New York.

The vast majority of Jews arrived in "steerage" or third-class (cost $30), meaning that they crossed the ocean sailing at the bottom of the ship in unsanitary conditions, crowded, with no privacy. While the large steamship would enter the New York

Harbor and berth at the pier, the third-class passengers were brought by barge to Ellis Island for legal and medical inspection.

First and second class passengers were not required to undergo inspection, with the reasoning that if one could afford a first or second class ticket, (cost $50-$60), they were less likely to become a burden on the state.

On a normal day, 5,000 people were processed, but one day in April 1907, there were 11,747 immigrants seeking the precious health certificates certifying that they were disease-free.

Between the years of 1892-1924, 12 million people passed through the immigration halls. By 1954, when the doors of Ellis Island closed, 16 million people had been processed. Now there is a wonderful museum with videos which shows the immigrant experience, and allows one to feel the excitement and anxiety that prevailed. It is truly fascinating to see the photos of those bygone times. A particular item of interest are the photos of people who later became famous, enriching the lives of the world with talents that would have languished into nothingness. Authors, artists, inventors, creative personalities in every field, gave vitality and uniqueness to America. The narrative of America would be far different if these millions of immigrants – Jews, Italians, Irish, Swedish and oppressed people from every corner of the globe – had not immigrated to the shores of the US. The variety of peoples is the underpinnings of "the American way of life." Each immigrant brought with him hopes, dreams and ideas packed in worn suitcases.

I recently saw the report of a census which stated that fully forty percent of the citizenry of America are immigrants. However, the fact is, that except for the American Indians, who owned and occupied the land that we know as America, all of its citizens descend from immigrants. We owe a tremendous debt of gratitude and *Hakarat Hatov* to the USA for the culture we absorbed, the education we received and the environment in which we lived our lives.

It is said that America is a melting pot. I believe that America is a vegetable soup, with each person keeping his own flavor and shape ... not being blended into the same nondescript flavor and color. Japanese, Mexican and French food are different, each has a distinctive taste and that is as it should be.

It is a far cry from being an immigrant to Israel today. The experience of immigrants from North America is not without its complexities. It's difficult enough to move to a new address within a city ... even harder to move to another state. But another country ... it certainly is far from simple. However, basically, one packs up the family and possessions, buys a ticket on El Al and in queenly fashion arrives at Ben Gurion airport. But that's another story and it must wait for later!

Baruch decided to join the flow and leave Europe. As with countless other immigrants, it was decided that the *Tateh* (Father) would emigrate first, as sailing tickets were costly. The *Tateh* would get settled, find employment and then send for the family, as money for the fares was raised, dollar by hard-won dollar. This was the formula to which thousands of families were separated for months to years until they were finally united.

The name Raja became Ray as the family crossed the ocean. Raja in Polish means Paradise. There are so many similarities to Raja, which is sometimes also translated in some forms of the word, royal; it would be hard to say that it is a total coincidence. In French, Rey means King, Roi in Spanish, Rajah in Turkish and Ra in Egyptian. I have always joked that I knew that the family was related to royalty and that I was a real Jewish Princess. (But, only in the best sense!)

Ben Ray arrived in America in 1918 and settled in Chicago, joining other *Stashovers.* He was 28 years old, tall, handsome, a natty dresser and an imposing figure. He had many talents; a learned layman who acted as an officiant at weddings on many occasions. He was the semi-permanent president of the *Stashover Verein.* His organizational talent was noteworthy; he never wanted to be a "paper" member, but was interested in every detail of any organization to which he became involved. This viewpoint appears strongly in every generation of the Ray family.

My grandparents endured three long years of separation. *Zayda* Ben was finally able to save enough money to bring over *Bubbe* Rose and their three children. The family settled in the Northwest side of Chicago and within a few years, two more children had been added to the family ... Manny or *Motele*, named after one of the *Rebbes* of the city of Ger, Rav Motele Kozmis and Joe or *Yossel*, as he was affectionately known.

Ben Ray's first formal job was selling burlap bags but that did not last long. He soon learned the intricacies of selling life insurance and became a representative of the New York Life Insurance Co. The rule was that the "Reps" could only sell life insurance to the clients. He forged his own path and was one of the first to sell general insurance as well. He decided to name the fledgling company after his eldest daughter Ruth and she, in fact, became the name on their famous calendars. For three decades, in hundreds of homes, the simple, white paper calendar, emblazoned with R. Ray & Co, printed in red letters, was a staple item and hung on the back of kitchen pantry doors, ticking off the weeks in the lives of his customers.

My grandparents' union lasted thirty-five years until Chaya Rasha, anglicized to Rose, passed away of Cancer in Chicago in 1941.

ZAYDA BEN WAS A UNIQUE INDIVIDUAL and like almost all of the Ray men ... stubborn to the core. He and the family were always dressed in the latest fashions. Looking at photographs, one wonders at the skill of the tailors and seamstresses who fashioned such excellent clothing. As a matter of course, buttons were covered, excellent fabrics were used, gloves were worn and the women's hats were worthy of a Queen Elizabeth garden party. But, interestingly enough, the pantry was not bare, but not the usual Jewish housewife's "Horn of Plenty." Not that the family went even remotely hungry ... but a car and fashionable clothing were of more importance. Until he entered the business world, *Zayda's* dress was composed of a black hat and *Kapota*; that was the uniform for observant *Klay Kodesh* in Europe. Polish

Ben Ray

noblemen of the fifteenth and sixteenth century were the originators of this type of outfit and until today it de rigueur for the entire *Chassidic / Charedi* world.

I've been told that it is worn so that the wearer will always remember that he is a Jew and should act in a moral way. Another reason is that anyone who is dressed in this outfit is advertising that he is on a higher moral plane vis-a-vis not listening to gossip or an off-color joke. Would that it always be so!

Of course, the children turned out exactly the opposite. In my father's home, food was always plentiful; he owned a grocery, a delicatessen and a restaurant at different periods in his life. Clothing was essential, of course, but not in the same category as food. Elegance was never a factor in our dress; need and practicality were the important items ... but even though we lived modestly in every way, we never felt deprived. Of course, all of the people with whom we associated were in the same boat; so how could we have known differently!

BUBBE ROSE WAS A GENEROUS big-hearted woman who spent her life caring for her family and doing acts of *Chesed* for her community. One time, I was attending a program which featured a mind reader. He collected bits of jewelry from the audience and told them facts about themselves. He was fingering my watch and said that my grandmother was a marvelous *Balabusta* and did many acts of charity. Well, not that I don't believe his talent, however, probably everyone in the audience had a *Bubbe* just like that. I wasn't too impressed and mentioned this incident to my Uncle Manny who parroted what the performer had said in almost the exact words!

Of course, being a good housekeeper was a totally different experience in the 1920s, almost a hundred years ago. There were no modern appliances, no washing machines or dryers, microwaves, dishwashers or refrigerators. At best, one owned an ice box and a faulty stove. There were also no furnaces, air conditioners, Mix-Masters, and believe it or not ... no home telephones. Until approximately 1940, people of modest means would get their emergency calls at the corner delicatessen or grocery store. One could not chat with friends at length, as it wasn't your private telephone. Then after phones were installed, many folks had a party-line. That is, that there were at least two apartments attached to one telephone line. One had to be careful what was said on the party-line or the entire neighborhood would know your personal business!

A CHARMING STORY OCCURRED recently concerning *Zayda* Ben and his connection to an event that happened 67 years ago. One Shabbat, Rabbi Berel Wein was delivering a sermon in our Jerusalem *shul.* It was a wonderful story about the fact that his grandfather had been the owner of a $20,000 life insurance policy. When he passed away, the family found that only $2,000 remained. It seems that the grandfather had donated $18,000 to a fund whose purpose was to help Jews in Europe. Rabbi Wein mentioned in passing that his mother had turned to the New York Life Insurance company representative, who held the policy, for information. After services, I asked the Rabbi if he knew that my grandfather was an agent for the company. He retorted , "Of course, the policy was bought from Ben Ray, everyone used him, A *Yid* shouldn't buy from an *Erlich Yid?*"

Two lessons emerge from this story. One, few things are more valued than an honorable reputation and the second is that observant Chicagoans stood together. They helped each other and gave charity in some cases that was more than proportionate to their income. Eighteen thousand dollars was a fortune in a time that the average salary was $10 per week. I've often wondered how widespread that practice was. *Kol Hakavod* to everyone involved in what was the most important subject at that point in history – the saving of European Jewry from extinction.

ZAYDA BEN WAS UNUSUAL in that he owned a car. He would travel his territory which consisted of the Northwest and the West sides of Chicago. He was a familiar sight, driving to an apartment house to collect the 25 cents per month fee from his clients. He would climb up the stairs mostly to the third floor to service his people. He used to joke that it appeared that all Jews lived on the third or fourth floor. There were no elevators in these apartment buildings and no one owned a freestanding house … that was for rich people.

To my knowledge, there were only three freestanding houses on the West Side (Douglas Park area). One belonged to Colonel Jacob Arvey, who was a powerful politician from the 24th Ward and was a stalwart of the mighty Democratic Party in Chicago. As everyone knows, the voting motto of Chicago is "Vote Early and Often!" Chicago is the first place in history that ever experienced *Tchiyat Hameitim* as each election saw thousands of votes being cast from local cemeteries! Remarkable!

Mrs. Helen Weiss and her three children lived on the West Side, not far from my grandparents. Unfortunately, Mrs. Weiss was an *Agunah* and her children, Estelle, Phil and King were growing up fatherless. Mrs. Weiss was a client of *Zayda* Ben's and for years, he made his monthly collection visits to this family.

After my grandmother, Rose, passed away, Ben often visited the family, spending time with them, teaching the children how to play chess, checkers and other pastimes. The children were delighted to have this friendly person taking an interest in them. Estelle, the eldest, told me how excited they were whenever he would arrive. Her eyes were still shining with pleasure, when she related these events that had occurred in their family eighty years earlier, when her mother was a middle-aged housewife with three young children in a difficult situation. One can only speculate what would have happened between Helen Weiss and Ben Ray had the vicissitudes of life not interfered. Unfortunately, in March 1943, my grandfather died of Cancer, two short years after his beloved wife.

THERE IS ANOTHER PRECIOUS Helen Weiss family story that happened in the early 1980s in Israel. My son, Uri met Shelli Weiss in Chicago when they were 14 years old. They went out together in groups and to *Bnei Akiva* functions. Once, I suggested to Uri that perhaps, they were a bit young to be so exclusive, even if it was in groups. Uri said, *Ima*, I like her face. I had no answer to that and the friendship blossomed into love. After graduating The Ida Crown Jewish Academy, both went to *Hachshara* and as they had planned, this was also their *Aliyah* to Israel. Shellie's grandmother was remarried to Rabbi Shmuel Stampfer, and lived in Petach Tikvah.

One day, Shelli decided that it was time to introduce Uri to her grandmother. During the introduction, noting that the name Karzen didn't connect to anyone that she knew of in Chicago, she inquired as to what was his mother's maiden name. When he said that his mother was a Ray from Chicago, Mrs. Stampfer was incredulous to believe that this young man was the great-grandson of her friend Ben Ray. Uri became one of her favorite grandsons ... a perfect match for her special and wonderful granddaughter. Of course, it was *Bashert* that two generations later, the Weiss and Ray families are *Geknipt un Gabinden*. (Tied together tightly) You couldn't make up stories with connections like this: Nobody would believe it!

Rachel

Rachel married and was the mother of a large family. She and her entire family were murdered in the Holocaust. Her parents, Avrum Moshe, Tzutel, along with dozens of sisters, brothers and cousins met the same fate. The reader should be aware that the Raja family was among the six million *Kedoshim*, including the one and a half million children that were murdered because they were Jews. Sadly, no other family information is available except that a second cousin, Nathan Cooper, was found and brought to the USA after the war. While I wish to set this story against momentous historical happenings, the Holocaust is so well documented that the narrative can be found in hundreds of books, articles and the personal stories of survivors.

Morris and Our Family in Toronto

Morris Ray immigrated to Toronto, Ontario, Canada. He was welcomed, married, reared his family, and lived the rest of his life there.

The Jewish community had grown and prospered, with Itchi Meyer Karollnick, his uncle, the titular head of the community, a legend in Toronto, who subsequently lived to a ripe old age.

It is said that Itchi Meyer would appear at every Orthodox wedding, and bellow out the *Sheva Brachot* in his booming voice. He had composed a special melody for the seventh blessing, *Asher Bara Sason V'Simcha*. In fact, a recording of this blessing was made in his inimitable style. Who knows how many copies are stashed in Toronto drawers, a precious bit of Jewish memorabilia. One wag jokingly quipped, "If Itchi Meyer did not appear to bless the bride and groom, were they indeed wed?"

Our Family in Chicago

The Karoll family, formerly Karollnick, expanded with some family members moving to Chicago. By the 1950s, the extended families of former citizens of Stashov, such as the Ray, Karoll, Brandzel (Cohen), and Helfand families, were established and thriving in The Windy City, as it is affectionately called.

The family became successful in a number of retail endeavors. The Karoll Men's Shops grew from one small to three large, modern men's stores. Cousins Marshall and Fred Helfand were the owners of a chain of lingerie and women's clothing stores.

Each year, when it was time to be outfitted for Camp *Moshava* the family would go to Marshall's original one on Harlem Avenue for our summer apparel needs ... we didn't have to go to different places; Cousin Marshal had everything that we needed. Similarly, when my sister Judy and I bought our lingerie trousseau, it was at the "Cover Girl" shop on Madison Avenue (West Side – Garfield Park) with Marshall suggesting and directing the purchases. Marshall, his wife Pearl and their family consisting of Phillip, Mark, and Abby were neighbors and members of our Synagogue when we lived in Park Ridge, Illinois. Marshall was a friend all of my life and, at his passing, the world lost a good, charitable person and I felt a vacuum that I knew that nobody else could fill; He was a wonderful family member.

Ruth Ray

Ruth, of the calendar fame, was the eldest child and the only daughter of Ben and Rose Ray. She was truly a great beauty. There exists a picture, taken by a professional photographer, where with her dark, soulful eyes and long, wavy, raven colored hair, could rival that of any movie star of the era. It appears that when she became of marriageable age, she claimed that there was no one suitable for her. Although the Rays were a family of modest means, it was decided to send her back to Europe to find a groom. This fact is hard to fathom. Today, it is not unusual for Jews to fly to Israel just to spend a few days for the High Holidays or attend a *Simcha*, but in the 1920s, I'm certain that it was worthy of comment. However, Ruth Ray did indeed sail to Europe and did find a groom.

Ruth and her chosen one were married in Chicago and moved to the Northwest Side of Chicago. Within a few years, two daughters were born, the eldest, Sharlene and Rochelle, the younger. The groom had arrived in Chicago, dressed in traditional *Chassidic* garb. He had been a star Talmud student, and dubbed worthy of Ruth Ray, who came from a family of *Yichus* (worthy family lineage, and Jewish prestige).

The 70s movie called "Hester Street" could have been custom-written for Aunt Ruth. The opening of the film depicts the main characters, a young couple who arrive from "The Old Country." She is dressed in the fashion of a young matron of the times, wearing a *shaitel* (a wig), and he is resplendent in a well-fitting *kapote*. At the dock, upon alighting from the ship, the husband pulls off his wife's *shaitel* and tosses it into the ocean. After a short time, the husband sports modern dress, has cut off his sidelocks, and shaved his beard. Little by little, he becomes less religiously observant and is finally "A Yankee Doodle," as the saying goes.

A short few years later found the new husband, who after marriage, was scheduled to sit and study in a *Yeshiva* learning to be a goldsmith, totally not religiously observant with Sabbath desecration and the eating of non-*Kosher* food, a part of his everyday life.

The marriage fell apart and they divorced. Sharlene and I were the same age and I lived with my Aunt Ruth and family for approximately a year. Why I was living there will be explained further on in the book. Dear Reader, you'll just have to wait. At any rate, Sharlene and I were approximately six years old, and were playmates. One day, we were exploring some storage boxes and we removed a piece of parchment that had a slash through it. We didn't know it at the time, but, it was their *Gett*, their official Jewish divorce document.

At that time, for a religiously observant Jewish woman to be divorced was most unusual and considered a disgrace. It wasn't the natural order of things. My Aunt Ruth was literally driven insane by the situation. She became more and more despondent, left alone with the girls, with no income, no marketable skills or education. Two years later, found her in an apartment with garbage piling up, bills unpaid, utilities being shut off, and my cousin Sharlene buying all types of *tchochkes* (miscellaneous unimportant small items) and toys that they would never use and for which they couldn't pay. It was a mess. My aunt was declared incompetent and sent to a mental institution where she spent five years. The exquisite-looking Ruth Ray existed no more. Now, in her 40s, she was an elderly-looking women, worn down by life, bitterly disappointed and she had, just about, stopped speaking. The newly married ex-husband took the children to live with him and his wife. Sharlene and Rochelle grew up on the South Side of Chicago, and received a minimum Jewish education.

Sharlene married, became an attorney, divorced, and lived outside of Washington D.C. I hadn't seen or heard about her for many years. Then, in 1983, she came to Chicago for her father's gravestone dedication. Unfortunately, Rochelle who had wed a Jewish man, who was happily married and had born three children, died young in her 30s. Cancer, always whispered, not said aloud, had claimed another Ray descendant.

Isadore Ray

Izzy (Isadore) Ray, the eldest son of Ben and Rose, was my father. He was born in Sandemierz, Poland in 1907. Sandemierz was his mother's hometown and from records it appears that all the three children born in Europe were born there, even though, nearby Stashov is considered the family's hometown. Few details of the family's life in Europe are known, with the exception of the fact that Baruch was a businessman, a teacher and a Cantor following in the steps of his father. In their passport picture, my grandmother is pictured with the three eldest children.

Izzy was 12 years old, just on the cusp of his *Bar Mitzvah* when he arrived. Because his father was the Cantor, though part-time, it was more than just a joyous family occasion. The congregation rejoiced with the newly-arrived family. He not only chanted part of the service and read the *Haftorah*, but gave the *Drasha* (scholarly presentation). The celebration was held in the local Synagogue on *Shabbat*. After the services were concluded, the congregation feasted on *Kichel*, herring, home-baked cakes and *Schnapps* (whiskey) ... lots of it!

Izzy attended the local school, but left at the age of sixteen. Always being an industrious person, and out of necessity, worked at any job that a youngster could find, such as the ubiquitous errand boy. He labored at menial part-time jobs, such as filling

Passport Picture – From Stashov to Chicago – Bubbe Rose
Ray with Father Izzy, (L) Uncle George and Aunt Ruth

orders for the business establishments of other people from Stashov, who had preceded him to America. Among other *Stashovers* who had joined the growing Chicago community were the families of Rabbi David Kaganoff, Rabbi Judah Graubert, the Merzels, Friedmans and Brandzel families. One of his first employers was the Brandzels, who owned a warehouse. He had the creative job of sweeping floors. He truly hated being an employee and at this point, imprinted in my father's character was the fact that one must be one's own boss. I believe that through osmosis, I absorbed that idea and passed it along to my children. True to his conviction, he always owned the various businesses during his life and never worked as an employee again.

A FAMILY STORY IS TOLD that when Izzy arrived in the United States, he had never seen a banana. He tried to eat it, peel and all, and loved it. This incident became a family story. I thought that this was a unique happening, until others told me the same story about their family. I guess none of them had ever a banana!

The Depression

October 29, 1929, the American stock market crashed. The financial world had been in a giant bubble. One reason is that because every person with a few dollars in their pocket became an expert in stocks and a capitalist with a portfolio. It was a fad and a game, with stocks climbing higher and higher, by the day. That day will live in infamy as all these "paper millionaires" became ordinary working folks when the market bottomed out. Some people lost all their money and the homes that were mortgaged to the hilt. There were people who became paupers overnight. Some of the losers could not face poverty and literally jumped out of windows committing suicide. Selling apples on the street became popular among these desperate people. Trickle up economy became the rule of the day. Because goods were not selling, they were not being manufactured and so on, up the chain. When you see pictures of that period, you will notice the shabby clothing, paucity of cars and a feeling of sadness pervades the very air. One of my life rules which has saved us money and heartache, is that, if something, a deal, is too good to be true ... It is too good to be true!

Over the years, perhaps, we have lost on a project in which we did not invest. But, I would never look back. You win some, and you lose some ... that is how the game of life is played.

Not that the infamous financier who is serving 150 years in jail, would even have taken my tiny investment ... but, had he offered, I would have said, "No, Thanks!" The people who believed that he could deliver seventeen percent on an investment, while the rest of the world was happy to get two to three percent on theirs, were greedy. Personally, I'm sorry that they lost their fortunes, and currently, many of his clients are in the same category as those in 1929, but greed is not an admirable trait. In a nutshell, they had it coming ... and there were many financially astute people who got burned! As in other important decisions ... due diligence is a must! Reader, be astute!

Shabbat

America was in the throes of the Depression and jobs were very hard to come by. Employment, especially, without working on Saturday (*Shabbat*) was impossible. At age 23, Izzy and his younger brother George left Chicago and moved to New York. This was done out of respect for their parents and their position in the community. As the brothers were unknown there, they were able to secure employment and unfortunately, worked on the Sabbath and Sunday, as well. It was not until some twenty-five years later, while owning a restaurant, he decided to close on *Shabbat*. My father made this crucial decision, and told it to me while we were taking a stroll one evening. I stared at him in astonishment when he related this to me. His face was shining and he appeared to be at peace with this decision. No, he was more than at peace; it was more a look of wondrous achievement.

While he had never allowed us children to work on the Sabbath or Holidays, we never realized how much it hurt him to do so. Children have a hard time thinking of their parents as people, and we, of course, were no different. But now, he was once again in his element. He joined a local Synagogue, and derived much pleasure from attending each Sabbath, as well as *Pesach*, *Sukkot* and *Shavuot*. He had always closed his business for the High Holidays of *Rosh Hashanah* and *Yom Kippur* but now the circle was complete. He was once again the Sabbath observer of his youth, and he was ecstatic with that decision. He became a member of Achei Yavnah Synagogue in Garfield Park, whose Rabbi was Shlomo Rappoport, the Principal of the Chicago Jewish Academy, where all the Ray girls had attended.

After a few years, the family moved to Hollywood Park, where he then joined the Synagogue, which was led by Rabbi Jacob Rich. There, the members of Ahavat Achim Congregation on Jersey Avenue in Chicago welcomed him and he enjoyed having a new circle of friends. Sadly, this ideal time in his life lasted only two years. He passed away on Friday, January 30, 1959 and is buried in the family plot at Waldheim Cemetery on Harlem at Roosevelt Road Avenue in Oak Park, Illinois. A plaque in his memory is affixed to the Memorial Board of that *Shul* and I will be forever grateful to them for the happiness that he enjoyed there.

There is a lesson to be learned in every happening. Thursday night after watching Masterpiece Theater on television, I called my parents to chat and to wish them a *Shabbat Shalom*. Speaking with my father, I inquired about his health, as he had seen a doctor the previous day, which in itself, was an unusual event. He was fifty-four years old and he had always enjoyed good health. I can never remember him spending a day in bed in his entire life. However, he had not been feeling himself, although the doctor did not find anything amiss. He had been a cigarette smoker since he had been a teen … what of it? Everybody smoked, it was nothing unusual. He was somewhat overweight, but his vitals appeared to be in normal condition.

The next morning, the phone rang at 7 a.m. I heard my Aunt Sylvia speaking, but at first, couldn't make sense of what she was saying. At that time, my father owned a luncheonette on Elston Avenue in Chicago. It seems that he had gone to work a bit earlier than usual, as it had snowed the night before and he wanted to shovel the walkway so that no one would fall and be injured. While shoveling, he suffered a massive heart attack and died immediately.

The funeral was held on Monday morning. The law in Illinois stated that no funerals could be held on Sunday. It has since been altered, however, it was as though we were "sitting *Shiva*" since Friday, which was a long three days. There is no history of heart disease in the family, so the lesson to be learned here is leave the snow shoveling to the young or the electric snow blower.

My father lived to see Judy and I married, not Rozzie and no grandchildren or great-grandchildren. After all he had been through, it did not seem fair, but that was his fate. His gravestone reads "He left after him the remnants of blessings to generations yet to come."

New York

Izzy and George arrived in New York determined to carve out successful lives for themselves. They set about seeking employment and as partners were the owners and operators of several businesses. Three enterprises stand out in my memory.

At one time, he and George worked in a small, neighborhood grocery store stacking shelves, waiting on customers and once again sweeping floors. After a short while, due to those economic Depression times, they were again out of work. They purchased a laundry service and drove the routes picking up dirty laundry and delivering the clean items in boxes. This was a time before plastic bags and I recall using the boxes as houses or helmets. They made wonderful toys and our imaginations were limitless, as we used these white cardboard boxes in every fun way. After the Second World War, the number of home washing machines and dryers made this business obsolete. Only diaper service survived and that ended with the invention of paper diapers such as Pampers in the 50s.

In New York, at that time and as today, many Jews were involved in the diamond business. My father became a diamond polisher. Each evening upon arriving home, he would empty his pockets of very small folded tissue paper. Inside were a number of small stones.

Being a very young child, diamonds didn't impress me and I never did believe that "Diamonds are a Girl's Best Friend", evidenced by Hollywood star, Marilyn Monroe, whose signature song it was, and who owned a large collection of gems, but suffered a tragic life.

Uncle George and Aunt Rose

George, two years younger than Izzy, were the closest of brothers. They shared everything; food, clothing, toys and even their mattress. They lived and worked together and were each other's best friend.

George married Rose (Richelson) and three children were born to them. Beverly, Joel and Rhoda grew up in a typical

Jewish, though non-traditional New York family.

When Beverly's son became a *Bar Mitzvah*, an entire Sabbath for the family was held at the Grossingers Resort Hotel in the Catskill Mountains.

Joel's *Bar Mitzvah* was a happy event for the family; it took place in New York in 1951. The Ray family arrived, en masse from Chicago and New York. When we stepped through the door of the hotel, a life-size cardboard cutout of the celebrant greeted us at the entrance, and the chopped liver on the buffet table was sculpted in the shape of a heart. To our surprise and relief ... the heart, at least, didn't beat! All the jokes about the excesses of a New York *Bar Mitzvah* were evident, but we all loved it.

There is a marvelous photograph depicting the four Ray brothers, George, the proud father of the *Bar Mitzvah*, and Izzy, Manny and Joe.

The picture depicts each brother and his wife. My father had married his third wife, Rose, just before the wonderful occasion and it was an unforgettable time for them. This treasured picture shows the importance of a real picture that you can hold in the hand and not one that is put in the computer, forgotten and never printed out. Print out your pictures or else don't bother taking them ... they will be surely lost in time and those important moments will be as though they never happened.

This was one of the few occasions that so many members of the family spent a wonderful *Shabbat* together. The family flew from Chicago to New York for the *Bar Mitzvah*. Flying in an airplane was not what it is today. It was a relatively new experience to fly domestically and people simply wouldn't trust an airplane to arrive safely. The last item one would purchase (no duty-free at that time!) was Flight Insurance. No one flew without this very necessary purchase. In every airport, there were machines that dispensed this protection. Today insurance is necessary in the likely scenario that luggage gets lost or one must cancel the flight for some reason such as a medical emergency, but at that time, it should have been called Airplane Crash Life Insurance, because that's what it was. The timid did not fly. From Chicago to New

York if taking the train, the timeline was two days, driving took 18 hours straight, or one just simply stayed home. Flying was for the brave and that idea didn't change very much until the advent of the jet engine.

At this point I must extend a *Hakarat Hatov*, recognition of an extraordinary good deed, to my Uncle George and Aunt Rose. When my mother was fatally ill and bedridden, I lived for a time with them. Joel and I were approximately the same age, perhaps two years old. Somewhere they had gotten hold of a twin buggy and with Joel and I ensconced within. My aunt would carefully lower us step by step down the stairs from their third floor home. Surely, no easy task, for her! Somehow that picture has stayed in my mind. It's fascinating how one retains a snippet of the past.

George, however, was not present to see his grandson being feted. He had been hit by a city bus a few years earlier. He lingered for two years and passed away. Beverly, herself, was smitten by Cancer and died when she was in her mid-thirties.

Recently Rhoda was admitted to the hospital for an infection and succumbed three days later. Now, Joel is the sole survivor of that branch of the family. To end this section on a happier note, Joel and wife Anne are the grandparents of several children – they are the State of Florida representatives of the Ray family.

Uncle Manny and Aunt Zira

Uncle Manny, the third son, and first native born American was born to *Bubbe* Rose and *Zayda* Ben, two years after my *Bubbe* immigrated to the United States.

Chicago was a bustling metropolis known for its famous Maxwell Street, stockyards, and Mafia. When I made *Aliyah*, upon telling people that I was from Chicago, their first reaction was to cock their hand as if to pretend to be shooting a gun and say, Al Capone … bang … bang! In the 1990s the reaction improved. They would be surprised to hear that Michael Jordan, the basketball star, was not an acquaintance of mine ... and then they still did the shooting bit!

Prohibition was in full swing, and graft was the oil that ran the local government. I was not privy to the huge acts of bribery connected to the building and other large industries, but on a smaller scale, it was well known that if a policeman stopped you for exceeding the speeding limit and if you handed him a $10 bill along with your license, the traffic ticket became non-existent.

I don't want to give you the wrong idea, but you must be aware that The State of Illinois has had at least four Governors jailed for various crimes in my memory alone. In the 20s, Chicago had the well-deserved reputation of being the "Wild West of the Midwest!" But, in spite of all these political shenanigans, Illinois absorbed millions of immigrants and a great metropolis was built. Because of its industrial diversity, there was always something for everyone who wanted to work. It was a well-known fact that if you could not find employment in Chicago, you really did have a problem!

Maxwell Street saw wave after wave of immigrants of different nationalities who got their start in America. Pushcarts for every imaginable type of merchandise lined the streets; and voices were heard in many languages. In the 1920s to the 40s, Italian, English with heavy Irish brogues and Yiddish with both *Galitzianer* and *Litvak* accents were common. Many a large department store had their humble beginnings on that colorful street. It lasted until the 1950s when the area was gentrified and the suburbs and shopping malls became the commerce arenas.

Manny took after his father, Ben, in appearance. He was tall, handsome and in temperament, stubborn to the core (which was always a true Ray family trait). When we got together, it was the noisiest of times. Whenever the group gathered, there seemed to be confrontation and a clash of ideas between the generations. A mid-size chaotic scene is the only way to describe those wonderful family get-togethers. Uncle Manny would raise his arms, shout and yell – and Rays were NEVER wrong. One time he bet $5 to his granddaughter that there was no ketchup in the refrigerator. There was … he was wrong (imagine!) and she was richer by five bucks! But, we all laughed together; we loved each other … we were FAMILY and it was wonderful!

Uncle Manny and Aunt Zira, his wife, would visit Israel periodically. In fact, I was impressed when the *Bar Mitzvah* of their son Barry was held in Jerusalem with the ceremony held at the Western Wall and the festive luncheon at the Tirat Bat Sheva Hotel. This was early on, years before it became fashionable for American Jews to celebrate here. They were pioneers holding their *Simcha* here, and many Chicagoans followed their lead.

There are memories that I will always cherish concerning Uncle Manny. Even though he had inherited a successful insurance business in his early 20s, due to the death of his young father, he was a hard worker, a canny businessman, and the business prospered even more. However, he was a bit prudent with money. Okay, he could be a penny pincher!

ONE CHARMING EXAMPLE was that since our *Aliyah*, one of the perks is that of living in Jerusalem and being the "Chicago Face" to many of our family and friends. One time, Manny and Zira were visiting. Unfortunately, Zira was hospitalized and Manny naturally wished to visit her each day. He was averse to spending the money for a taxi and requested Jay to ferry him there and back. We had recently made *Aliyah*, were not employed and the cost of gas for the car was horrendous. Americans were spending $1.79 per gallon and we were paying $3.50 per gallon, not unlike the ratio of gasoline today. After a few days, Jay casually suggested that perhaps he would hire a cab for the next day as he had an appointment in the morning. Manny, totally nonplussed, told him that he would wait until the afternoon when Jay was free, because *taxis are so expensive!*

A few years later, when the summers in Israel seemed to be getting hotter by the year, we wanted to install central air-conditioning, but we simply couldn't afford to do so. My aunt and uncle were to be coming to visit for a few weeks, and I decided to ask them for a loan. Air conditioning had become crucial, not a luxury item, as the temperature climbed higher each summer day. It was always a joy to have them in Israel visiting with us and once, while having a lively conversation with him in our overly warm salon, Manny became uncomfortable and suggested that we turn on the air conditioning. I then informed him that the house was not air conditioned and asked for a loan to do so. He didn't reply, and I jokingly said that if he couldn't loan us the money, perhaps he would like to donate it and we would put up a plaque dedicating the unit to him. He subtly changed the subject and that was that!

But one time the scene was different. Manny and Zira were blessed with three children, the eldest of which was a daughter, Roberta, who married Erwin Katz, who became one of the youngest judges in the Illinois court system and was a nephew of Rabbi Moshe Feinstein (z'l). She followed faithfully in her parents' community service work. Even though quite young, she was elected the President of the PTA of the Arie Crown Hebrew Day School. Roberta insisted on attending the School End of Year Dinner, in June 1973, even though she had just learned that she had been stricken with Cancer. She fought the disease valiantly and every avenue for a cure was explored. Along with traditional medicine, Manny traveled the globe and visited famous Rabbis in the hope of a *Bracha* that would help their daughter. But, it was not to be. She passed away at age 31. She was the mother of three young children; it was one of life's unbelievable tragedies.

Manny and Zira were in shock, felled by the loss. Previously, when the Ray clan would gather for a family occasion, the laughter and especially the friendly arguments about any subject, could be heard, probably even on the next block. But then there was no shouting, no yelling and no waving of hands by Uncle Manny, who sat silently and jokes were not heard from Aunt Zira. The *Balagan* was sorely missed and the feeling of loss was palpable. It took a few years until Manny's booming voice and Zira's kidding nature was heard again. Like so many other parents that lose children, they never wholly recovered from that blow.

While still a young man in his 20s, Manny found his niche in the insurance business, and made another life choice. He met the love of his life, Zira Siegel and married her. This time in their young lives was a dizzying round of events, for the Ray family, America and eventually the entire world.

Within seven years, the following occurred: The Second World War was raging in Europe; America was pulled in after the attack by the Japanese on Pearl Harbor, an island on the Pacific Ocean, a half world away. My grandparents both passed away. Their youngest son, Joe, came to live with Zira and Manny. Zira became pregnant just before Uncle Manny was drafted and sent to Europe on a luxury liner converted to a troop ship, which sailed with 10,000 American soldiers aboard. In New York, Manny's elder brother, Izzy, my father, had married Minnie Gartner, and two daughters were born to them, Judy and Ruby. Minnie passed away and Izzy married her younger sister, Jean and the union produced another daughter, Roslyn. Then Jean died from the now eradicated disease Tuberculosis, and left Izzy with three young daughters. In the meantime, in Chicago, Roberta was born while Manny was overseas and Zira also was in charge of running the insurance business, until her newly-married husband returned. Also, don't forget sister Ruth, whose marriage was falling apart and who slowly became more and more despondent. If you, Dear Reader, become cock-eyed from just reading this account … can you imagine what stamina and courage it took for the principals who lived it?

In 1945, US President Franklin Delano Roosevelt died and Harry Truman became the leader of the Free World. The troops were coming home, and Manny, like thousands of other soldiers, was given permission to search the hell hole of Europe for survivors of the Holocaust. He found two survivors of the Ray family, Nathan Cooper and his sister.

The Ray family was in a turmoil situation. Uncle Manny had been gone three years and he had never met his newborn daughter; his younger brother, Joe, was an orphan, and his brother Izzy and sister Ruth were in situations that were at best unstable.

Manny was being discharged in New York. There was a joyous reunion between the brothers, but the pall of family troubles

muted the celebration. A plan had to be drafted in light of all
these unusual situations. The following was the outcome of the
deliberations. Manny was on his way back home to Chicago. He
took me with him and I went to live with him, Zira and the baby.
My Uncle Joe, then 18 years old, would come from Manny's
home in Chicago and live with my father and Judy in New York.
Roslyn, two years old, was sent to a children's home, not far
from the family home in Borough Park. The plan was carried
out and the families thrived, although, not under the most ideal
conditions.

After being "Over There" for three years, with no return trips
to the US ... as there was no furlough schedule, Manny returned.

One of the most difficult parts of being in the army was
"Keeping *Kosher*." It was during the Second World War that
Jewish soldiers, who wished to eat *Kosher* food, were aided by
a new army service. Upon the request of the Jewish Chaplain
in charge, soldiers could receive food for Passover and a few
other special items. However, mostly the men survived as
best they could. Manny to the end of his life could not stand
eating potatoes, especially mashed, and would eat them only in
an emergency situation. But, his absolute nemesis was *Peanut
Butter*. Even the opening of the jar would send him to another
room. He was so nauseous with the thought of consuming it.
He had spent his entire military service subsisting on these two
products, along with the limited supply of fruits and vegetables
that were available. Thinner, but still jaunty, he reunited with his
family, Zira and baby Roberta, resumed his business career and
interrupted life.

At this point, I must tell you about a most marvelous and unique
individual, my Aunt Zira. Many times I have thought about
her courage and bravery in the face of adversity. The beloved
daughter of Doris and Rabbi Samuel Siegel, affectionately known
as S.S. or "Steamship Siegel." Her father was a striking looking
individual, silver-colored hair, a natty dresser and he spoke
eloquently. He was the Development Director or fund-raiser for
the Hebrew Theological College, which was the largest and most

important *Yeshiva Gedola* outside of New York. Doris, his *Rebbetzin*, was a tiny lady in stature, always fashionably dressed and shod in high heels. To this day, I believe that the magnificent hats that she wore to the Synagogue inspired me to write in my Chicago Jewish Academy High School Year Book, that my ambition was to be a millinery designer. Zira followed in her mother's footsteps, not only in her wardrobe, but as a "fixer" in everyone's affairs.

Both Rabbi and Mrs. Siegel were pillars of the community, well known for their open house policy. Every Sabbath found their home on Independence Boulevard a gathering place for any traveler who needed home hospitality while visiting Chicago. When I became part of Zira and Manny's household, I was accepted like a member of the family, made welcome and spent many a Sabbath there taking part in the delicious meals that Mrs. Siegel prepared. She was a *Balabusta* of the highest order, and probably one of the best cooks I have ever had the privilege in partaking of her food. Mrs. Siegel was an old-time cook. Her recipes which people recorded for their own use, had direction such as "mix a little of this and a dash of that, or three fingers of something else." However, whatever she cooked or baked was deemed a success. To this day, whenever I taste sweet gefilte fish, I think of her and her culinary artistry.

After each elegant Sabbath lunch, it was the job of the female contingent to clean up. I usually had the task of drying the gold-rimmed special china that was used at those meals. Well, one time, I dropped a dish and it broke in two. Of course, I was mortified. It was their beautiful, special set for eighteen guests and I had the honor of breaking the very first piece. Immediately, it became very quiet in the room, but the six-year-old guest was not scolded. However, from the next time on, I became the chief silverware dryer. I guess I had been demoted!

Years later, a while after her mother had passed on, Zira and I were chatting in her living room. We were reminiscing and she told me a very strange story. Zira wanted to bake a certain cake that her mother had baked for special occasions for many years. Like so many of the family's favorite, Zira had the recipe written down. She looked high and low and couldn't seem to find it. She figured that it was gone forever. Early one morning, she enters into the kitchen and behold, there is the recipe card for that particular cake sitting on her kitchen table. Believe it or not, that is what happened, and the family continued to enjoy that cake.

Another very difficult-to-believe story happened after Roberta (*z'l*) had passed away, leaving three children, the youngest Eli, still a baby. The housekeeper came upon Roberta's photo and asked who was the woman pictured. When told that she was the deceased mother of her charges, she looked at my Aunt Zira and commented, "I could swear that I have seen her in the bedroom, sitting on the rocking chair, holding and singing to a baby – now I understand." There are dimensions that we cannot fathom and I firmly believe that they exist.

Aunt Zira was always a spiritual person. When she told me these happenings, I hardly blinked an eye … she was that type of person.

Roberta became my little sister, in place of Rozzie, who had remained in New York. She was the first child born to Zira and Manny, as well as the first granddaughter to the Siegels. One bedroom in the Siegel home became a virtual child's dream-come-true with toys and playthings just waiting for her to grow into. She was still a baby and couldn't appreciate any of it. I had been sent to Chicago with no toys or games with which to play. My father hadn't thought to do so – no doubt survival of the family was uppermost in his mind. A mother would have thought to send things, but as I had none … it was a no toy time for me. Roberta, too young to be aware of her largesse, had a doll house with electric lights that went on and off and a whole tiny family to enjoy their home. She also had a doll with real hair, which for years I desired one just like it. It was my dream gift, but I never received it. Those were two things that I played with all the time. Interestingly enough, I was never envious of her, and I truly enjoyed myself in that room. You could say that I was the "Tryer-Outer" making sure that everything was in order and ready for her to enjoy, as she grew up.

There was one Jewish Day School in Chicago which was situated on the West Side of Chicago. However, by the time Roberta was ready to enter Kindergarten, the Jews were again on the move ... this time to the North Side of Chicago. Albany Park became the desired area for Orthodox Jews including Zira and Manny. They, along with like-minded friends, began to work toward forming a Hebrew day school in that area. Establishing a school is a most difficult task, with meetings upon meetings that must be held. Teachers, students, venue and money ... and lots of it, must be considered. Zira ended up being one of the powerhouses of the *Torah Umesorah* Organization, based in New York. She was also President of the PTA a number of times. Manny was Chairman of the Board for 14 years. Even many years later, their efforts were noted and appreciated. It was a labor of love for the committee who achieved the establishment of the Central Hebrew Day School, later to be known as the Arie Crown Jewish Day School of Albany Park. The school exists and thrives up until today. Thousands of students owe their Jewish education to that small group of pioneers with the Rays among the leaders.

Aunt Zira was a medical marvel and unfortunately, suffered from health problems her entire life. She was an expert on illnesses and knew the floor plan of hospitals in the Chicagoland and Florida areas. She joked that her medical history file had just a few pages less than the Tolstoy novel, War and Peace.

The times that she visited with us were treasured times, and we were able to speak thoughtfully about the Ray family and its bizarre history. I asked her once if she knew why I and my sisters have no *ketubah* or wedding ring or any item from my parents' union. She related that my father had entrusted some valuables to her for safekeeping. As luck would have it, the box which contained the few pieces, was stolen from her home in a robbery. One day after her last trip to Israel, she sent me a box of treasured family pictures. Many appear in this document, some over eighty years old, picturing the Ray family of the past.

Zira passed away at the age of 73. While she could be critical

JEME: (serves 6 hungry people)

Ingredients: Small pieces of *Cholent* meat
5 lbs whole grated potatoes ~ 5 raw eggs ~ 3 sliced potatoes
2 grated onions ~ Salt ~ Pepper ~ 1 teas. Sugar ~ Oil

Put oil in bottom of pot, heat.
Put sliced potatoes in heated oil; add the
rest of the ingredients; meat in last.
Bake at 300 dgs. (F)

Don't Bother It Until Next Day.

At family celebrations, there was a dish that was often served. It is called "Jeme." Aunt Zira passed the recipe along to me and I now to you. Enjoy!

to a fault, she was a touchstone for the family members. Though we had not lived even on the same continent for years, on the morning after her passing, it was surreal for me to see that the sun rose and the earth was still in its orbit. The impact of her life, not only on her children, but her extended family was extensive. She was the arbiter of taste, in dress, manners and most other subjects … and let everyone know it. But with all her foibles, she was loved. Zira was a unique individual and will be remembered fondly by all who were touched by her.

Manny lost his best friend when Zira was passed away. They had been together since their teens. In the waning days of 1998, at age 77, Manny contracted Pancreatic Cancer, suffered its pain for three months and joined his beloved partner of 53 years. They were laid to rest in the new Ray section of Waldheim Cemetery in Oak Park, Illinois.

Manny was the first family member to attain the age of 60 and it was fully celebrated. When he hit the age of 70, we were ecstatic. No Ray in the family's memory had attained that golden age and we all reveled in the fact that it could be done. Manny was also the family's medical history expert. Did arthritis, heart trouble, or high blood pressure run in the family? The answers Yes, Yes and No were given by Uncle Manny. Upon his passing the patriarch of the family became Joe or Yossel, the caboose of the five children.

The last child born to Rose and Ben was Joe. At this time, the family was living on the Northwest Side of Chicago, on the corner of Division and Kedzie Avenues. Joe attended the local Public School, but when it was time for him to attend afternoon Hebrew School classes, he was enrolled in the Grenshaw Talmud Torah on the West Side, located at Grenshaw and Kedzie. His father Ben, would drive Joe to the school five days a week. It became a *shlep* (Joe's quote to drive him every day, and it was decided that the family move to the West Side). The building at 1103 Independence Boulevard became their home, and it was two doors from the office of the Hapoel Hamizrachi Organization. That building would figure in the Ray family's tableau for many years. They began to take part in the prayers at the Makarover Rebbe's Shtiebel (a small Synagogue usually found in a renovated family home), located at 1241 S. Independence Boulevard. *Zayda* Ben became a leader in the Synagogue and Joe became best friends with the Rabbi's son.

As noted previously, when his parents died, Joe became an orphan at sixteen years old. He went to live with Manny and Zira. After two years, Uncle Joe and I then changed places. He traveled to New York to live with his eldest brother, Izzy, and I came to Chicago and took his place with Zira and Manny.

In New York, Izzy sent him to the school which was the future high school of Yeshiva University. He was always an enterprising person and worked at various and sundry jobs. He met a beautiful, religiously observant young woman named Sylvia. Their dates were unusual. For example, while they were courting, Joe was working as a diamond polisher. After the Sabbath, Joe would go to the factory to put in a few hours and earn extra money. Sylvia would sit near him while he was working on the stones. The system was that the stones were polished under a bright light, but the problem was that it was against the code of polishers to work late hours. So they put a dark piece of material over the cone-shaped light and sat together working and talking under their home-made tent! Sylvia and Joe were married in Chicago, in the basement social hall of a West Side Synagogue. A movie of their wedding exists and it's surreal to see all of us cousins as tots and young children.

We were living in Chicago when I was ten and my sister Rozzie was six years old. One summer, we were invited to visit with Sylvia, Joe and their family who lived in Dubuque, Iowa. That was the time that much of the *Kosher* packing houses were located there, and Joe was working as a *Shochet, a* ritual slaughterer. We very excited to travel there on the Burlington Railroad all by ourselves. Roz and I boarded the train thrilling to this adventure. During the ride, I decided that we should have a cola in the dining room. As in the elegant trains of yore, the dining room tables were covered with starched, white tablecloths, gleaming silverware and a vase with a fresh flower. After we finished, I paid the bill and left a tip, as I thought proper. As I was walking down the aisle leaving the dining car, Rozzie, following, cried out, "Ruby, you forgot to take your change." As I returned the tip, in my best older-to-younger sister look, I told her that I would explain later, and shepherded her back to our seats. Younger sisters can be so trying!

Sylvia and Joe were blessed with four children, namely, Burton, Rhonda, Alan and Yale. One summer Burton and Alan were sent to a summer day camp in the Chicago area. Jay, my boyfriend, at the time, was one of the counselors at this camp. One day, just before the season started, Jay received a phone call from my Uncle Joe. It appears that his boys were to be in Jay's group. Joe wanted to alert Jay to the fact that Alan was a bit wild. He was a #1 *Shovav* and had the reputation to go with it. Joe reasoned that as it appeared that Jay was on the way to becoming a part of the family, he would give him a heads up. Jay kept an eye on him and Alan, true to his fashion, was a terror. It's amazing how children straighten out. He is married to Sari, who while retired now, was an honored staff member of the Ida Crown Jewish Academy for over thirty years. Their eight daughters are married and they are grandparents many times over. Burton and wife Leah made *Aliyah* a short time after us. For years, we both were the Ray family representatives in Israel. It was wonderful to share their children's weddings and numerous happy occasions with them. Not long ago, Rhonda and her mate, Ephraim have joined the trips "To Israel to see the Kids," as their son and family have taken this important step. Yale and Rochel's welcoming home is our base in Chicago, at times, but we are looking forward to having them be here with us and the rest of the family.

THE FOLLOWING STORY ADDS to the picture of Chicago Jewry in the 1950s. Jay was not only a counselor, but he also drove the van to pick up the youngsters. He lived in Albany Park, not far from where the camp was located. His route extended from Humboldt Park to Highland Park; the furthest South to the furthest North. He traveled first to Humboldt Park and the mother would be standing on the corner alone, as the child wasn't feeling well that day, and so was not coming to camp. He would then travel to Highland Park. Same story. No kid, only a mother, with the same report. Neither of them had called him earlier to tell him not to come and cell phones were yet to be invented! Then he drove to the campsite to begin the day with a dozen little terrors! One more thing, just an unimportant little item … the brakes on the van were not the best, in fact, they would have never passed a test today. Jay was constantly stopping and starting. That summer was a bit of a nightmare, but he did have a summer job and for a nineteen-year-old, that was pretty good!

Uncle Joe was a constant presence all of my life. He had many wonderful qualities. Among them, he was a *Baal Tzedakah* and appeared on every organization's donor list. More than once, I was the *Shliach Mitzvah* when he handed me a very substantial check to give to a person in need.

In 1963, Joe became a charter member in the Chicago Board Option Exchange. It developed into the largest options exchange in the world. In fact, he and a few other entrepreneurs had this idea from its inception, and developed it to what it is today.

Uncle Joe has been gone three years now and there is a daily void. We would receive e-mails every day, sometimes two or three a day. Most of the topics concerned President George Bush, who he called and emailed a number of times a day depending on the current political hot potato subject of the hour. He was a passionate citizen and believed in making his voice heard. He would write lengthy answers to any political questions, and as far as we were concerned, he was usually correct.

But, my favorite personal memory is when he and Sylvia would visit Israel to visit with their numerous children, grandchildren and great-grandchildren, he never forgot Jay and I. We were always included in this wonderful group. He called me his favorite niece. I reveled in his warmth, but as I would kid him back saying, "I bet you tell that to all of your nieces!" A smile would slowly emerge on his face.

Uncle Joe passed away, surrounded by his family, while they sung favorite family hymns. He said that he had no grievances to G-D. He had been blessed with a special wife, a marvelous family, had enjoyed good health, and a wonderful life. What he said was true, but to that, I add that he was an example of an exceptional *Mentsh*, which he repeatedly exhorted his beloved family to emulate. In Hebron, a "Jewel of a Synagogue" has been dedicated in his memory by his family. Recently, I had the privilege of praying there and introduced my great-grandchildren to their Uncle Joe – May his memory be for a blessing.

The Family of Manny and Zira

The marriage of Manny and Zira produced three children. Roberta, Barry and Shimmy (Sherwin). Barry met Harriet Weintraub, a native of Charleston, South Carolina, complete with a charming Southern drawl, at a Summer NCSY Conference, when they were young adults. Harriet, a beautiful, vivacious teenager, had broken her leg, and Barry, a handsome, terrific guy had gallantly offered to help her navigate. He navigated her right into his heart and by the end of the season, a new couple was created. This was the start of a wonderful relationship. Their decades long marriage, successful in every way endures, and is replicated in their own children and grandchildren.

Shimmy and his wife Helen are the parents of four children, two of whom have joined us in Israel. We were seventeen first cousins. Unfortunately, there are only twelve remaining, but we are happy at any time to welcome them to Israel and enjoy a warm family reunion.

The Gartners – My Mother's Side of the Family

Until this point, this story has concerned the Ray family. Of course, there is another side, my mother's family, the Gartners, who hailed from Kolbeshov, Poland, a town of consequence. It wasn't a village or just another small spot on the map; it was large enough to have the train stop there. This was a point of pride to the community.

In my research, the towns of Stashov, Sandemierz, Kolbeshov, and Kohlbehom kept appearing over and over again. In Kolbeshov, there was a *Rebbe* who had a large following. He was known as the *Kolbeshover Rebbe*, and after World War II, a community of his sect was established in the borough of Bronx, a section of New York City. Also, frequent mention is made of belonging to the *Gerer Chassidim* and to the court of the *Trisker Rebbe*.

IN LIGHT OF THE PRACTICES OF observant youth today, where separation of the sexes is the desired goal, you'd be amazed at the activities of those observant teen-agers in that era.

Among the Kolbeshover children, there was a son named Sender who was a youth at that time. There were groups which engaged the religious young people; very much akin to the *Bnei Akiva* of America to which all observant teens were members, not only in Chicago, but in every major city, in the 50s and 60s. Sender, the Rabbi's son, was very much a part of these happenings such as enjoying hayrides and other activities, which were not gender-specific. Both guys and gals (my future Aunt Gussie, for one) enjoyed these outings and a good time was had by all.

Sender, mixed gender hayrides not withstanding, became a renowned Orthodox Rabbi. It seems that at one memorable Synagogue convocation a question of Jewish law arose. Many Rabbis gave their opinion and then Sender, the Kolbeshover Rebbe spoke. When he concluded, the room remained quiet – it was his opinion that was the deciding factor.

Marriage and the Family

As the family expanded, Raja cousins were married to Emmers, Gartners, Lass, and Waxpress, as well as other local families. (Note: I include all the various maiden names, as presently unknown cousins are welcome to join this illustrious group!)

Sandemierz, also known as Tzozmier, was a small town not far from Stashov. Most probably, the matchmaker was acquainted with all the available young men and women in the area and deemed them suitable for each other. There is a *Midrash* that 30 days before the birth of a child, an angel announces who is its *Bashert.*

Sandemierz was the sister city to Stashov as far as the Raja family was concerned. Quite often, marriages took place between the two towns, with the interwoven families becoming one big cousins club.

The Lineage of Our Great-Grandparents

The earliest event that is recorded was the marriage in Poland of my great-grandparents, Shmuel Gartner to Toba, (nee Meyer). He was the owner of a seltzer factory. They had seven children. The eldest was Shimon, who died in childhood in Europe. Dovid married Bluma (Laufer), Chaim married Fradel (Ande,) Pinya (Phil) married Helen (Blitzer,) Sara Itel married Elimelech Kornbluth, Mendele married Malka (Lesser) and the youngest, Yisroel, married Chaya Rivka (Waxpress,) who were my maternal grandparents.

The Gartner family was fortunate in that they moved to the United States in the 1920s, settling in various parts of New York.

Six children were born to Yisroel and Chaya Rivka. Eliezer married Minnie (Krill,) Esther Malka married Max Adams, Gussie married Max Schwartz, Chaim Simcha married Manya, Chana Mindel (Minnie) married Isadore (Izzy) Ray; and after she passed away, Izzy married the youngest daughter, Shaindel.

Izzy (Yisroel Tzvi) and Minnie were my parents. Jean (Shaindel) was technically my aunt, but for all intents and purposes, she was my mother, as she was a loving parent. I was blessed with three mothers in my life, but that fact must wait to be explained later.

I record the maiden names of family members on purpose. Once, upon casually meeting a new neighbor and hearing that his family name was Wachspress, I mentioned that the name Waxpress is found in my family. As a matter of fact, Chaya Rivka Waxpress is my great-grandmother, and I am named after her. After playing "Jewish Geography," we are pretty certain that we must be related, coming from the same area in Poland. So, I found an unknown, new cousin, and if not a cousin, certainly a new friend!

Eliezer and Minnie Gartner

The eldest child Laizer (Eliezer) and Minnie owned a grocery store on East 41st Street in the Lower East Side of New York. They spent their lives working together in that small neighborhood store. In their 70s, they decided to fulfill their life's dream of *Aliyah*; they officially retired and sold their business. In 1970, they sailed to Israel on the Queen Elizabeth and moved to Netanya. It was a very brave move. This was the time before the Jewish Agency was of help to *Olim*. Jay and I had occasion to visit with them during our early visits to Israel. They always said with a smile, "We are so happy and satisfied and we are enjoying our lives here in the sun." Their biggest regret was that they felt that they should have done it sooner. Laizer spent hours studying Talmud and other sacred texts, and my Aunt Minnie, who had shown her talent as an artist in her earlier years, now had the time and energy to follow her dream. One of her paintings hangs in our home, and looking at it, I think of them, and remember their wonderful sense of fulfillment.

Their three children, Judy, Yaakov and David, have all been blessed and their families have grown to include both grandchildren and great-grandchildren. Judy has children in America as well as Israel, where her progeny have distinguished themselves in various fields. Her daughter, Malka, is a professor of linguistics at Bar Ilan University. Her brother, Yaakov, moved to Israel in 1966. Now retired, he spent 22 years as a Professor of Talmud also at Bar Ilan University and has published books on Jewish Law that we are proud to have in our personal library.

Esther and Max Adams

Esther and Max Adams appear to have always lived in Staten Island, while the rest of the family lived mostly on the Lower East Side or in Williamsburg. They were the parents of two girls, who when they married, also lived in Staten Island. It was classier than living on the mainland. In the early 40s there was no bridge and one had to take the ferry to the island. You had to get there on the "Watah", as the word is pronounced in the Empire State.

Gussie and Max Schwartz

Gussie and Max Schwartz were privileged to have three highly intelligent children. Toby, Harvey and Ira. They lived within a short walking distance from our family, which made the two units interdependent – the sisters were very close and they discussed everything together. Toby, married to Joel Skurnick, had three children. Toby and I were the same age, and enjoyed being with one another. When I moved to Chicago, we wrote letters, and "caught up" with each other's happenings periodically when I visited her city. She was a truly special person. She taught in various schools and was a dedicated professional. She contracted Cancer and passed away in her 60s.

Ira, the youngest, has been a Professor at New York Medical College for many years. He married Arlene Ebner. They have three children. One day we received a wedding invitation from one of the cousins. As is my normal reaction, knowing that we would not be in the United States at that time, sent a congratulatory card along with a nominal check as a wedding gift. Speaking to my sister, Roz, a few days later, she asked me if we had received an invitation to the wedding. I answered in the affirmative and she asked, "Do you know who the *Machatanim* are? I was flummoxed and answered, "No, what am I missing?" Thus, I found out that Richard Joel, the President of Yeshiva University, has become part of our extended family! We are happy to have him … but does he realize what type of a *Chashuva* family he has joined!

Invariably, people make remarks about the child in the middle of the family structure and how unfortunate he is, because it is the older child who gets the privileges and the youngest is petted by virtue of being the last to be born. Well, my answer is … a family is like a sandwich and the best part is most certainly the meat in the middle. The top and bottom are just bread! The filling is the best and most interesting ingredient of any sandwich. So there!

Harvey is the "filling" child in that family. Harvey married Sarah Morgenstern and it was one of his best decisions! They have six children and over thirty-three grandchildren with more hopefully, to come. Harvey graduated law school, and has a flourishing law career in New York, which keeps him traveling to and from his office. He is too young to retire and he has become one of the phenomenons of business travelers who fly for business purposes on a monthly basis. Four years ago, they made another wise decision and made *Aliyah*. Even better than that, they decided to move to Jerusalem and the best of all, is that they are our neighbors!

The Wedding of My Parents

The wedding of Minnie Gartner and Izzy Ray was held on Sunday, November 1, 1931. Their wedding photo depicts a young couple beautifully outfitted. My father looked exceedingly handsome and elegant in a formal tuxedo, while my mother was attired in a lovely dress and her hair covering was a lace cloche, which is a close fitting headdress, in the style of the day. A smile played on her lips, and her eyes seemed to look forward to a charmed life of blessings, the prayer of every bridal couple.

Interestingly enough, my father is not smiling, although he had a friendly disposition, loved interacting with people and his general demeanor was pleasant. In this picture he appears to be on the lookout for something, as though he is expecting something to happen. It is not the look of the average groom. Could he have had a premonition that their lives were not to be the stuff of dreams and marital bliss? I doubt it, but he does have rather a strange look on his face.

Wedding picture of Izzy and Minnie Ray

Working to make a living, socializing with family and friends, the young couple was busy building a foundation for their new life together. Within two years, the first child, a girl, was born on Sunday, July 4, 1933. The cute, blond baby was named Judy and with her birth the family was firmly established.

War Clouds

By 1938, the world was again on the brink of another World War. The world-wide Depression of the 20s had not made a recovery and the economies of the European countries were in shambles. Life became more difficult with each passing year. History has proven through the centuries that a scapegoat to blame for bad economic conditions is always needed by the masses. The Jews, without a country of their own, have been a handy target and the world's whipping boy for centuries. Conditions for the Jews of Europe were worsening with restrictions of their movements, and life became harsher with each passing day.

America was a different story. Franklin Delano Roosevelt (FDR) was the President of the United States. In 1932, Roosevelt had created a policy of "The New Deal" putting Americans back to work via programs such as the WPA, which had the people build roads, highways, railways and every type of infrastructure. America knew very well what was happening in the rest of the world, but chose to be Isolationists. There was a huge amount of water, an entire ocean, between the two continents, and they felt that they could afford to ignore the world's problems. They had fought in World War I, helped defeat the enemy then and now, they felt that it was their turn to just prosper, have peace, and enjoy their time in the sun.

Of course, there were Americans who recognized the danger of Germany and the maniac who led them, Adolph Hitler … May his name be blotted out. However, these voices were drowned out until December 7, 1941, a day that will live in infamy. The Japanese, in a surprise attack, bombed the US Naval Base at Pearl Harbor scuttling most of the ships and bringing about the deaths of hundreds of personnel. It was a devastating experience. Today, the ship "Arizona" has become a museum and is well worth a trip.

It was probably a brave thing to do on my parents' part, at that time in 1938, but at any rate, May 9th found a new little person on the planet. I probably looked like Sir Winston Churchill, as many babies appear to resemble him at birth. But as I grew, blonde hair appeared and I guess I was as cute as any other baby girl. The blonde hair was a trait of all the Ray female cousins; even decades later and I stand by it honestly. OK, so I've had a little help from my beautician friends, but the blonde hair is (was) for real!

When I was two years old, and Judy aged seven, my mother passed away after having suffered from Cancer for a few months. Unfortunately, of the woman who gave me life, I have no memories whatsoever.

Decades later, Judy and I were in New York attending a *Simcha*. We decided that it was time that we visited our mother's grave. We drove to New Mount Zion Cemetery, which is located in New Jersey. We searched for the plot to no avail. Finally, I noticed a separate section where a good-sized tree had grown, it's roots buried deep in the grave. The tombstone read ... Minnie Ray – Wife, Mother and the date of 1940. We had located it. Neither of us had ever been there and it was an eerie feeling seeing that tree. We decided to have it removed. Ten years later, we again visited the grave only to discover that a small tree was now growing from the grave. We decided to just leave it to grow. It is the only plot that has a tree growing out of it in the entire area. Judy and I venture many spiritual thoughts as to why it was growing only there, but it is an absolute eerie fact that the tree exists until today.

Within a year, my father re-married. The happy bride was Jean, my deceased mother's younger sister. It must have been a natural changeover. My father had the same in-laws and family, while Jean had spent much of her time caretaking us children during her sister's illness.

Father Izzy, Sister Judy and Curious Ruby in the park

There is a charming photo of my father, Judy and I. It was taken in a park. We were dressed 40s style. (I do love the red and white dress that I am wearing.) I am at the bottom of the line looking up at everyone. I probably wanted to know what they were saying and itched to be part of the conversation. I don't think that I have changed much! We appeared to be a typical happy family on an enjoyable outing.

Within a year, Roslyn was born. Another cute baby girl entered the family. Judy was nine and I was four years old and of course, it was nice to have a real live doll in the house.

JUDY AND I LIVED, LOVED, PLAYED and fought together as siblings normally do. One time there was a child photography scheme in that if you took portraits of a child, the picture was then entered into a beautiful child contest. My parents fell for the scheme and you can see a picture of me seated with a bow (+ Jewel!) in my hair. That bow created much havoc as Judy for the last 70 years has claimed that the bow was hers!

I vividly remember wearing that same hair bow while we were sitting in the back of the family car arguing, while my father drove. I was so frustrated and angry at Judy that I took the blasted thing out of my hair and threw it out of the window. You can well imagine what happened next. I'm not quite sure that she has forgiven me until today! She has mentioned that incident a few times when we were reminiscing. Perhaps I should buy her a new one and repay the debt!

Another memorable incident was when we were playing ball in the living room. The ball hit a standing lamp, fell over and broke the glass bowl. Of course, we thought that the end of the world had come, expecting that our father's anger would be unbearable. But, we are still here to tell the tale. Is there anyone who doesn't have a story like that in their life?

My father was enormously talented in so many ways. He could fix anything, even standing lamps with glass bowls! He had no formal training, but was a whiz at electricity, plumbing, painting and even tailoring.

Whether it was a shortage of money or just the desire to try his hand at tailoring, I'll never know. But, one winter my father sewed two winter coats. Judy's was green and mine was red. He also made us matching leggings and hats. They were a hit and perhaps that was one incident that sparked my love of one-of-a-kind clothing creations and uniqueness in fashion. Too bad that I never won the lottery to be able to carry out that wishful thought!

I thought about that incident while attending a poetry reading. A friend, Dr. Bayla Schor, wrote a slim volume of verse in Hebrew, called *Hashira Hazot* (This Song). Every page is related and dedicated to a chapter in the Bible. In the book of Exodus, the portion of *Tetzavah* relates the required dress of the Priestly Family.

Bayla related that when she was a young girl, her mother sewed all her clothes. In the poem it tells how she lovingly chose the pattern and spent time finding the perfect material, matching thread and buttons. Her mother spent many hours at her sewing machine expertly fashioning a fine outfit for her beloved child. When it was finished, Bayla wouldn't even try it on because it was home-made – she wanted a store-bought dress. Children can be cruel and thoughtless. Whenever I think about Bayla's presentation that ended with tears not only in her eyes, but much of the audience, it comes to me loud and clear that, Thank G-D, He gave us two ears and only one mouth. Speech can do much damage; the truism, THINK BEFORE YOU SPEAK, cannot be reiterated enough.

But my dad's overriding talent was his ability in mathematics. He was akin to the best calculator, which hadn't even been invented yet. He could do any math problem in his head. Poor Dad, he was so frustrated that none of his girls even liked math. We all hated it and it was our collective worst subject. The many hours that I sat with him and he drilled me in multiplication or "time tables" could have been better spent at any subject, but not math!

In high school, when we were forced to take algebra and geometry, I truly didn't know which side was up. I couldn't grasp the principles, no matter how I tried. It was fortunate that I had the same teacher for both subjects. He knew me and understood my difficulty. At the end of the marking period, when he saw that all the rest of the subjects were graded excellent, he called me into his office and exclaimed, "Ruby, I'm going to give you a B – not that you deserve it. However, I truly think that you could take these math courses ten times and know no more than you do now." The man was correct. He didn't want to spoil my grade point average for the Honor Society, which he suspected that I would achieve. When I was inducted into the Honor Society, I kissed him chastely on the cheek for his largesse. Thank you, Mr. Newman ... I'll never forget you!

That wonderful period as a real family with Father, Mother and three children was a halcyon time. We were an Orthodox Jewish family, living on Bedford Avenue in New York and life was good. There is a sign which hangs in our home which reads, "Grant Us The Treasure Of A Normal Day." We were finally, just an everyday normal family.

The family was closely woven and spent many good times together. My Gartner grandparents lived just across the Williamsburg bridge and I recall being in a stroller and pushed across the bridge.

Zayda was the Cantor of his Synagogue, and we spent many holidays with them. Our grandfather delighted in his two blondie granddaughters and was always good for a tickle and kidding around. He called us his *Ketzeles* and made mewing sounds that sent us into giggles and boisterous laughter.

One of the morays of the time was "Going To The Catskills." Because there was no air conditioning, as it was yet to be invented, people sought cooler surroundings. New York had days that you could fry eggs on the sidewalk. August was known as "The Dog Days" while the heat and humidity climbed to unbearable heights.

The Catskill Mountains was the answer at that time. Bungalow colonies dotted the area and they were known as *kochaleins* (cooking for oneself). That meant that each family *shlepped* a few favorite kitchen utensils, pots, dishes and silverware. Everyone tried to bring as little as possible, but in the 1940s, there was no such thing as paper plates or throw-away utensils. So, a family required a supply of their kitchenware. Also, clothing for the entire stay had to be brought. There were no washing machines available on a regular basis. Perhaps, wealthier colonies had them, but for the regular folk, not even the quarter-fed machines were installed yet.

So, the ritual went thusly. During the spring, before Pesach, one had to figure out where the rest of the family was renting. The chatter centered on length of stay, cost and all the other details required for a family vacation. Then, on the appointed day, the family and all their needed possessions would be stuffed into the car or taxi.

Ferndale, in Sullivan County, was our destination that sticky, hot day in July 1943. The long drive, no air-conditioning, kids teasing each other in the back seat, and the baby crying was a common sight on the highway. When we finally arrived at the bungalow, the children immediately ran outside and probably except for sleeping, never saw the inside of the primitive structure.

The weeks passed in this manner. Family taken to the Catskills; Father returns to NY and lives a bachelor existence from Sunday to Thursday night; Returns for the Sabbath and then the process resumes. Mother takes care of the family in the bungalow colony, spending her time outside as much as possible. There were no organized programs for adults or children and there wasn't much to do, except meet with the neighbors and talk, with the ever present card game in progress. Everyone waited for Thursday night when Daddy would arrive to cool himself off and spend some vacation time with his family.

The kids had a great time playing outside not only when the sun shone, but still together when dusk fell and into the night. One of the highlights of the day was when the ice man came to fill the ice-boxes (electric refrigerators, no such thing yet). He would stop at the house, take his tongs and spear a chunk of ice. Then he would lug it into the house and put it in the ice-box. But, the best part of all was that there would be chips of ice on the ground and we were in heaven. I can still taste the ice-cold treat on my tongue. Of course, the contest was … who could suck the chip the longest without having it melt. If I ever won that contest, I don't remember it.

During the Fall of that year, my mother began to feel ill. She was diagnosed with Tuberculosis, which was a dread disease at that time. I overheard my father reiterating time and again, that he was certain that she had contracted the disease at the bungalow during the summer. I remember her only as a shadowy form lying in bed. She lingered an entire year until the holiday of *Simchat Torah*, when she passed away.

We, the children, did not attend the funeral. Even until today, I remember being in a place with giant objects surrounding me. I sensed that something important was taking place. As an adult, I realized that it appeared to be a place with standing rolls of linoleum. I asked Judy if she remembered that incident. She told me that we were being baby-sat during the time of the funeral by our Great Uncle Chaim and Aunt Manya Gartner, who owned a linoleum store.

My father had a desperate situation on his hands. He was in mourning for two wives and had the sole responsibility for his three daughters, all under nine years of age. While the family tried to help, it was a losing proposition. The old canard that says, one mother can take care of many children, but, numerous children cannot take care of one mother is so true.

Rozzie was a baby, I was five and Judy, nine years old and we needed the attention of a person who cared about us. A number of housekeepers were hired, but Mary Poppins never showed up. One was sloppy, another ignored the baby, a third was dishonest; it was a nightmare for my Dad. A solution had to be found.

It was decided that my Uncle Manny, the new ex-soldier, who was returning from Europe, would take me with him to Chicago. I was to live with him and his family. Judy would remain with my father. But Rozzie was to go to a home for children whose parents were unable to care for them. Interestingly enough, I accepted my position and went willingly. But, I was so concerned about Roz, as I thought it was an orphanage, in the Dickinsonian fashion, and I remember crying whenever I thought of her.

Many years later, Roz told me that she had a wonderful time. She became the darling of the home. There is a picture of her as a toddler, which shows a cute, blonde, well-cared for, smiling tot with a small bike apparently enjoying her playtime. She has no bad memories of that period in her life. When I heard that, of course, I was delighted, but I cannot forget her six-year old sister who was always so concerned about her.

In Chicago, I would receive letters from my Dad with a little gift enclosed. The gift was a tiny package of gum. I would write notes back in my childish handwriting, always with the request that he visit and bring my sisters with him.

The day before we began the journey to Chicago was my sixth birthday. I went with Uncle Manny to Radio City Music Hall which was akin to a palace in Xanadu, made famous by the poet, Samuel Taylor Coleridge's epic poem Kubla Kahn. It had been built in the style of the times which was to create a luxurious fairyland. They certainly succeeded. Until today, the theater with colors of red and gold, gilt carving on the walls and stars twinkling in the ceiling is one of the most beautiful and enduring attractions in New York City. The stage show was the Rockettes and their precision dancing. But they didn't impress me. I don't remember that part of the program, but the movie Dumbo made such a lasting impression on me. It's no wonder that Walt Disney was the King of animation. I vowed never to forget that memorable day, and I haven't.

That marvelous outing with an ice cream soda finishing off the day was my farewell to New York for a number of years. The train took more than two days to chug its way to one of the nation's largest transportation centers.

Chicago – Jewish Style

Chicago was another huge, bustling city. We had lived in a pleasant section in New York and I moved to a wonderful neighborhood in Chicago, The Windy City, as it is known.

The West Side deserves to have a lyrical poem dedicated to it and I intend to add my voice in praise of it. Meyer Levin, author of *The Old Bunch*, grew up in Chicago and used the city as a backdrop for his prize winning novel. He loved the city and spoke of its diversity, feeling of electricity and excitement in the air. But, I was just a small child and his description was of the outside world. My love letter is to The West Side that I knew. It was special and you must understand it to appreciate its dynamics.

Lawndale District was bordered by two large parks with a wide strip of green running from one end to the other which was known as the famous Douglas Boulevard. Douglas Park was a neighborhood park with a lagoon for boating; the boats were rented in the field house at 25 cents per hour.

In the winter, the water froze, so that ice skaters could enjoy themselves as music played in the background. Playgrounds with slides and climbing facilities dotted the park, while day camps were popular and there were activities for all. I attended these summer camps and there I not only learned to swim, but became a Red Cross-certified Life Guard.

Garfield was a more elegant park with a lagoon, stocked with fish for actual fishing and boating, beautiful formal gardens and other activities which were popular with the residents. But the jewel in the crown was The Garfield Park Conservatory, which was one of the largest under glass flower and fauna gardens in the world. The exhibits were both outdoors and inside; the riot of colors that were maintained were unforgettable, so much so, that the marvelous, unique, memory has remained with me.

The "Vest" Side was the largest concentration of Jews that Chicago ever had or will have. At one time, 110,000 Jews lived in Chicago; some 40% lived in the Lawndale District. The 24th Ward Democratic organization led by Col. Jacob Arvey brought in the Democratic vote, election after election. In 1936, President Franklin Delano Roosevelt called this ward, "The Number One Ward in the Democratic Party."

The boulevard was an extension of our homes. Air conditioning was a thing of the future and an enormous amount of time was spent there. At that time, people rarely locked their doors and during those hot, sticky, humid Chicago nights, families would sit on the grassy boulevard. It was a child's paradise, playing endless games of tag, hide-n-go-seek and jump rope, and then going to sleep on spread-out blankets. Children would then be carried home, sleeping on parents shoulders on the peaceful West Side.

Crime in that area was a rarity and police vied to be assigned there. Officer Friendly walked his beat and was indeed a buddy; he was not anyone to be feared. I don't remember a single officer being Jewish, but I do remember that before *Rosh Hashanah* we would give slices of honey cake to the, probably, Irish cop on the corner.

All activities centered around Douglas Boulevard, which became Independence Boulevard at the "Statue." This was a large bronze sculpture which featured two boys and two girls celebrating the Fourth of July, America's Independence Day. The phrase "Meet you at the Statue," was a part of our everyday language.

There were forty-two Synagogues, many built in the Masonic Style, which was the fashion of the day. They were tall, large structures with the Synagogues elegant, gilded and formal. World famous Cantors could be heard chanting the High Holiday services. At times these "stars" would be right across the street from each other! Leibele Waldman, Moshe Koussevitsky, Pierre Pinchuk, Richard Tucker and others, all held sway to appreciative audiences. There were other Jewish communal buildings along Douglas Boulevard. The Hebrew Theological College fronted the boulevard and across the way the JPI (Jewish People's Institute) stood, which was the model for Jewish community centers for decades to come.

On Independence Boulevard, the continuation of Douglas Park Boulevard, were found more Synagogues and many *shtieblach*. Temple Judea, the only non-Orthodox house of worship on the West Side happened to be third in a row following the Makarover Shtiebel and The Hebrew Parochial School.

Walking further, a few blocks over, was The *Lishka*, the head office of *Bnei Akiva* of the Midwest which was housed in the Religious Zionists of America building.

The West Side was modeled on the *Kehila* system. There were services and institutions for every need recognized at the time. Within a few circular blocks was found The Douglas Park Library. Public schools dotted the area where the majority of the students were Jewish. The High Holy Days appeared on school calendars and many were closed for the Jewish holidays. There were other community facilities such as The Orthodox Home for the Elderly as well as an organization which serviced the Jewish blind. The Marks Nathan Jewish Orphan Home was another unique institution. It housed 300 girls and boys at any given time and many of its graduates became successful and prominent citizens. I have met people who grew up in the home. Almost to a person, they were satisfied with their upbringing. Even words of praise were dedicated to the staff who dealt with these difficult situations on a daily basis.

Mount Sinai Hospital, originally established in large part to circumvent the quota on Jewish doctors and medical students, became a world class facility. Established in 1912, it served the rapidly expanding Lawndale District. By the 1950s, there were few Jews in the area, but it was still supported in part by Jewish funds. It had expanded its facilities numerous times, and was so forward in its approach, that it even conducted medical research, which was a rarity at that time.

Anshe Knesseth Israel (The Russische Shul), The First Roumanian Congregation (The Roumaineshe Shul), and Kehilath Jacob Synagogue among others were important elements of the neighborhood. Rabbi Zev Wein was the Rabbi at the Bnei Jacob Anshe Lutnik Shul, where the Hebrew Parochial School of Chicago was located in its early years. In the basement, (lower level!) we, the small amount of pupils of the only Hebrew Day School west of the Hudson River, sat in the bleak, dark school rooms eager to study. In spite of the surroundings, we did learn. In the morning, we learned Torah subjects largely taught by dedicated Yiddish-speaking immigrants from Europe. The afternoon sessions were devoted to secular subjects. The students who understood Yiddish learned the language from their grandparents. The rest of us, myself included, were caught in the web of learning in three languages, which is totally against pedagogic fundamentals and a nightmare. Here we were in the first grade and were supposed to master Hebrew, Yiddish and the fundamentals of English. The miracle is that in large part, it was accomplished. More on the HPS to follow.

The Hebrew Theological College (HTC), the *Yeshiva,* was an anchor in the neighborhood. It enjoyed an international reputation. There, young men came from not only the Midwest of America, but Kentucky and California as well as numerous other US states. There were foreign students from Canada, Panama and points south. The school also sponsored a number of young men who were Holocaust victims, and had to be treated in a special manner.

Ben Shandalov, a longtime friend, was a student at the HTC. I asked him to write his impressions, lest you think that I wrote this with very old, rose-colored glasses. This following is Ben's addition to this narrative. It is evident that we wear the same glasses!

"I was just a teenager when I came to the HTC in Chicago from St. Louis, Missouri. I met the GVS (Great Vest Side) in September of 1949. If anyone saw me getting out of the cab that took me from the train station, they probably thought that I looked lost. I kept looking around at all of the young people on the streets walking around actually wearing *yarmulkas* (nobody used the word *kippot* in those days). I had never seen so many religious kids in one place at any time back home … and walking in public with a *yarmulka*? Who are you kidding?

"Within a few days I had calculated that there were more Orthodox Synagogues between Homan and Independence (or "Indepants" as it was pronounced by the immigrants) than in all of St. Louis. But I also learned that the people were warm and welcoming to all newcomers.

"In the days to come, I would experience new worlds

and unique events. It was 1:00 a.m. on a Sunday morning, just a few minutes after the *Yeshiva* had completed saying *Selichot.* It was warm in the dorm and the windows were open. I suddenly heard singing and recognized the sounds as being part of *Selichot.* I looked out the window to see where these sounds were coming from. If you knew the West Side, you realize that the HTC, located at Douglas and St. Louis, was a full block away from the Russische Shul at Douglas and Homan, but that is exactly where the sounds were coming from. It was also warm in the *shul* and its windows were also open. The melodious voice I heard … a full block away … was actually the world famous Cantor Moshe Koussevitsky!

"Just about eight days later, I again stood with amazement as I tried to cross a street on the way to *Tashlich* at the Douglas Park Lagoon. I saw hundreds of Jews streaming along with me. Imagine, so many Jews that the police had to control traffic to let us cross the street. This may sound common and mundane today as we stand on Peterson, Devon, Lincoln, Touhy and Howard for *Tashlich,* but it was a new world at that time for a teenager from out of town. The West Side is long gone … but, never forgotten."

Whenever I think about the West Side, what comes to my mind is the High Holidays – *Rosh Hashanah* and *Yom Kippur.* The Synagogues were bursting at that time of year. Whether one was observant or not, if you were not inside praying, you were in front meeting family and friends.

The ceremony of *Tashlich* is held on the first day of *Rosh Hashanah* and it was an event we waited for all year. Whole families, dressed in their finery would walk along Douglas Park Boulevard toward the parks that were like bookends of the boulevard going toward one of the lagoons. After the recitation of the prayers, it was such fun turning our pockets inside out and spiritually throwing our sins into the water. The ducks didn't seem to mind that we did not bring any real food.

Simchat Torah was truly joyous. Beginning with *Hakafot* at the *Yeshiva*, which had the Rabbis and their students dancing and the women and girls on the sidelines clapping along – no dancing, just cheerleading. After the dancing, streams of merry people were seen on the boulevard going from home to home lifting a wineglass for a *L'Chayim* in open houses, with the goal of ending the evening at the home of Rabbi Oscar and Janette Fasman. He was the beloved president of the *Yeshiva*, very personable, but a disciplinarian when he had to play that role.

Mrs. Fasman was a perfect first lady, with many communal achievements to her name. On *Simchat Torah*, she would outdo herself. Everyone was invited to their home for the premier open house of the evening. The table was laden with every type of cake, cookie and her specialty of a seven layer cake which tasted heavenly. She always took the time to speak to us and made everyone feel welcome, and that she was happy that they came. She was a most gracious hostess and a role model for all of the future Rabbis' wives that she inspired.

At the time when her son, Chaim, was to leave Chicago to study in Israel, she became ill which, indeed proved to be fatal. He wanted to postpone the trip, but his mother implored him to leave then, in order to have the great *Zechut* of studying Torah in *Eretz Yisrael*. I can imagine how she begged her son to go and his guilt at leaving. But that was Janette Fasman; a most memorable woman.

Years later when Rabbi Fasman passed away, my husband and I went to pay a condolence call at Chaim's home. We entered the apartment where the brothers were "sitting *Shiva*" in the salon, but there didn't appear to be any other women in the room. So, I went into the kitchen and there were three granddaughters preparing meals. I started to reminisce about their grandmother and they were fascinated. Then I realized that they never met her, and that I was a historian for their family and that they were unaware of their illustrious grandparents' achievements.

After a while, the mourners came into the kitchen. My husband had told them that I was there as I also wanted to pay my respects to the family of the Rabbi. Of course, we had all known each other – we were all members of the Orthodox community in the "Old Country." I was humbled that they would seek me out, but the graciousness of the parents evidently rubbed off on the next generation. After this incident happened, I met those "Kitchen Friends," who again bewailed the fact that they know very little about their family, as no one has ever seen fit to write their story. It would be a most inspiring one. I trust that it will be written some day.

In Chicago, I went to live with Manny, Zira and Roberta, the baby. They lived on Independence Boulevard surrounded by the institutions that marked the West Side as a truly Jewish area. A few houses down lived the Neiman family. Their eldest daughter, Faigie, and I became close friends. Every *Sukkot* holiday, they would build the largest *Sukkah* I had ever seen. Every inch was decorated with holiday posters and plaques and the *schach* covered a magical display of decorations. Besides the usual hangings of Jewish stars, fruit of many kinds, tiny *shofrot* and colored paper rings, there were tiny boxes of candy and wine. It was a shining, fantasy display. The best part was that I was always invited, and sitting next to Faigie, it was like being part of a real family.

In the three-story brownstone next to them lived Cantor Kipper. He was a jolly gentleman who always had a smile for the kids living on the block. We were fascinated by the comings and goings in his apartment.

The buildings were built in the same style and they all had an extended indoor porch off the living room. These porches were used for many purposes. Sometimes they extended the length of the living room. At times they were converted into bedrooms, as in my uncle and aunt's home, which is where I slept. But in Cantor Kipper's home, it became a permanent Bridal Canopy and the traffic in and out was one of wedding parties. Once in a while, we would sneak in to watch the ceremony. As Faigie was a bit taller than me, I would have to be the one to scrunch down, so

that she could also see. What is more thrilling for little girls than
to see real live brides so close up? They appeared to be princesses
in their wedding costumes. Other kids played "wedding"; we
were lucky enough to often really be there!

I'm not certain how long I lived with my aunt and uncle
on Independence Boulevard, but I then went to live with the
Kesselman's on Millard Avenue. Their youngest daughter was
engaged to Aunt Zira's brother, and they had a larger apartment,
though I shared the bedroom with Faigie, their daughter. They
were an older couple, very kind and I was treated well.

It was there that I picked up the habit of having milk and
cookies before I went to sleep. I was a bit pudgy, but I guess then
it was cute. I think that at that time when I was seven years or
eight years old, I became a sugar addict. The psychologists could
argue that I used sweet food to allay my feelings of loneliness for
my family. But, whatever the basis, I know that the addiction to
sugar is a real factor in my life. Over the years I have probably
tried every fad diet from nothing but cabbage soup for three days
to drinking cases of Slim-Fast and every other known appetite
depressant. It has taken me many years to recognize this. In
truth, I still fight it every day.

SCHOOL WAS ALWAYS MY PASSION. When after the
searing heat of summer and the scorching heat of August passed
and with the thought of cooler September days ... it meant one
thing ... going back to school. I was excited to see the ads in the
newspapers and store windows. September meant new clothes.
Two new outfits for the *Yom Tov* season and three outfits for the
school year. We always received two pairs of new shoes ... one
for the Holidays which would then become my Sabbath shoes
and one pair for school.

To this day, I love to meander and shop stationary stores.
Picking up a brand new notebook with the smell of its pages
just about intoxicates me. Buying school supplies to put in the
new pencil box was an art. Required was two #2 pencils (yellow)
with erasers on top, one pencil sharpener, one additional eraser

that became rock hard and never worked after the first month, one blunt-edged scissors and best of all, a box of new Crayola crayons (eight) with vibrant colors. The red crayon was always the first one to be broken as it was used over and over again until it became a nub. The dark brown crayon would be almost in perfect shape when all the others had gone to crayon heaven.

In the first grade we learned and perfected our reading. I became so proficient that I was asked by the teacher to tutor other students who needed a bit of help. We were seated alphabetically and Neal Rothner was always seated behind Ruby Ray. Neal, because of illness, had missed quite a bit of school and I was asked to help him as we were seated close to one another, thus began a lifelong friendship. From first grade through college we were connected. When we were both attending Wilbur Wright Junior College in Austin, I attended class in the morning and Neal was a student in the same classes in the evening. He attended the HTC during the day. We worked out a system where we shared the same hall locker and would leave notes and books for each other. In the two years that we shared the locker, we rarely saw each other. But, it was a great system for us and it worked. I never heard of the same arrangement between anyone else.

Neal married Beata Glickman. They made *Aliyah* and our families are friends to this day. When our children were living in Israel prior to our arrival, the Rothners were lifesavers in that both Uri and Tammy were Sabbath guests in their home. The many times that Uri, on weekend leave from the army, would step through the door, have a *nosh*, put his dirty laundry in the hamper, and sleep for hours, became a family anecdote. Beata would manage to have his uniform ready for wearing, bright and early Sunday morning when he left to return to his unit. Tammy would be able to spend *Shabbat* with a caring family and not fend for herself in the Bar Ilan dormitory, which made her move to Israel definitely more pleasant.

Second grade brought a lifelong friend into my life. Rachel Babad and her family were fortunate to have sailed on one of the last ships to leave Vienna, before the gates of the European hell were sealed. Her father, Dr. Joseph Babad, became the Dean of Students (with an ever present pipe in his mouth) at the Hebrew Theological College. They lived on Douglas Park Boulevard, near the campus. Her father, mother and sister, Ada, who was older by two years, appeared to be a perfect family and best of all, they had brought a piano with them. They appeared to be well off financially, especially to a little girl living without family and toys.

Each school day, Mrs. Kesselman would give me three cents for milk money. The milk came in little bottles and you could pay two cents for white or three cents for chocolate milk, and drink it as you ate the sandwich, fruit and cookies for lunch that was brought from home. But, I had a better plan for the three cents!

Every month there were song books that were published with the printed words of the hit songs of the day. "Hit Parade", "The Songbird", "Hits of the 40s", etc. (10 cents each) were much coveted magazines among my crowd. My secret plan was that I do not purchase milk and save up the pennies in order to buy the song book magazines. This worked well and I had the up-to-date lyrics to the latest songs. I always loved to sing and possessed a pleasant voice. It was good enough for school choirs. At least I never was embarrassed by the teacher asking me just to mouth the words in place of singing out loud like friends of mine who shall remain nameless!

We were in the age group of seven-eight-nine years old when your "Best Friend" could last as little as twenty-four hours or years. There were also "Better Friends" and "Friends." Nothing was as important as your friends. We spent our time together in school, and then played outside until called for dinner. But one could safely say that most of our waking time was spent with each other learning both formally and the ways of the world, informally.

My two best friends at that time were Vivian Reiss and Beverly Branden. We three would walk together down the street, arms linked, singing the latest hit songs of the day. Not only did we love popular songs, such as "Somewhere Over the Rainbow," but as it was wartime and we also sang ...

Whistle while you work ...
Hitler is a jerk ...
Mussolini is a Meanie ...
And the Japs are worse!

AND ...

There'll be blue birds over
The white cliffs of Dover
Tomorrow, when the world is free.

There'll be love and laughter and
Peace forever after
Tomorrow, just you wait and see

The Shepherd will tend the sheep
The valleys will bloom again.
And Jimmy will go to sleep
In his own little room again.

We played tag, hopscotch, drawing the boxy form on the sidewalk, marking the numbers from 1-10 with a tiny piece of chalk. Did you ever know of a new piece of chalk not breaking immediately, leaving only little pieces with which to draw? Skipping rope, particularly, Double-Dutch was our favorite. We spent hours on this exercise. One chant that is forever burned into my mind is ...

My mother, your mother lives across the way ...
1516 East Broadway ...

Every night there is a fight
And this is what they say ...

Boys are rotten, made of cotton
Girls are dandy, made of candy.

Ishkabible soda cracker ... Ishkabible boo!

Ishkabible soda cracker ... Out goes Y-O-U!

The Douglas Park Library was one of our favorite places –
a solid, brick, small square of a building not far from school.
A series of books of the adventures of Betsy, Tacy and Tib by
Maude Hart Lovelace was a popular girls' series. Bev, Vivian and
I adopted for ourselves the characters in the books. I was Tib, as
she was blonde and the youngest. I was definitely a blondie, and
younger than my buddies by six and eight months.

One of the rooms was designated as a Youth-Fiction room.
We were zealous readers and each took out the maximum of six
books per week.

One time we made a solemn decision that we would begin with
the letter A and read every book in the room. We didn't finish, but
I think we made it to "M." It was an important undertaking and
we took it very seriously. To this day, my good friends are readers.
I try not to buy popular novels, as I go through them quickly. As
one friend remarked, "You don't read books, you swallow them."
Nevertheless, our personal library is extensive. Between the *seforim*
and non-fiction books that line the shelves, they have pushed
themselves beyond any possible future shelf space. Perhaps I
should figure out how to attach books to the ceiling!

At times, after school, we were asked to do errands. One of
our favorites was the spooky egg store. Vivian's mother baked
continuously and needed eggs frequently. On a side street in an
ancient building, down three broken, unsafe stairs, in a basement,
underneath a 40 watt bulb sat Mr. Yankel. He would choose an
egg, hold it under the light and check it for blood spots.

We would sit and watch him, fascinated by the gentleman,
sitting in the dim room, with shadows playing over the unpainted
walls. It was a dreary place.

The Three Musketeers – Betsy, Tacy and Tib (That's me on right), 1949

Chills ran up our spines with every sound that we heard. We would try to get away from the building as fast as we could, but how fast can you run carrying a bulky, square carton with two dozen eggs?

During this time, I was moved from the Kesselman's to the home of my Aunt Ruth and her soon to be ex-husband and children. It was not a happy place. My aunt, who had been so beautiful in her youth, was now a careworn, sad person who spent her time listening to the soap operas which I suppose removed her from her own plight, at least temporarily. She was dressed in the same house dress and "old lady" shoes every day. Years later, when I saw earlier pictures of her fashionably dressed in colorful clothing, it was hard to believe that this was the same person. I picture her cooking or ironing with ever present red-rimmed eyes. She became more and more depressed as the divorce loomed.

My two cousins, Sharlene and Rochelle, were just about my age and we enjoyed each other's company. My aunt was kind to me and it was as if she had three girls instead of two. But her husband did his best to ignore and exclude me. Sharlene and my birthdays were within a few days of each other. One time, we had already gone to bed, when he came into the bedroom carrying one gift-wrapped box. He sat at the edge of my bed, with his back to me, gave Sharlene the box, kissed her and wished her a happy birthday. This was his attitude toward me. Perhaps this whole experience with him was a valuable lesson, good for a lifetime. Never ignore anyone, no matter whom … no matter where … no matter the circumstances … especially not a seven-year-old child in a difficult situation.

The giving and receiving of gifts is an important element to me. I believe that it shows unselfishness on the part of the givers. Not only the time spent considering something that will be a welcome addition to the life of the giftee, but the purchasing or creating the object, the choosing and wrapping of the item. The money is truly beside the point. In my kitchen, as in millions of other kitchens of proud grandmas all over the world, there are pictures created by my grandchildren and great-grandchildren, which are priceless. I love to give gifts, in fact, I always thought that at a birthday party the honoree should give presents to his guests!

My granddaughter, Noa, brought this facet of my persona to light recently. Noa is the mother of three of our great-grandchildren. She asked me recently if I had a bicycle when I was growing up. I wondered why she wanted to know. She answered that every time we come to visit, we bring the children gifts. When they each became four years of age, we had asked if it was OK with the parents if we bought the children bicycles. I thought back to the days of our grandchildren and realized that we had been doing that for years. As each child grew to a larger bike, *Saba* and I would keep them all stocked with bikes. Besides those gifts, we would never forget a birthday. I could not fathom not celebrating birthdays or anniversaries or any *simcha* and gifts are always part of the celebration. And to my mind, a pretty wrapped box with a bow and ribbons is another way of saying ... I love you!

Of course, the answer to Noa's question was that I never owned a bike until I was thirteen. My father bought me one for that birthday, and I learned how to ride, but it was already too late for that activity. I was becoming a young lady and at that time in history, bikes were geared towards boys and were considered juvenile.

On Douglas Boulevard stood Theodor Herzl Junior College, a most imposing and important building in the neighborhood. This was a time before it was both fashionable and believed necessary to attend higher education. But, as Jews have through the ages worshiped learning, so too, was it in the 1900s on the West Side. The norm for the American population in that period was that at the age of 18, upon finishing high school, the students left the classrooms and searched for employment.

Two major Jewish institutions stood on Lawndale and Douglas Boulevard. One was the Hebrew Theological School and the second was the JPI (The Jewish People's Institute). What a great place that was! It was a very large, solid brick building and contained every leisure activity possible at the time. There were many rooms for conferences and lectures. There was also a dairy restaurant (no *kashrut* supervision and opened on the Sabbath), a regulation gym with saunas and dressing rooms, and an Olympic-sized swimming pool. There were educational courses offered, a choir and many social, educational clubs. But the best part was the roof garden, surrounded with flowers, where dances were held and the music wafted over the neighborhood on summer evenings. Many a Jewish couple met at the JPI; it was a great matchmaker venue! Some 70 different clubs met in the building. In 1932, it was made a national Historical Landmark.

The truth was that the Jews were on the low rung of the

economic ladder. The community was hard working i.e. when my father owned a grocery store, the store was open from 6:30 a.m. to 11 p.m. and he was present those hours every day.

Upon my graduation from high school, almost to a graduate, the thinking was geared to attending college, so as to assure a bright financial future. However, there were a few students who set out to find employment as their parents needed the income from an additional worker in the family.

Herzl College, with free tuition, sat smack in the center of the West Side, directly across from the "I'll meet you at the statue" fame. The percentage of Jews attending was high. The school was almost entirely Jewish as was John Marshall High School and other public grammar schools. In the 1940s, it became a training center for Navy officers. I recall seeing them in their beige uniforms and visored caps, in neighborhood stores or sitting on the grass, smoking and having a bit of R&R (rest and relaxation).

It was either VE Day (Victory over Europe) or VJ Day (Victory over Japan) as I was too young to actually remember them, but I remember an occasion, perhaps it was a Memorial Day parade, with flags flying and the uniformed Navy guys leading it down the boulevard, along with impromptu parties and loud cheering.

In April 1945, the one day that stands out clearly in my memory is of the day President Franklin Delano Roosevelt died. It was weird as all the adults were crying bitterly. It was as if the entire world was "sitting *Shiva*." There wasn't a household that wasn't engulfed in deep grief. He had won an unprecedented four terms, and many Americans knew of no other president. Because of him, even today, the Jews vote overwhelmingly Democratic, although the grip is lessoning as each American election takes place.

Roosevelt was a father figure, having led the country through the Great Depression and World War II. As far as the children were concerned, rumor had it that if he should lose the election, Thomas Dewey, his opponent, would institute school on Saturday. What could have been a worse fate? We were depressed about the whole situation.

Of course, many years later, when the fact became known that Roosevelt a WASP (White Anglo Saxon Protestant,) and a perfect example of the American upper class, which meant that his worldview was historically tinged with anti-Semitism, his actions in Jewish-related situations became clearer.

Jewish leaders begged him to bomb the train tracks leading to the death camps, but he never gave the order. In 1939, when the ship, The St. Louis, approached US shores with an overflowing cargo of displaced Jews, he refused permission to land in America. His wife, Eleanor Roosevelt, was a true humanitarian and understanding the plight of the homeless Jews, tried in every way to persuade him to give a Presidential Order to save this floating jail. But, it was not to be. The ship was sent away, back to Europe. Except for the Jews who somehow fled to England, by 1940, all of the passengers found themselves once again under Nazi rule. Their fates unknown, but it can be surmised that they perished. This was not only an indelible stain on America, but the world. There was no place for Jews … anywhere. In Canada, the saying of "Even One Jew Is Too Much" led the thinking of the day. Thankfully there has been a sea of change in the Canadian outlook and the country is a stalwart supporter of Israel.

I must share with you another institution, which was located just off the boulevard, and received little notice at the time, but played a major role in changing the religious thinking of American Jewry.

Escaping from Europe, the famed Hungarian *Chassidic Rebbe*, Rabbi Meisels and family arrived in Chicago and opened a *shtiebel*. It was a red brick, two-story building with a bay window fronting the living room on the first floor. The family living upstairs had many young children, which made it a noisy, but friendly and happy place. There was even a crystal chandelier hanging in their dining room!

The family of Vivian Reiss were followers of the *Rebbe*. Many a Sabbath afternoon, Vivian and I would spend with their children playing appropriate games in the small garden surrounding the house and having a wonderful time.

The daughter became engaged; the marriage to be performed in their garden and all the youngsters were to accompany the wedding party and take part in the procession. If that wasn't the most exciting thing to have ever happened ... I don't know what else it could be!

As explained before, we had been furtive witnesses at weddings in Cantor Kipper's home, but this one was different. Firstly, we were part of the wedding party and secondly, something else that I had never seen before. As the bride was led to the marriage canopy, her bridal veil was a piece of thick satin. She could not see where she was going! Her parents steered her toward her groom, as one would handle a boat. Very unusual goings on and I forgot this bridal veil incident until years later attending other weddings in this mode, where, it seemed to be the accepted veil style. In the interim years, the impact of this group and the Orthodox way of following the Torah went from singular incidents to mainstream behavior. In the 40s, Orthodoxy in America was moribund. Today, the Orthodox (from Latin, *Orthos Doxo*, meaning the correct way) are strong and are major players in the Jewish religious world.

In the 40s, the Hebrew Parochial School (HPS) became the first and only Hebrew Day School west of the Hudson River. In order to establish a viable school, pupils were required. This appears to be a simple statement, but it isn't. A goodly portion of the Jewish community in Chicago were comprised of immigrants; the pupils being first generation Americans. But, everyone aspired to be AMERICANS, with a CAPITAL "A", or as I have phrased it "Yankee Doodles." The people who settled here were generally from Orthodox backgrounds. However, religious practices waned in the face of lack of employment if one refused to work on the Sabbath and "Since this was a New World, did one truly have to keep the old country ways?" Of course, my answer is that the Torah is for all time. Yes, there are adaptations to modern life, but within the Torah guidelines. I am so thankful that from my great-great-great-grandparents to my great-grandchildren runs an unbroken chain of NINE generations of Torah-observant family members on both the Ray and Gartner sides. Unfortunately, this fact cannot be claimed by the average Jewish person. I consider it one of my personal blessings from The Good Lord; may it continue to be so.

At any rate, I was enrolled in HPS in the first grade. The early days of the school were held in the basement school rooms of the Bais Medrash Hagadol Anshei Lutnik Synagogue, on Douglas Boulevard. The rooms were dark and the entire place was dreary, but I guess that was the best that they could do for a first effort. By second grade, the educational building of Kehilath Jacob Synagogue, on Hamlin Avenue, led by Rabbi Meyer Kagen was the school's venue. At least not being in a basement meant that the rooms were light and airy and there were windows that you could look out with green trees in view. It felt absolutely wonderful to have classes in such luxury.

All of my neighborhood friends attended Public School. The parents were fearful that their children's education would not be on par with the public schools. Another fear, commonly heard, was that if the kids only attend school with other Jews, how will they learn to act towards non-Jews?

Nothing has changed in all these years concerning the tuition. To send two or three youngsters was and still is a big undertaking. Parents sometimes have to choose between wants and needs, such as a new family car or the children's education. It is a long term commitment. I am fairly certain that the majority of students were then on scholarship grants, but money was and still is a consideration. So, the classes were small and perhaps, that is one reason why the education that we received was good. Another was the dedication of the staff who were unappreciated, underpaid and never received salaries on time. Rabbi Eliyahu Bloch was an example of a *Tzadik*. He was the Hebrew teacher for the girls in my class for years – and I blush when I think of the problems that we gave him. We were just normal students and treated all teachers the same. Whatever we could get away with, we did; which is a universal attitude for pupils everywhere.

In fourth grade, I was living with the Kesselman family and I was, no doubt, a scholarship student. However, by that time, the school had purchased a building on Independence Boulevard. It was situated smack between the Makarover Shtiebel and Temple Judea, the only non-Orthodox house of worship in the entire West Side. The school was situated in a red brick, two-story building with a bay window jutting out from what was planned to be an extension of the living room. If the reader thinks that this description sounds familiar, it is, as most of the buildings in the area were built exactly on the same layout!

As one entered the building, there was a dark hallway. There were hooks for coats that ran the entire length of the building. Every year, there seemed to a be a forgotten dung-colored sweater left, hanging on a hook the entire school year, and it hung and hung. I wondered who had extra clothes to be able to forget such an important item. Now that I think of it, the sweater was probably forgotten on purpose. It was always so unattractive. I wouldn't have wanted to wear it either!

On the right was the salon, which became the schoolroom for the largest sized class. One semester, my class was located there and I spent much time sitting in the back of the class, in the bay window watching the seasons change. Not that I was being punished, but again, we sat alphabetically and I was an "R" for Ray, so it was back of the room for me.

Across from that room was a girl's bathroom, with the bathtub still in place. It had been covered with a heavy board. We used to scare the younger kids, by telling them that there was a body in it. I always loved scary stories and I half believed it also!

The rest of the building was converted into classrooms. In the winter, the roof leaked and we had to watch out for pails. If a window pane cracked, it stayed cracked. The desks were obtained from somewhere and there were odd initials and unfamiliar names carved into their tops. There were also some desk tops with "bad language" carved on them. It seems that the troublemakers sat at these desks. So the question is … did the words have influence and create "bad" kids, or did those kids change the desks so that they could see those carvings? I never sat in one of those places.

I was too embarrassed by the words!

The bathrooms had not been adapted to a school setting and were still family conveniences so that there was one toilet downstairs and one toilet upstairs. I can still remember youngsters hopping up and down on their feet saying … "Come on already … Ya' paying rent?"

Playing outside was great! Besides the small yard behind the school, we had the courtyard of Temple Judea. It had two sculptures and a pool with a fountain. However, I remember no water in it. One big problem was that the playing area was not large enough to accommodate all the students at one time for recess. So as the clock ticked toward 10 a.m. it was as if someone said, "On your mark … get set … go!" And we all raced to get the best spots to play in for our circle of friends. Now, that was pressure!

A Family Reunited

After three years, the big day finally arrived. My dad, Judy and Roz moved to Chicago. We were together once again, and I had a real family.

Judy was now a young lady of fourteen, I was nine and Rozzie five years old. My father bought a grocery store and we lived in three rooms in the back. Having brought no furnishings with him, he pieced together whatever he could. For the years that we lived there, my dresser was an orange crate, storage were milk crates and we used whatever we could find at hand.

I remember that first Passover when we went to Woolworth's Five and Dime Store and bought dishes, pots, pans, silverware and whatever else was needed for the holiday. The Passover Plate was a serving dish with pictures of Colonial Americans on it and there was a little boy playing a flute. I never quite put that picture and Passover together, but it was a fine plate and served the family for years.

Very interesting was the fact that there were no dairy foods served. Our custom was to eat only meat or *pareve* dishes. We children sat at the end of the table with the tablecloth pushed to one side and enjoyed our glasses of milk for the week of Passover.

Celebrating Passover has always been a mountain of work. But the weeks leading up to the holiday when you owned a grocery store were nothing short of back-breaking labor. Manishewitz and Streits *Kosher* manufacturers and distributors both had order blanks. They were printed on a large size pad of paper and every hand in the store helping with the Passover orders was valuable. I would read off the items … "Mrs. Nettie Cohen, 5 pound box of Matzah, 1 Farfel, 3 Matzah Meal, 2 jars of Gefilte Fish, 2 jars Nyafat." My dad or another worker would collect the items and put them in a cardboard box on which the name of the customer would be marked, plus the address and the floor number. Of course, third floor seemed to be the norm, and for certain, there were no elevators in our neighborhood! Then each evening, my dad and his helper would deliver all these cartons. It was amazing that he had the strength to enjoy the holiday.

The memories of our *Sedorim* are special. My dad, Judy and I read the entire *Haggadah* and would sing much of it, and once Rozzie learned to read, we were quite a choir. He taught us melodies that were written by his father and grandfather and like sponges, we soaked it all up.

Jay learned these melodies and we taught them to our children. Now when we are with the family and I hear them sing the same familiar melodies, I feel a rush of pleasure and *nachas* and of course, "*Savta* is crying again, pass her the (always available) tissues!"

By us also living on the premises, the arrangement worked well as my dad was able to care for us and work in the store at the same time. Each day, when returning from school, after Judy and I finished our homework, we would be recruited to help. I was the little girl in the long white apron and we both became adept at marking merchandise, filling in stock and waiting on customers. In the beginning, only my head and shoulders could be seen above the counter. I imagine that there were customers who were annoyed to see two youngsters working in the store. However at that time, it was not unusual as families worked together in many enterprises. We did pretty well for being a couple of kids! One thing emerged from this experience, Judy and I were never interested in having any part of a retail establishment; and this has never changed.

Of historic interest were ration books. Because it was wartime, various items were needed for war production. Goods such as rubber, steel, nylon stockings, sugar, tires, cars, gasoline, appliances of every kind and shoes were rationed. There were ration books and a stamp for each item. One was entitled to two pairs of shoes per year. You had to give a stamp for a 5 pound bag of sugar to the grocer and so on. Family cars were put up on blocks for the duration of the war, as people did not have enough gas ration stamps to make it worthwhile to run a car. Of course like in every other situation, "Vitamin P is vital." My father always had extra ration items under a special counter. If a good customer needed additional bags of sugar to bake for a wedding or *Bar Mitzvah* party, the mother of the celebrant would collect stamps from her friends and the sugar would appear like magic. It's like the old adage says ... If you know someone ... you don't need "Protekzia!"

Pussy Katz

As far as I was concerned, the best part of the entire grocery store experience were the CATS. We had two of them. They were good "ratters" and kept the premises rodent-free. I grew to love them and became a true cat lover. Most of my life we were the "parents" of a playful kitty. I know that people think that dogs are loyal and there's nothing wrong with them. I like dogs, but, *I love cats*!

When we moved to Des Plaines, a neighbor couldn't keep her cat. We adopted her and Pussy Katz lived with us for twenty years. She had a personality of her own, independent and proud, but very loving. One morning, I opened the door and there she sat with what looked to me as the "Cat who swallowed the Canary!" She looked so proud of herself as she had brought me a gift. The gift was a dead bird that she was presenting to me. I dared not scold her, this situation is akin to the psychology of raising children. It was very thoughtful of her, but not the kind of thing that you want to happen again.

Our frequent trips to Israel were of much concern vis-a-vis Pussy. Twice she was kenneled; both times were disasters. She became ill and kenneling, therefore, was not an option. So we decided to leave her at home and planned that Jeffrey Schoenberg, a *Ben Bayit*, would come to the house and check up on her. One time, as Jeffrey entered, Pussy Katz ran out. It was nighttime and for an hour Jeff chased her all over the neighborhood. He was distraught, thinking if she was not to be found, he would leave the country rather than face me. As happened, she came trotting up the walk, all by herself, when she was finished visiting her friends.

Pussy Katz

On another trip, when I returned home, I found her dried feces on my bed; two weeks worth. It appeared that she was so angry with me for leaving her alone, that she was going to show me what she thought of the situation.

She was truly angry and would not "talk" to me for a couple of days. She got over it, but afterwards upon leaving the house for a few days, I would cover my bed with plastic sheeting!

Daughter Tammy reminds me of the time that I had waxed the top of the television cabinet. All TVs at that time were enclosed in wood furniture cabinets. Pussy took a flying leap wanting to perch on top of the TV. But because of the wax job, she couldn't stop and went sailing over the cabinet, landing on the floor ... Was she surprised! We still laugh over that one.

I notice that most of what I have recorded concerns problems with her, but I believe that having and caring for a pet is a valuable lesson in kindness for children as well as adults. As a kitten, she brought much laughter watching her with a length of string or even chasing her tail. Fully grown, she brought a sense of calm and love to our home.

Son Uri, always had something "live" in his room. There were turtles and hamsters, a tank of goldfish, snails and all types of oddities; everything interested him. He wanted a bird in the worst way. One birthday that was his gift. We purchased a parakeet with cage, swing and all the accessories that a little bird heart would desire. There was only one problem ... that was our wonderful Pussy Katz who was the resident pet in the house for over ten years. What to do? The birdcage was placed in the middle of the Family Room far from any furniture where the cat could climb up and even touch the cage.

However, Pussy Katz must have sensed, or smelled that a living creature was there and would sit at the bottom of the cage for hours. The bird must have been so frightened, even though she could not see the cat that we believe that she died of a heart attack from fear of the unseen danger. That was bird #1 and when it happened to its successor, we decided that it was cruel and unusual punishment for the poor things; so no more birds. Pussy Katz remained the Queen of her turf. Jay also conducted numerous turtle funerals when they got out of their cages and got roasted by the heated radiators.

One hectic time, before *Rosh Hashanah*, I noticed that Pussy Katz was coughing, and didn't look well. The day after the holiday, I took her to the veterinarian. This same doctor had told us that if folks treated their children as well as we treated Pussy Katz, it would be a better world. At any rate, after examining her, he gave me the terrible news that she had Cancer and should be put down immediately. I was aghast at the news and couldn't accept it – Cancer ... a Jewish disease for a Jewish cat. However, she worsened quickly and a few weeks later, it was decided to follow the Vet's suggestion.

While the Vet prepared the injection, I held her tightly in my arms and looked into her eyes and whispered goodbye. She looked back at me with her beautiful yellow-hazel eyes as though she understood what was going to happen, but she trusted me.

She had been a wonderful pet and if there is a pet heaven … she deserves to be a queen there.

BACK AT MY FATHER'S GROCERY STORE on Roosevelt Road. We girls were growing up. On *Shabbat*, Judy and I would walk to our youth group, *Bnei Akiva*. It was a minimum of a kilometer walk each way, but every week we would hike there to meet our friends and spend the day with them.

Our group was named Raananah. There was another group called Techiya, which consisted of our same age girls. There was always competition between the two. In truth they had the more popular girls, but we had spirit and that counted for a lot. My group consisted of the following persons. Beverly Brandon (Serlin), Renee Goldberger(?), Phyllis Hertz (Drazin), Ethel Kagan (Tarshish), Shoshana Nadoff (Nadov), Ruby Ray (Karzen), Sharlene Rosenbaum (Balter), and Naomi Sobel(?). Malkie Ginsburg (Eichenstein) was with us just for our freshman year at the Academy, but left a lasting impression on the group.

Techiya was composed of Rachel Babad (Bruckenstein), Judy Primack (Silver), Rashi Reifer (Shnell), Timna Sharon (Lieberman), Verne Siegel (Ganz), Jackie Spark (Green) and Cissy Warshawsky (Shakowsky).

I was "good" friends with both groups and we spent the years together learning academically in the classroom, as well as from each other becoming the people that we would be as adults.

There have been so many friends that passed away young, mostly from Cancer, that I have wondered if we were exposed to asbestos in the walls of the school. As of this writing, Judy died in a car accident with her husband of less than two years at age 22. Jackie, Shoshana and Rachel succumbed to Cancer in their middle years. Phyllis recently died, Rashi and Ethel are widows. At least four of the fellows in the class have also died, mostly from the big "C" which again brings to mind the subject of a lethal ingredient in our past. However, these sad moments will occur in the distant future and we were busy growing up and having a marvelous time while we learned, laughed and loved.

Mom

I was ten years old, living with the family in the back of the grocery store. Mother's Day, was just a few days away. In class, the assignment was to make a Mother's Day card. I did my best and brought it home and gave it to Judy. She promptly burst out into tears crying, "I'm your sister, not your mother!" I felt terrible that she was so hurt. Of course, I knew that she was my sister, but she did most of the cooking and in many ways had stepped into the mother role. I was bewildered. Here, I had created this beautiful card and I had no one to give it to!

A few months later, this dilemma was solved. My father was to marry again. I knew that he was lonely and needed a wife, not only to help raise us, but for companionship. Every few months, he would dress up, looking so handsome, and go to the movies. I know that there was at least one woman who had been interested in marrying him. Sally was a divorcee with two children who lived near the grocery store. She was pretty, vivacious, but not Jewishly observant. That relationship, as far as I know, went nowhere. My father once mentioned this woman to me, as well as her not being observant, which was the reason that he would not contemplate marrying her.

Rose Lass, a woman in her 40s, blonde, petite, observant lived in New York. She had been married for a short time, but was childless. Immigrating to the US as a teenager from Poland, she originated from the same area as my sister Rozzie's in-law family.

A short while after the marriage, my father sold the grocery store. We moved to the heart of the West Side, on the corner of 15th Street and St. Louis Avenue. He purchased a delicatessen on the Northwest corner and a few feet away stood an apartment house where we rented a nice apartment on the first floor. It had three bedrooms, with Judy, as the eldest, having her own room, of course. Roz and I always shared a bedroom and come to think of it, I went from her to my husband and never had my own room. But that's a blessing and I never complained. However, on another second thought … after we married … Roz did indeed have her own room until her wedding! Hmmmm … so, she did have her privacy for a few years … never thought of it before … well, it's much too late now for any complaints!

Mom, as we called her, fit right into the family. There were never any comparisons with anyone else as she was the only mother that any of us had really known. She tried to cook healthfully, introduced us to wheat germ and vegetables of which we had never heard, (New York Stuff!) and made a home for us. My father was a more amiable sort of fellow and she was rather quiet, but, he seemed to be happy and satisfied, so who were we to complain?

Among my friends, there were times that I witnessed arguments and fights with parents. My friends would speak rudely and out of turn to them. That behavior to us children was an oddity. We were grateful to live in a normal home, and though it took a while to get used to having someone, a mother, to care about us, we would never dare to raise our voices and finally, my father would have killed us! My dad was wonderful and thankfully he was a disciplinarian. Of course, we were girls, not hyperactive boys and except for some rare incidents, we never had raging fights … never. We three girls quarreled, but the age difference between all of us gave us the space that we needed. We were at different stages in our lives and friction was not an intruder as it was in other homes.

At this time in my life, my world was school, where I was an eighth grader — and nothing was better than being a VIP! In April, after the Passover vacation, the perks of graduation began. We wore graduation ribbons for two months until they became tattered, and for the actual graduation, they had to be replaced. Autograph books were carried all over and everyone wanted the popular "cool" people to sign yours personally.

In the Hebrew Parochial School graduation class of 1951, there were four boys and three girls, Beverly Brandon, Vivian Reiss and Ruby Ray – a.k.a. Betsy, Tacy and Tib. Sadly, graduation was the end of the trio. While Bev and I went on to be lowly freshman at the Chicago Jewish Academy, Vivian moved with her family to New York and matriculated through the Bais Yaakov School system. Every year, to this day, my friends receive birthday greetings from "Tib." We have kept in touch (bless e-mail) and manage to even see each other from time to time, though they still live in America. As someone wrote in my autograph book ...

New friends are silver ... Old friends are gold
Enjoy the silver ... But treasure the gold

On the home front, we were responsible for household chores. One of mine occurred every Friday. I had to dust the wooden slats of the Venetian blinds that covered every window of that home. (THERE WERE FOURTEEN BLINDS! ... OVER 200 SLATS!) I swore that I would NEVER, NEVER have those blinds in any home that I owned ... AND I NEVER HAVE!

When we were teenagers, we did our own clothes ironing. I would faithfully iron the cotton blouses that were the style I wore each day. Roz and I shared a closet and she would borrow and wear my freshly-ironed blouses quite often, without a smidgen of guilt! She told me that on the days that she "borrowed" my clothes, she would spend a lot of time on the lookout for me in the halls of the Academy, where she was an eighth grader and I, a Junior (3rd year high school) and she never even got caught! Roz confessed to me just a few years ago. As I mentioned before ... younger siblings can be a trial!

The delicatessen that my dad owned was two blocks from the Hebrew Theological College. I was too young to appreciate the fact that the guys came for sandwiches and a bit of fatherly guidance that was served up with the food. At any hour, there were out-of-town students gobbling up the sandwiches of salami, bologna, or corned beef served with potato chips, pickles and a bottle of soda pop. Joe Shechter was one of the guys that was hired to help out during rush hour and it was always rush hour. My sister Judy had a fine time while helping in the store. I never remember her complaining about working then ... it was a good deal for her. Every Sunday morning my job was taking the streetcar and traveling to Lazar's Kosher Sausage Factory / Store and *shlepping* back salami and bologna, one of each under an arm. Judy never wanted to leave the store to do errands … can't imagine why!

Chocolate covered bananas were a specialty in my dad's store. At that time there was no factory that produced them, so we made them on an ancient stove in the back of the store. A huge iron vat was placed on a medium flame in which pounds of dark chocolate was melted. While the chocolate was melting, Judy and I would peel dozens of medium ripe bananas. Judy would then put a Popsicle stick in each one and drop them in the vat while Ruby, wearing a long white apron, standing on a stool, would stir the chocolate. When the bananas were coated, we would remove them with a tong and put them on a wax-papered covered table, then into the freezer. A couple of times, we tried to put on crushed nuts, but the task became so messy, with trying to turn them and have the nuts distributed evenly, that we reluctantly abandoned the nut idea. They were a delicacy and folks came from all over to feast on them. I can still taste them … Yum!

One day it became apparent that the neighborhood was changing. African Americans were beginning to appear in the neighborhood and the crime rate began to climb. The area changed rapidly as the Jews began to move to places like Albany Park, Austin and further to areas North, South and West.

One day, I was twelve years old, manning the counter, and standing next to the cash register, when a young fellow walked up to me, pointed a gun and requested money. I was paralyzed with fear, all I saw was a black, ugly object in front of my nose. I gave him the money and looking around he noticed my brand new, leather "Bomber" jacket. He picked it up and then I started to cry. It was a beautiful, brown colored jacket, all the rage. Everyone was wearing them and I wanted my jacket back. He looked at me, saw the copious tears, dropped the jacket, took some bread off the counter, and ran away.

My father had been trying to sell the store for a while unsuccessfully. However, after this happening, he put a padlock on the door and we left. It was simply too dangerous for us to walk to school and life became hazardous.

I was summoned to court and testified against the robber. He was jailed, but for our family as well as thousands of others, Jewish life in the West Side was essentially over.

Curious to see what happened to the neighborhood, we decided to return for a tour. The numerous beautiful Synagogues have been converted to churches, but many a Star of David and Hebrew writing is still visible on the buildings. The parks and green areas are uncared for and sections have become slums. It is heartbreaking. The Jews are historically known as the Wandering Jews. It is factual that Jewish neighborhoods are built up with every amenity ... Synagogues, community centers, ritual baths, schools and after fifty years or so, a new area catches their fancy and they are off. Almost without exception this has occurred in every State in the Union. There is the "old" and the "new" Jewish community. In Monsey, New York, there is a Synagogue built of wood, less costly than the brick and mortar buildings. The idea was that it is cheaper to leave when the Jews abandon it. A disturbing thought perhaps, but painfully true.

Camp!

When we attended *Moshava* Summer Camp in Rolling Prairie, Indiana, we had no idea the impact that it would have on our lives. It was a three-week period of intense Jewish living among our peers. We lived in tarpaulin tents, eight girls plus a counselor in each one. There was a communal dining room, the head office, and the *Bet Shimush* (archaic Hebrew word for toilets) as well as green lawns, trees, Hog's Lake where we swam and a working farm next door. The food was fine; some of it donated, which reminds me of a story.

ONE SUMMER, THE FARM just down the road had a surplus crop of watermelon. They were charitable people and the camp was the recipient of the surplus. Thus, the campers ate watermelon for breakfast, lunch and dinner and snacks. By the end of that camp period, I was so sick of eating watermelon that I didn't touch a piece for over twenty years!

However, no one went there for the food, that's for sure. The beauty of the experience was the Zionist spirit that pervaded even the air that we breathed. There were night activities with "Color Wars" being a favorite, sing-alongs around the bonfires and all manner of sport activities.

But there was one activity that was so special, that if you were fortunate enough to be part of it, it never left you. The observance of the *Fast of Tisha B'Av*. In the early evening, a mock-up of the Holy Temple, which King Solomon had built in Biblical times, was put on fire. After watching the flames go higher and higher, the campers filed into the dining room. The room was dark, everyone sat on the floor, a candle was lit for each group, flickering shadows played on the walls and ceiling, while the appropriate prayers were read in a mournful voice. The experience touched each soul and since then, whenever Camp *Moshava* is the topic of discussion … the experience of that shared hour is mentioned. Every *Tisha B'Av*, no matter where in the world I have been, whether in a humble or sophisticated setting … camp comes to mind. The leaders created an unforgettable experience that I have come to appreciate greatly.

High School

I've known many people who hated high school. They felt embarrassed and shy and teenage angst ruled their lives. But not me … I loved it!

The Chicago Jewish Academy (CJA) situated on Wilcox Avenue was my school. We spent four years studying, and growing up. It influenced our lives to the utmost degree. The day began with a coed *Minyan* at 8:15. But the Freshman girls had to scramble and finish as it was our responsibility to serve a light breakfast to the "Minyanaires" on Monday and Thursday. Classes began at 9 a.m. sharp and the long day ended at 5:30 p.m. I would arrive home at 6:00 and the family would then gather for dinner.

Now that I have stated that I adored high school, I stand unequivocally by the statement … with the exception of any class in which Rabbi Hirsh Eisenberg was the instructor. He taught the girls' classes in Torah and the highest Hebrew language instruction class. I was terrified of him … there is no other word for it. He was a born teacher and a decent person, but he conducted his classes entirely in Hebrew. He wouldn't tolerate even a partial explanation in English … and it was rough. The only person who sailed through his classes was Judy Primack (*z'l*). Being Hebrew teachers, her parents spoke the language at home, and we never cared that Judy was smart to begin with, plus the bonus of being fluent in Hebrew. She was the "Teacher's Pet." We didn't envy her, we just wanted that type of help at home also. Judy played the piano, sang publicly, was talented in so many ways and was voted Most Popular Girl in more than one election.

At the CJA, as well as every other high school, being "popular" was the buzz word of our lives. Nothing was more important than being an integral part of a group of guys or gals. Being a member of a group in *Bnei Akiva* was the fulcrum of that popularity wheel. But other spokes in the wheel included sports and school activities. There was a volley ball team, but it was very unsuccessful. Each year we would play against other private schools and we ultimately ended up in last place. There was no time allotted to practice and I guess that we weren't very skilled, but we certainly enjoyed it. Beverly Brandon and I took turns being Captain … she one semester, and I the next.

There were clubs such as the publishing of the *Bnot Torah* Newsletter. I always loved to write and was the editor of that hand-out for two years. Rabbi Meyer Juzint was the long-suffering faculty advisor of the newsletter. Meeting him in the halls, he would say in a soft voice, "Please, can I have the articles, we're a week (or two weeks) overdue!" The fact that we published five issues a year, I considered a miracle. Finally, the idea took hold that we should publish a *Tu B'Shvat / Purim* edition and a *Pesach / Shavuot* edition. Even Rabbi Juzint was happier that we were able to publish it (almost) on time. We couldn't help it if the holidays fell so close together!

There was also a Girl's *Minyan* for Afternoon prayers. We would take turns acting as the prayer leaders. When I am in the Synagogue for the Afternoon prayers, there will always be one of the men, who thinks that he is a joker and wants to know if I would lead the service. His eyebrows inevitably raise when I say that I'd be happy to, as I am knowledgeable – but it's not a good idea. I'm not sure if the jokers believe me, but the CJA (in the person of Rabbi Juzint) prepared us well.

I was always interested in the workings of the Student Council of the CJA. When I was a Junior, I decided to run for the Council and wanted to be an officer. Now, at this time in history, girls couldn't be president or vice-president; those were only male-oriented positions. Being a treasurer was also verboten as everyone knew that girls were not "good with money." So, I ran for secretary. In all the years of the school's past existence, there

Ruby and Staff of Bnot Torah Newsletter, CJA, 1954

was never a male secretary; that was a female position. That was not only just conventional wisdom, but reality. It was not until years later that the male-female idea was overturned. But I was not a rebel, so I ran for School Secretary and won the position. There is a picture of me hanging up an election poster and being helped by a little kid handing me a roll of Scotch tape. That "Little Kid" grew up to be Dr. Jeffrey Buckman. Many years later, Jeff married Myrna, they lived in Des Plaines and were not only among the best of members for our Synagogue, but the closest of friends and both were presidents of our Synagogue. A lifetime, lots of children and experiences later, we are still like family. The Buckman home is literally our Chicago area home and "our" bedroom suite of rooms stands ready for us at any time.

Speaking of teenage rebels, one of my very good friends decided that as part of her religious observance, she would like to don *Talit* and *Tefilin*. She did wear a *Talit* once or twice at the morning *minyan*, but it was a very quiet rebellion. The rest of us were not really interested, but felt that if she wanted it, why not? However, the powers-that-be felt that it was totally out-of-the-question and her protest was over quickly.

Another protest that went nowhere fast, was the study of Talmud for the girls. It had been the practice of Jewish Day Schools to teach the subject only to the boys. Every once in a while, we would sign a petition and meet with the Principal, Rabbi Rappoport, but to no avail. It was not in our best interest, they intoned. And the fact is, that instead of a *Blatt Gemorah*, we studied the Bible and are versed in the Prophets. Torah, the Hebrew Language, Prayers, Jewish History, and *Halacha* were our other subjects, but never a *Blatt*. It is noteworthy that in today's world, it is common for women to study Talmud intensively, and they excel in it. I guess that they thought that we were either not smart enough to study it or that it was "unladylike," for some reason.

As Orthodox observant young people, there were situations that occurred, which would never be a consideration in Public School arenas. There was the great "Marriage" scandal. One

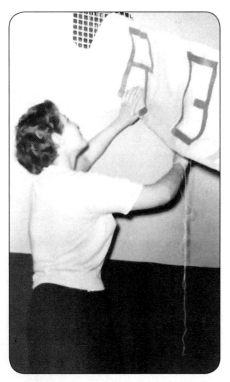

Ruby Wins Secretary Position of Chicago Jewish Academy Student Council, 1954

day in the lunchroom, one of the guys stood up on a chair, with a wedding band in his hand and declared *Harei At Mekudeshet Li* to one of the laughing girls sitting there. In front of the seventy-five students watching this "joke", she accepted his gold band. According to Jewish law, they were truly wed. Of course, the whole spectacle was meant to be taken as a practical joke, but, in truth, they were *Halachikly* wed and would have to have a Jewish divorce from each other when they wanted to legally marry. This was a real problem that secular school administrators would never have. However, it was no joke, no joke at all!

Petticoats were a fashion must for every well-dressed high school girl. The ritual was that every Sunday afternoon, a five pound bag of sugar was added to a bathtub of cool water. One by one the slips were dunked in the sugar water, hung on a hanger on the shower bar to dry. When they were dry, they were able to stand by themselves. This was fashion at its apex.

The Petticoat Revolution is a wonderful example of what passed for student disobedience in the 50s. Wearing a petticoat slip was the fashion; one wasn't dressed "au currant" unless it peeked out under a skirt. It began with wearing one and slowly graduated to wearing four, five and possibly six slips under our clothing. To exaggerate the "hour glass" figure ever more, slips with hoops were also worn. One afternoon, entering into the Rabbi Rappoport's office, two of us were caught in the door frame and because our skirts were so wide, they flew up. When "Rappie", as he was affectionately known, saw more leg than was considered proper, he issued a proclamation that no student was to wear more than two slips at a time. The students thought that it was an infringement on their rights, they protested a bit with a lame petition, but lost the argument. Fortunately, fashion fads are limited in time; petticoats were out and mood rings were "in."

One of the best ideas that I ever dreamed up was the event of the "Snowball Festival." There, of course, were no mixers or dances allowed at our school and we ached to have a fancy dress activity. I was the chairman of the Outside Committee which planned activities outside of the school. We thought up the idea of a dinner in a restaurant. There were only two *Kosher* restaurants downtown in the loop (or anywhere in Chicago) and we wanted it to be an elegant affair, so we chose Barish Kosher Restaurant, as Sigel's was too small and we guessed correctly that it would be a sell out!

The invitations, place cards and table menus had a dark blue shiny cover with the information printed on very thin onionskin paper in gold lettering. Each item sported a gold tassel. Styrofoam snowballs were the centerpieces and the room was decorated with blue and white chains and balloons. It never before or since looked so smart! Part of the entertainment was Judy Primack (*z'l*) playing the piano. Singing with her was a fellow that I had recently begun dating, Jay Karzen. He could hardly refuse then, but more about him later! Even though Barish's was on the lower level (the basement) and the piano was not exactly tuned properly, the tradition of the Snowball Festival continued for many years. Reading the Academy Alumni newsletter, I noticed that the name of the event was changed a number of years ago. But, to have that same idea being a success over fifty years is a long run that any play would envy.

History was being made in Washington. As I lived literally

across the street from the Academy, and televisions were not part of the schools property, my family TV became the venue for the current affairs class. While the McCarthy hearings were being played out on the screen, my class would sit on the living room floor watching the TV, fascinated as the politicians tried to make us, Americans, think that the Communists were everywhere and probably lived next door. Especially in Hollywood, there was a witch hunt and reputations of directors, actors, and screenplay writers were ruined. Many of the victims were Jewish – they were fired and unemployed for years. There were at least two suicides attributed to this shameful chapter in American history. And no, there were no Commies in our building and the teacher wouldn't allow me to serve popcorn!

The school was just a few short blocks from the corner of Madison and Crawford Avenue. Situated there was Goldblatt's Department Store and a few blocks of decent and reasonably priced shopping. There were trendy small stores which today we would label as boutiques. Cover Girl, one of a small chain of lingerie shops owned by the Helfand cousins joined with Madigan's Department Store and a whole host of shoe stores which carried the fashion dreams of teenage girls.

It was a time of no inflation in prices. The price of school shoes were $3.99 and "Sabbath" shoes, $4.99 per pair, but they had to have low, thin, curved heels known as "Kitten Heels"; only that type was acceptable. School shoes were of the "Penny Loafer" style. A small opening on the top of the shoe which had room for a penny coin; hence the name. We bought mostly dark brown, so that dirt was hardly noticeable. The only person who wore shoes in pastel colors of yellow, pink or light blue was Celia Schoichet (Mussman). Her mother was the cook at the HTC and Celia was a definite fashion plate in school. She was always dressed smartly in the latest fashion.

Having shopping so close to the school was a definite perk for us … but the school authorities thought differently. We were not to go there on school hours, however we never considered study periods and lunch breaks truly school time. Over the years, with all the hours we spent browsing, we probably were more knowledgeable of the location of items in the stores than some of the personnel! The only time that this system faltered was the time that I was shopping with a friend at Madigan's Department Store, when over a counter my eyes met one of our teachers. Well, win some, lose some!

One day it was announced that we were to be tested on our "Aptitude", or what career would be best for us to pursue. After the test, the teacher met with us individually. She furrowed her brow and made a statement that I have never forgotten. She didn't suggest what path I should take, but uttered those infamous words, "Whatever you do, don't marry a farmer!" Believe me that was the very last thing that I was planning to do. Farm work? That was one thing less for her to worry about! Me, a farmer's wife, never! Notice that she didn't suggest a career or even just simple employment. I was a seventeen-year-old young lady and was expected to get married and "just" be a housewife.

For religiously, observant young women, the entire subject was a joke, anyway. There were three professions open to us, either a teacher, or a teacher, or a teacher. Secretaries had Sabbath problems, early Friday exits and holiday absences as did most other choices. The thought of a career in law or medicine was not even on the radar. But, the times they were a'changin and not only were my peers interested in working out of the house, but, wanted an education.

A college education was important to us and those who desired having one, managed to obtain it. To a middle class young adult in the 40s and 50s, it was a foregone conclusion that they would "do better" financially than their parents and grandparents. A college and university education was the key and we were willing to learn, work and earn our share of the pie.

Hakarat Hatov (recognizing of a good deed) is a basic principle of Jewish teachings. It is so important to appreciate and verbalize to the people who have made a difference for good in one's life. Having been an "orphan" in a sense of the word in

Chicago during my formative years, I was aware of how much influence the community had in my life. In many respects, the Chicago Orthodox Community were surrogate parents to me. The Associated Talmud Torah, the Hebrew Parochial School, the Chicago Jewish Academy, *Bnei Akiva* and other agencies were the influences in my life and I know that I would not have been the person I am without them.

Abraham Buckman, a teacher at the Academy, had been a favorite of mine. He was a disciplinarian but it was paired with a shy smile and I always felt that he loved and respected his students. A few years after I had graduated, I learned that he, at a young age, was terminally ill. Very saddened, I decided to write him a letter and tell him how much I had enjoyed his teaching and that he had greatly enriched my education. While I was penning this note I thought about other individuals who by their ideas and untiring labor had not only added to me as a individual, but had actually created the persona of Ruby Ray. They had given me values, ideals, education, friends and an entire life. I wrote also to Rabbi Leonard Mishkin, who had headed The Associated Talmud Torahs, and Rabbi Menachem B. Sachs who were two of the many people who were responsible for the success of the Orthodox Jewish community in the 1940s and 50s in Chicago. *Todah Rabbah* sounds inadequate for such important achievements, but know that it is straight from my heart.

Jay Karzen

It was the fall of 1954 and I was reading the local Lerner Life newspaper, when my eye fell upon a picture of a fellow that I had seen in *Bnei Akiva*. He was wearing the garb of a Cantor dressed in a white robe and tall Cantorial cap. He had a wonderful voice and had spent years being part of, as well as leading choirs and had performed in numerous presentations. The High Holidays found him acting as Cantor in Synagogues not only in Chicago, but other locations further field, such as Denver, Minneapolis and Wisconsin. His name was Jay Karzen. He lived in Albany Park and he was three and one half years older than I. I had noticed

Jay, but had never spoken with him ... didn't have the nerve. He was from the North Side and everyone knew that the Northsiders were a "Fast" crowd. I was just in high school and he was a college man – at that time that difference was significant. When I saw that picture, I said to my mother ... See that picture, he's a really nice guy and popular! (The mark of a winner!) Little did I know that I was looking at the picture of my *Bashert*.

A few months later in June, a call came out from the *Bnei Akiva* office appealing to the older *Bogrim* to spend a weekend preparing Camp *Moshava* for the campers. This meant setting up all of the tents and performing other tasks which constituted hard labor. Even so, there was never a lack of volunteers as it was fun, and we could envision ourselves pioneers in Palestine (as Israel was then known) doing the work of *Kibbutzniks* to which we aspired.

We traveled to Hog's Lake, Indiana in an open truck. We sat on the sides of the open vehicle and never gave the lack of safety a thought. On Thursday evening, a scheduled *Kumzitz* with songs and the laughter almost made us forget our aching muscles. Friday morning, when the labor detail for the Sabbath meal was announced, I was in heaven. There were four of us "privileged" to be on kitchen duty ... my friend Florice Tannenbaum and I, and two young men. One was a fellow whose name I cannot recall and Jay Karzen. Well, why was I so excited? Very simple ... it was traditional for the Kitchen Committee to go for a walk after lunch. Very cozy situation as the guys would ask the girls and if you were asked, that meant that you were POPULAR; nothing else better, right?

As it happened, Jay Karzen asked Florice Tannenbaum to go on the walk! Now, Florice was in my group. She was my friend and I liked her, but not when it came to Jay Karzen! I couldn't believe it! But, guess what happened? It rained, no it poured BUCKETS, and the walk had to be cancelled. Oh well ... I don't think that I was ever so happy as to see sheets of rain turn the entire campsite into a mud field. Florice remained my friend, but to my delight ... she never did go out with Jay Karzen!

Sunday evening and it was time to return home. We climbed

into the open truck and there just "happened" to be one seat left and it "happened" to be next to me. Now, Jay Karzen is NEVER late to anything. He would rather be a half hour early than be five minutes late, but he was the last one on the truck and he sat down next to Ruby Ray.

I cannot recall the details of the conversation, but the situation was that Jay was "going steady" with a lovely and nice young lady, Judy Blumofe. She was even wearing his Friendship ring. But heavenly plans prevailed and four hours later, it was decided that Jay retrieve his ring and that I was to wear it proudly on a long chain, as was the fashion. And that Dear Readers, is exactly what happened.

We began to date and our first one found us in the Riverview Amusement Park. We had a fun time. Little did we know that the evening was the beginning of a lifetime journey together. There is a photo that we took that day, sitting together on a paper moon. It pictures two young people, he, 19 and I, 16 years old dressed in the latest fashion. I, in my favorite blue suit and "Kitten" heels, while Jay wears an ugly flowered Hawaii-like patterned shirt. His mother would buy these shirts from Mr. Aaron Teitelbaum who was a Customer Peddler and periodically came to her house lugging two packed suitcases. She would buy the family's stockings, underwear and awful shirts for the boys. I'm not certain if she disliked shopping or because she felt sorry for him, but men in his profession were fixtures of that time.

The end of the Mr. Teitelbaum story is an Israeli classic. When we moved to Israel, *Ohel Aharon*, a neighborhood Synagogue, was donated by and built in the name of the Karzen family's old friend, Mr. Aaron Teitelbaum, whose picture even hangs in the lobby. It's a certainty that only Jay knows who he was. But now, we joke that at least, the boys wore those horrendous shirts for a good cause!

Why did we go to Riverview on a date? It was a large amusement park on the North Side of Chicago and holds fond memories of happy times for thousands of young and oldsters alike. It seemed to be a fairyland of dreams, kind of place. There was a wonderful merry-go-round that was built for the Chicago Exposition in the early 1900s with its galloping horses, but included benches for the timid. "Aladdin's Castle" was a place where you could see yourself in weird mirrors, and the exit was a roll of drums that rolled you down and out of the building. There were exciting rides such as "Shoot The Shoots" where the boat would slide down tracks and you were always wet when alighting from the craft. Roller Coaster rides such as "The Bobs" and "The Silver Streak" elicited shrieks of excitement. Of course, there was the old standby, "The Tunnel of Love" with canoe-like boats sailing through a tunnel. That was the most erotic idea in the whole park and symbolized the times. It was a period of such innocence, which is even hard to imagine today.

Many booths such as "Lady Nina," who told your fortune, games of skill, where winnings were stuffed dolls, as well as freak shows and oddities of every genre could be found. Food of various kinds was offered for sale, but not *Kosher* and we always had to bring our lunch and even snacks. But for the rest of the world, ice cream, donuts and cotton candy were on the menu. It was a child's garden of delights, experienced in bright and garish colors. It was fun and every youth group would go on a day trip a few times a year. Monday, Wednesday and Friday were two cent days and Tuesday and Thursday cost five cents for entry. Seventy years later, Jay remembered these prices and was able to rattle them off without any hesitation. The park closed in the 60s, but the memories are priceless. It was an ideal venue to spend a pleasant evening and that's why we probably spent the first few hours of our lives together in Riverview Amusement Park.

School started again in September and I had the world on a string. I was a senior with all the privileges that went with it. Best of all, senior year in Illinois does not have Regent Tests clouding it like in New York. Graduation loomed and a good part of the year was spent in preparation for the big day. We were busy publishing THE ACADEMOCRAT which is the senior yearbook and all the activities connected with leaving the school where we had truly matured. We had entered at the age of thirteen, green behind the ears, and left at seventeen, mature adults, or so we thought at the time.

I also had a "steady," and nothing did more for your self esteem and popularity (there's that word again!) than a boyfriend who took you to not only movies, bowling and parties with his "older" friends, but to the Chez Paree, an actual nightclub, which was a product of the 40s and 50s and today can only be seen in the movies. And he had a car! No traveling by bus or streetcar ... my guy picked me up in his own green Chevrolet and that was impressive!

Our courtship was conventional, but exciting to me. I soon met my steady's best friends, Burton Wax and Maxima Schwartz among others, with whom he had been lifelong friends. We would double-date by attending movies, bowling, miniature golf, live theater performances and get-togethers at each other homes. Every Saturday night we would go out, that was Date-Night. In the winter we would have a long evening to be together, but in the summer, I would oftentimes arrive home at 2:30 a.m. This infuriated my father, but I would tell him that Jay wouldn't get home before 3 a.m. as he had to drive to his home in Albany Park. It never mollified him, but frankly I couldn't think of anything else to say except the truth!

The times that Jay and I spent an evening at my house, my mother would pass the living room doorway every half hour. She was *shlinging* aspirins, as she called it. How many aspirins can you take in two hours? Of course, she was keeping an eye on us ... this was dating 1955 style! We still laugh about this.

Jay was supplementing his income from teaching Hebrew School with private *Bar Mitzvah* lessons. On Sunday evenings, he was teaching a pupil nearby my home and would join us for dinner. My mother had a new toy; it was an electric bar-b-que, known as a Rotisserie and she would broil tenderloin steak every Sunday night. Unfortunately, she liked it WELL-DONE and it came out dry, stringy and overdone. The family was used to it and we enjoyed it tremendously, but Jay couldn't tolerate it. The problem was that he was at his girlfriend's house and her mother was so proud of her new appliance, but the meat just stuck in his throat. What to do? So he ate it and then would go into the bathroom and vomit it back up. Not a happy meal for him. Luckily, however, the Kid's big day came in a few months and the Sunday evening torture sessions were over. Jay was very thin and my mother always wanted to fatten him up with a good, hearty meal. I was unaware of this problem until afterwards and of course, never told her what happened with her "hearty" meals.

There was good news and bad news during this time in the Ray household. My older sister Judy had married a young man, Aryeh Levin, from Louisville, Kentucky, who was at the HTC studying for Rabbinical ordination. He fit into the family immediately and was welcomed like a son. Over the years, Aryeh, who became a pulpit Rabbi, served congregations in Manitowoc, Wisconsin and Memphis, Tennessee. When they moved back to Chicago, we were happy. As it happened, it was the only time that we were to live in the same city as adults.

The sad news was that after Judy married, Aunt Ruth who had been living in a mental institution became ill with Cancer and came to live in our home, occupying Judy's girlhood bedroom. She lived with us until the severity of the illness required hospital care. By that time, our wedding was coming up and I never did have a room of my own … I was trading Rozzie for Jay … can't complain about that! At least, he would never wear my freshly ironed blouses!

Among the most stressful times in life is meeting the prospective in-laws. Jay and I had been "an item" for a number of months, learning about each other and happy with the knowledge. He had met my parents when he would pick me up for a date, but I hadn't met his as yet. Then I received an elegant formal invitation to his brother's *Bar Mitzvah* party. Not only would I meet his parents, but the entire Karzen "Klan." The party was to be held on Saturday evening at a hotel and I was terrified. I sat on the couch all day and the amount of tears that I shed were only dwarfed by the rainstorms that fell all day. It was an absolute *mabul* outside, but I couldn't worry about riverbanks flooding over or flooded basements … I was miserable and my parents could not convince me otherwise. I felt like I was being led to the gallows as my dad drove me to the affair.

Of course, what happened was that his parents, brother and sister became my family that evening. They took me to their hearts and it has remained so until today. After the wedding, Max became Dad and Yetta became Mom. Sandy was the younger brother that I never had and Ilene, another younger sister. Ilene was thrilled to finally have a sister and our families welded together beautifully.

Dad and I had a very special relationship. I was his daughter-in-law for over 25 years and there was never a cross word between us. The one disagreement that we had concerned my going back to work. Dad was a product of his generation who considered it demeaning to the husband for a wife to go out into the world and work or have a career. But, that was the time that women began to be serious about their careers and jobs, and the old thinking wouldn't fit the 1960s young women. Every year for my birthday, he would buy me a bottle of L'Air Du Temp created by Nina Ricci perfume because he knew how much I loved the scent. He was a gentleman of the old school, dressed well and rarely lifted his voice. He reminded me of the film stars Fred Astaire or Clark Gable with their elegant demeanors and I loved him without reservation.

Yetta / Mom had a totally different personality. She was a product of her generation and had never worked outside the home. She was a marvelous baker and cook, looked after and reared her children to the best of her ability. For countless years, as a Sabbath gift, she would send over a honey cake at the appropriate season or an upside down pineapple cake. The problem was that no one in our family liked honey cake and we were tired of the pineapple cake.

After some years, we tried to hint that perhaps she should bake something else, but she never caught on and our neighbors became used to and looked forward to her cake each week. But she truly was a magnificent cook and baker, and when I heard

Parents, Max and Yetta Karzen with "Young" Karzens

that one of the local organizations was printing a cook book, I sent recipes to be printed in her memory. Over the years she shared many recipes with me in her own handwriting. They are preserved and I intend to hand them down to the next generation. I consider them treasured heirlooms.

Employment

The year of 1954 was a pivotal year in my life. I was a graduate of the Academy, was searching for a real job, and was scheduled to attend Wilbur Wright Junior College. It was the first time that I was in the world of non-Jews, interacting with them on a daily basis.

When I first started college, it was September and immediately I was faced with the problem of my non-attendance during the High Holidays. I went to the Dean of Students, whose name was Dr. Sabat. I started by telling him that I was Jewish and needed a pass for those days. I also added that I was engaged to a Rabbinical student in order to emphasize how important it was to me. He smiled and said, "How are Rabbis Regensberg and Rogov?" I stared at him dumbfounded. He then told me that he had been a student at the HTC for some time, but had left to pursue his chosen career. Of course, his name was Shabbat originally, but had been Americanized. Like so many Jews at that time, their names were changed as they sounded "too Jewish." Especially famous people and many Hollywood stars, producers, directors and others were "Of The Tribe," but the fact was generally unknown. Everyone wanted to be a "Yankee Doodle" (a real American) in every facet of their lives.

P.S. As to the Dr. Sabat story ... of course, I received my holiday pass!

Teaching Sunday School was the employment of choice for our crowd until we graduated from high school. One year, I was teaching at Rabbi Starr's South Side school and happy to have the job. But, only a 16-year-old could survive this schedule. I was dating Jay and date-night was only Saturday evening. In the summer months, by the time he traveled from his home in the Albany Park neighborhood to Garfield Park area to pick me up, it was a minimum of 9 p.m. I would return home at 2 a.m. and enjoy fours hours of sleep. Arising at 6 a.m. I would then proceed to take a bus to the Loop, catch the subway (the "EL" in Chicago speech) then take another bus to the Synagogue. After classes, I would reverse the trip and return home about 2:30 in the afternoon. I earned the princely sum of $25 which included the fares which I paid.

Finally, it was time for me to be seriously employed. I searched for an afternoon or evening part-time job which would allow me to attend college in the morning. It was tough finding one. I answered an ad for an opening in an insurance company. As I was being interviewed, the phone rang and I heard the gentleman say, "But she doesn't look it." I inquired whether the question pertained to my being Jewish. The answer was yes. I arose from the chair and said to him in a frosty voice filled with a 17-year-old's righteous indignation that I would never work in a place where race or religion were a factor in one's employment. I knew that insurance companies particularly were racist, but here was the first-hand proof. I flounced out and that was that.

I finally found a real job with a boss, a desk and responsibility. I was a part-time secretary for the Board of Jewish Education in the High School of Jewish Studies Division. Dr. Yosef Schub was the head of the school. He was a gentleman of the old school, very kind and fair to me. The students were a good group. The school was downtown, meaning that I traveled to the Loop each day. But the worst part was that in this old building, in the evening quiet of the offices, I could hear the rats scrambling up and down in the walls. That was creepy and the fact is that my worst nightmare is and has always been rats and mice. I am surprised that I lasted as long as I did.

However, the next year I began teaching Hebrew School and taught at the Torah Center which was located in the Lakeview Jewish Congregation near Broadway and Lake Shore Drive. Herman Davis (*z'l*), the Rabbi, was a fine person and was devoted to his congregation, as well as to Jewish education. He would make an effort to meet with me and point out interesting facets of Judaism with which I shared with the students. Most of my friends also became Hebrew teachers. It was a natural for us and it was perfect for our schedules. We were attending college in the morning and teaching in the afternoon.

But, truthfully, what did we know about teaching? My class was the highest grade. They were *Bar* and *Bat Mitzvah* age, which meant that they were 12 and 13; I was just five years older than they. They spent the most responsive time of their day, from 9 a.m. until 3 p.m. in Public School and then tired and resentful, they were forced to sit for two more hours in another classroom, learning what most of the youngsters couldn't care about in the first place. It was a difficult situation for both the students and teachers. I had the normal amount of discipline problems, but I do remember that period of my life pleasantly.

Mr. and Mrs. Jay Karzen

Jay and I became engaged the following year in January 1956. We were to live in Albany Park and I decided to find employment closer to our new home and was fortunate to be employed at the

Bnai Shalom Congregation. The congregational Rabbi was Alvin Kleinerman (*z'l*) who had been my teacher and principal at the Hebrew Parochial School on the West Side. Again I was given the highest class, which is probably why I am inordinately familiar with the *Bar Mitzvah* portion of the service.

There is a joke that Allan King, the comedian, used to tell about the time that his son became a *Bar Mitzvah*. The family heard his son practicing over and over for months. By the time the celebration arrived, even the maid and the family dog could recite it!

That school year passed pleasantly enough especially as our wedding was on the horizon and I was presented with wedding gifts. There are bowls and a few items that I am using until today – 58 years later. I haven't seen any of these students and lost track of them. But know that if you are reading this and were once a student in my class in the school year of 1955-56 and your mother had you gift us turquoise-colored oval serving dishes for a wedding gift, you share our lives in Israel. You most certainly received a thank you note from the newly established Karzen family, but again *Todah Rabbah* on your mom's thoughtfulness.

The year 1956 was a time of attending school, teaching school and being engaged to Jay Karzen … what could be better than that? I would write MRS. JAY KARZEN over and over again listening to lectures in class. I could never fathom not taking his name, not joining it to my own. I was legally Ruby Charlotte Karzen until I decided to drop the Charlotte and become Ruby Ray Karzen. It sounds lyrical and currently appears on my business literature. It was fun showing off my new diamond engagement ring, and like other engaged girls who would run their fingers through their hair, all the while splaying their fingers so that the ring was visible! It was a thoroughly enjoyable time!

It was a true-to-form Chicago winter, with cold weather, snow, icy sidewalks and dangerous driving conditions. But January 1956 was the worst of times and the best of times. Two weeks into the new year, Jay's maternal grandmother, who had been living with Jay's family, passed away. We had decided to marry and were planning on becoming engaged at the end of the month. His parents not only approved of me, but had taken me to their hearts.

Jay's extended family of paternal grandparents, Aunt Dorothy who made her home with them, and the various aunts, uncles, cousins became my family.

To Jay's paternal grandparents, I was known as Jayzie's girl. He was the apple of their eye and I was happy to go along for the ride. Jay had already purchased THE RING (I only peeked at it once!) and my future in-laws gave their approval wholeheartedly.

On January 31, 1956, Jay graduated from Roosevelt University. There was to be a get-together at his house and the guests included my parents and siblings. I knew that this was it! Finally, after all the waiting and deliberating ... I knew that he would formally propose. On the way back from the graduation, he stopped the car, took out the ring and shared this beautiful thought with me.

The Rabbis relate the interpretation of *Chut Hameshulash*, which is a tri-braided rope. Three things happening concurrently bring blessings. One, he graduated college, secondly, he was to enter the Rabbinic school program of the HTC and third, we were to be engaged to marry. I was delighted with his proposal ... it was spiritual, fitting and beautiful. I would have hated to fish out a diamond ring from a cup of yoghurt or pudding or something else runny. The ring was beautiful ... just what I wanted – a marquise diamond with two baguettes, one on each side and a matching wedding band that encircled the engagement ring.

There were no words to describe my happiness. I was engaged to a wonderful guy with every attribute that I thought would ensure a perfect life. He was kind, considerate, generous with his time and money, and I thought that he was marvelous. I loved him so much. One time I was speaking of him to someone with the ever present stars shining in my eyes, and the cynic asked, "He does put his pants on one leg at a time, doesn't he?" Nuts to him! I was 18 years old and in love with Jay Karzen and truth to tell, in love with love itself. Nothing could dampen my attitude!

Everything fell into place as planned. We counted the days until the wedding. The 11 months, and 29 of our engagement days did pass, but slowly.

February 22nd was President Washington's birthday and it is well known for its sales. A few days before, my mother suggested that we *shlep* to the South Side of Chicago, where there was a Margie's Bridal Store. The ad in the newspaper claimed that unbelievable sales were to be held to celebrate the holiday. So, off we went ... the three buses that we took meant that we were traveling for two and a half hours each way. But we did find THE DRESS.

The lace and seed pearl confection is pictured in our wedding portrait. It helped fulfill the hope of every female on earth ... to look like and to be "Princess For A Day." Grace Kelly, the actress, who had recently been married to the Prince of Monaco and who my mother always claimed that I resembled, had nothing on Ruby Ray. The dress was ON RESERVE for ten months. Jay drove me to pick it up, but, of course, he never got a sneak preview of it.

Interestingly enough, after I wore it once at our wedding, the dress hung in the closet for 30 years. When we made *Aliyah*, it was given to a *gemach* for newly arrived Russian brides. I hope that whomever wore it was as happy as I was ... Now that is a blessing!

Planning a wedding is always an interesting time in one's life. There are discussions about every aspect of the evening and every bride looks forward to the PERFECT wedding. Couples should spend more time thinking about what happens after the six-hour party than color schemes, menus and whom to invite – but they don't. I've often thought that if a couple is able to maneuver the shoals of the rocky strewn river of that supposedly perfect affair without recriminations on both sides of the family, they should receive a medal of diplomacy.

I had the PROBLEM with the dress, my future mother-in-law's dress, that is. The color scheme and style for the bridesmaids and other female attendants that I was dreaming of (brides are like that!) were planned to be short, calf-length pastel-colored dresses. All the attendants agreed and purchased short cocktail dresses in colors of pink, yellow, light blue, light green, and so forth in accordance with the bride's wishes. After all, why not?

We were all to go through the same exercise eventually and I was prepared to accede to my friends' preferences when their time came. Perfect, I thought. However, one day my future mother-in-law excitedly showed me her choice. I think that I blanched and turned white. She held up a full length long, deep purple frock! *Oy Vey!* What to do? There went my perfectly color coordinated bridal party! Sometimes, once in a while, we do the right thing. I just smiled and said that it was beautiful and that she would look lovely in it. Of course, she wore it. It did look magnificent and she was happy. My girlfriends who knew the situation gave me an "A" for diplomacy. *C'est La Vie!*

The Sabbath before the wedding Jay was called to the Torah. Candies are thrown at the celebrant to wish the couple a sweet life. The solemnity of the Synagogue service was broken when he took out his handkerchief, waved it at the crowd in a gesture of surrender!

Besides the hiccup with the purple dress, all the rest of the *Meshugas* occurred as planned. The men wore Midnight Blue, Tony Martin style, with satin collar tuxedos and indeed were a handsome lot. There was a least one *shidach* made that evening. Phyllis Hertz and Avrum Drazin saw each other in a new light and married a year later. Could it have partly been their appearance or clothing? They had known each other for years, but they had their "Eureka" moment at our wedding.

The wedding party was large and consisted of our parents, siblings, Jay's grandparents and chosen friends. The bridesmaids were Eileen (Levin) Braverman, Phyllis (Hertz) Drazin, Rashi (Reifer) Shnell, Maxima (Schwartz) Wax, Judy (Ray) Levin, Matron of Honor and Roz (Ray) Zuckerman, Maid of Honor and lastly Ilene (Karzen) Pondel, Junior bridesmaid. Rachel (Babad) Bruckenstein was in the year of mourning for her mother and she was an honorary bridesmaid, fixing my train and other tasks before I walked down the aisle. The ushers were Zvie Liberman, Willie Lewis, Burton Wax and Marvin Zissman. Sandy Karzen was the Best Man and they were indeed a distinguished looking group.

December 30, 1956 finally arrived. It was a beautiful, mild Chicago winter day with an azure sky and fluffy white clouds dotting it. The room was set up beautifully, but the aisle was placed on the diagonal creating a shorter walking distance. To this day, Jay remembers this detail that irked him, but I was immune to any criticism. The guests were seated and impatient since we began one hour and a half late. Why, I have no idea, but the taking of pictures and the signing of the *ketubah* must have taken longer than we anticipated. Finally we were lined up to begin the procession. The music began and our friends began walking slowly down the aisle.

The music then changed and I stood at the head of the white, flower-strewn aisle as the white wrought iron gates slowly opened. I surveyed the room and saw all of the upturned smiling faces and then it hit me … Did I really know what I was doing? I was 18½ years young, but I did love him with the starry-eyed kind of love. He was a great guy, but forever is a long time. Nevertheless, with all these thoughts running through my head, I approached the *chupah* and just went with the flow. The ceremony was traditional with the Rabbis, who were Jay's teachers, officiating. One humorous moment was when the blessings were being chanted. The Rabbi made an error reciting the one after exiting the lavatory instead of the wedding blessing. He immediately corrected himself, but that gaffe brought forth chuckles which softened the solemnity of the ceremony. Jay's breaking of the glass brought forth the traditional cheers of *Mazal Tov* from the exuberant audience.

After the ceremony, everyone was kissing and hugging and all of a sudden, it became silent. A space opened in the crowd and it was apparent that someone had fallen and was lying on the floor. Jay's grandfather had suffered a heart attack and was surrounded by gawking guests. He was rushed to the hospital – four months later he passed away. Thankfully, there is picture in our wedding photo album which shows him and the *Bubbe* happily walking down the aisle smiling at their favorite grandson, their "Jayzie." Our wedding had been the primary topic of conversation between them for months. I will forever be grateful that they both lived to participate in the festivities of that wonderful day.

In Times Square, we bought a mock newspaper with the bold headline ... Karzens Hit New York On Honeymoon. We were scheduled for two weeks, and they were filled with activities every minute. Jay wanted to sample every *Kosher* eating place, as restaurants in Chicago were

The Magic Day!
December 30, 1956

scarce. We did a pretty good job of it and sampled Ratner's, Shmulke Bernstein's and Poliakoffs, but Lou G. Sigels was our favorite, and I can still taste the sour pickles and sourkraut that were served at every meal.

We went to the theater and saw "Candide" (thumbs down) and the huge hit of the year, Cecil B. DeMille's "The 10 Commandments" starring Charleton Heston. That movie and its depiction of G-D writing the Commandments with a fiery finger and the parting of the Reed Sea left such a deep impression on viewers that truth to tell, even today, it is believed that those scenes were realities and that is the way in which it must have really happened. Also, there was a sign which brought a chuckle. It read ... *Thou Shalt Not Smoke.* The movie won every award that year and even the sign was mentioned.

Why was the sign unique? Because this was the era of the 50s; people acted properly and humor in public places was unknown.

There were no stores with clever names – this idea would not evolve until the 60s. It is a fact that the 50s was a dour generation, being and acting "Proper" was a full time consideration. Headed by Dwight D. Eisenhower, the elderly President of the United States, people acted in a conservative, even stuffy, fashion. Women wore hats and gloves on every occasion. Short gloves in every color of the rainbow to match the outfits were worn even to the Synagogue. Long white gloves were a must and even into the next decade, they were donned along with full length frocks that were worn to formal occasions. In my Academy yearbook, next to my photo under "ambition" is written the words "millinery designer." The movies of the time glamorized hats, especially with large brims. To this day, as I have a "Hat Face" I enjoy wearing them tilted to one side – it is my trademark. In the Synagogue, over the years there have been women who copied my style. Well, as "Imitation is the sincerest form of flattery," I just chuckle to myself, and enjoy the moment.

The two weeks of our Honeymoon passed rapidly. My aunt and uncle, Laizer and Minnie Gartner made *Sheva Brochos* for us. It was a marvelous event with the gathering of the Gartner clan. They honored the memories of both my mothers, who had been sisters and maiden name had been Gartner. The situation was a bit odd, but the warmth that exuded from the gathering was certainly a way to be *sameach* the Bride and Groom.

I had another important task to perform as well as to enjoy my "Bridal" status. We had chosen the wedding date because it was part of college winter vacation and I had final exams two weeks after we returned. I dragged my textbooks and tried to study a bit, but it was a lost cause. Honeymoons and finals don't mix very well … but I did try (not too hard, I admit!).

Frankly, I couldn't wait to return to our jewel of an apartment, to begin playing house for real. We had fixed it up with care and each item was chosen lovingly. Places were found for the numerous wedding gifts that guests had sent. Prior to the wedding, once the invitations had been mailed out, it was a joy to return home. The delivery man from Marshall Fields Department Store knew the way to our home without an address. Each day, upon returning home, festively wrapped gifts were waiting for me and I had a wonderful time unwrapping all the presents. It was uncanny as if guests sensed that we would have an "open home" and many serving items were to be needed. We received serving trays in every material from silver-plated to ceramic to wood, a crystal punch bowl, pitchers, candy dishes as well as religious items. Boy was that fun … it was like having a birthday every day! Most of the gifts are still in use today and I have recently decided to pass some along to be used in the newly established homes of our grandchildren, as they marry one by one by one.

We received no sterling silver pieces, but many items that were silver plated. The unique process of silver plating, known as Sheffield Silver and very much resembling sterling had been invented in the late 40s and was popular. The pieces were luxurious and made elegant gifts. Years later, in Israel, we found that one of our neighbors, Simon Krause had actually created the process and that he was from Sheffield, England. Thanks to the brainchild of Mr. Krause, who was an octogenarian when we met, we have enjoyed the use of these luxurious items that we never would have owned without his expertise. It is a joke on Diskin Street that so many of us who married around the same time, owned identical pieces, whether we hailed from New York, Chicago, or London. Mr. Krause was well aware of his achievement and smiled as he accepted the accolades of us all.

Too young to know better department: Among the gifts that we received were a set of tea cups / cake plates in soft pastel colors in an antique style. I thought that they were ugly and couldn't appreciate the beauty of the design.

I returned them to Marshall Fields (where else?) and bought an electric frying pan which was a brand new kitchen item, which had recently entered the market. What a mistake! Not too many years later, it became known that frying food is the least desirable method of cooking. In addition, when we lived in Iowa, I became aware of antiques and regretted my folly with the frying pan, which by then had been relegated to a rummage sale. It appears to be fate that I now actually own a set of cups similar to those that I foolishly returned. After the passing of my father-in-law, and Yetta was to live with Ilene, their household items were dispersed among the family. I requested nothing but the set of twelve cups and saucers, each individually styled, that were presented to my in-laws upon their 40th anniversary. The cups also made *Aliyah* and are in a place of honor.

Prior to the wedding, when we were in the process of fixing up the apartment to suit our needs, Jay, shoeless, was standing on a small ladder trying to fix a closet shelf. The phone rang and as he alighted from the ladder, hit his toe on it and the toe smarted. He picked up the receiver and when his mother found out that he was without shoes, said that she was coming right over. What could we be doing alone in our apartment and he shoeless! This was a week before the wedding. Indeed, how times have changed!

At 4925 North Albany Avenue, in the neighborhood of Albany Park, Chicago, we found the perfect apartment. It was one bedroom and one bath, but it had a small eat-in kitchen, a formal dining room and a good size living room. Perfect for a couple starting out. One problem was the old-fashioned refrigerator and stove that were in the kitchen. When the landlady heard that I taught Hebrew School, she enlisted me to give her daughter, aged nine, Hebrew lessons. In exchange, we would receive new appliances. I was delighted with my new toys and was happy to reciprocate with the instruction. The daughter was totally uninterested in learning anything and after a very few lessons did not want to continue. So, the upshot is that I had sparkling new appliances and no student. It was her choice and the landlady never held it against me. The daughter should have been in Hebrew School in the first place where she belonged!

The kitchen was outfitted, but we did buy some furniture. Unbelievably, those pieces for the most part are still in service. We bought a sofa that opened up to twin beds for the company that we expected. That sofa has been upholstered four times in fifty-six years and is an essential part of the décor of our living room. The desk and chair that was bought at the same time as the sofa, stands next to me, right now, at my elbow and is still bearing its load of papers and other paraphernalia. The black-stained Mahogany bedroom set is one that we use each night and I still admire its sleek lines all of these years later. The point is that if you buy decent pieces they should last many years if treated with care. I must add that this furniture was not costly. We had little money, but they were looked after lovingly. As a new wife, one of my favorite activities was waxing the new furniture even though it didn't need it. I dusted and waxed until I was afraid that the wood would disintegrate and I would be waxing just wax!

We also bought two side tables and a coffee table to match our sofa. However, they were the exact height of the two toddlers whose favorite activity was gnawing on the wood. The finish disappeared and when tiny tooth marks became the design, it was time to purchase new ones.

Cooking was a challenge which I had to master. The first dish that I wanted to prepare for my brand new husband was to broil a steak ... that was and remains his favorite meal. I removed the steak from its wrapping and looked for the broiler. I couldn't find it. Not that the new oven was so overly complicated, but I didn't know the first thing about cooking! All my life, I was busy at school or work while my mother prepared my dinner. I didn't know a thing! But I did figure it out. It must have been tasty and my husband was happy.

However, it didn't always work out so well. My sister Judy had given me the all-time bestselling cookbook, "The Complete American-Jewish Cookbook." I spent time perusing it trying to find simple recipes that I could handle. One evening, I prepared a casserole that included the ingredients of lox, potatoes and milk, (p.280). What could be bad? We liked them individually ... BUT NOT TOGETHER! It was absolutely awful and until today when we discover that a food is uneatable, we compare it to that early concoction ... that awful tasting casserole comes out the winner every time!

The casserole was a disaster, but after it was tossed in the garbage, that was the end of it. Not so, the CHOPPED LIVER fiasco. After a few months of spending the Sabbath with my family or his, we decided that it was time to spend Sabbath by ourselves. I was going to prepare a proper meal beginning with chopped liver.

Jay arrived home after the Friday Evening Sabbath services and we sat down for the traditional meal. After waxing divine over the chopped liver and declaring it the best that he ever ate, Jay casually inquired how long had I broiled the liver? Broiled the liver? Why would I do that? Mr. Fleisher, the butcher, *kashers* everything. I don't have to do that. "I don't even know how," I exclaimed. Well, needless to say, my new frying pan was *treif*, as well as the utensils that I had used. Luckily, the liver was cold, but I had to put the plates away for a year. Now, not only did I come from an observant home, but I had been in religious Jewish Day Schools all my life. How could I not have known? Very simple … In my time there was no instruction in how to keep a *Kosher* home and no teaching of a practical course in *kashering* meat, an act that was still very much performed in the home. A number of years later, the CJA, introduced a home economics course for the high school students. A little too late for me, but at least it does now exist.

On occasion, when a Synagogue would need a Rabbi to officiate at an occasion, they would send an older Rabbinical student to fill their needs. Many times, Jay would be chosen to lead a congregation as Cantor for the High Holidays. He had an illustrious career as a youngster in the choir led by Cantor Tevele Cohen. He led High Holiday services in Tzemach Tzedek Congregation, A.G. Beth Israel, Roseland, Illinois, and Cheyenne, Wyoming among others.

One year, he was billed as "The Youngest Cantor," (aged 17) and was leading the services at a Synagogue on the Northwest Side of Chicago. A congregant approached him telling him that the legendary Cantor and Opera Star, Richard Tucker was officiating a few blocks away and offered him a ticket to hear Tucker. This instance notwithstanding, he was an excellent Cantor and chants to this day to a most appreciative congregation.

The first High Holiday season after we were married, I accompanied him to Roseland. It was the beginning of many interesting High Holiday experiences, venues and bizarre happenings that we experienced throughout the years. Roseland is the town that Mr. Pullman of the sleeping rail cars built. It is a small, true company town – everybody and everything revolved around its activities and all the members worked for the Pullman Company in some capacity. We were ensconced at the Pullman Hotel, a place built in the 1930s, at the height of popularity for the sleeping cars.

It seemed to come out of Central Casting in Hollywood as its faded, elegant interior would have been ideal for a Western or period piece movie. The Rabbi was an elderly gentleman who never realized that there was a balcony and thought that the entire congregation was sitting in the main floor. He looked and acted like the cartoon character Mr. McGoo, complete with round eyeglasses. Roseland was an experience. There were probably a few thousand of these small congregations at that time – today they barely exist. Pullman is a part of the history of the Vanished small Jewish communities, places that nourished the Jewish soul for decades and are no more.

Graduation Day from Wright Junior College arrived seemingly quickly. The past two years had been a tumultuous period for us. But there was a big problem looming on the horizon. How would I be able to finish my college education? There was no way that we could afford the tuition. Equally, our parents were not in financially comfortable positions. The only answer was to secure a scholarship. Roosevelt University, Jay's alma mater was a logical choice, as I was already teaching afternoon Hebrew School in the vicinity.

As my class standing was number thirteen out of over three thousand graduates, it was not difficult to join the Scholarship process. At the ceremony, a Karzen family joke was born. My mother-in-law was disturbed when she saw the program with my name at number thirteen. She wanted to know why I couldn't have come in twelfth or fourteenth, as thirteen is such an unlucky number!

The scholarship process was divided into three parts. First, there were approximately one thousand hopefuls tested in a huge gym. The second part consisted of one hundred graduates and I passed that test, also. The third test was a beauty! There were five students who made it to the finals, three men and two women. We were asked to come to the school and were questioned behind a one-way glass wall. Then the waiting began. When the letter arrived from the university, I opened it with shaking hands. My future was written on that single piece of paper. Had I retained that letter it would have been a wonderful exhibit in the Smithsonian Museum in Washington, a star in the SHAMEFUL ANTIQUE IDEAS section.

Why? It said that the committee is sorry to inform me that because there were three scholarships to be awarded with three men competing and since men need an education to make a living to support a family ... the awards were given to the three men and the two women were out!

I was so upset that I believe I cried for three days. I thought that it was my fault. It didn't even occur to me that the system stank and gender discrimination was at play. There was no concept of that, as yet, and I lost.

To think of that situation in the current year of 2013 is to see the truth in the saying ... You've come A Long Way Baby!

CHERRY ON THE TOP

Part Two

Vanished Communities

JEWS HAVE BEEN PART AND PARCEL OF AMERICA since its founding. Was Columbus a Jew? He could have been, but we do know that his cartographer was a Jew. There were Jews in the Colonies and Haim Solomon played a definitive role in the time of George Washington. It has been said that without Solomon, who raised and lent money to the Colonists, they would have never had the money to finance the War of Independence in 1776. There is a bronze statue dedicated to this patriot in downtown Chicago. Jews played prominent parts in America's history and when the West had to be won, the Jewish peddler was a familiar and welcome sight as he carried the necessities of life across the plains. These peddlers were the forerunners of the department stores which can be found in every populated area.

Most Jews settled in New York. Stories about the tenements, sweat shops and inhuman living conditions are numerous. The person most connected with the start of Unions was Samuel Gompers, a Jew, who spent his lifetime trying to better the life of the worker. However, there were Jews who personally wanted a better life and they would strap a bag across their backs and with another one in each hand, would set out for the world beyond the shores of New York. They carried merchandise of every kind, from clothing to safety pins and would extend credit to the farm-women. It was a difficult existence. After a while, a trading post was built and when the village became a town, the trading post became a general store. The next step was the opening of a small department store and with luck, a city was developed and the peddler was the owner of a retail establishment with high earnings. Of course, I am describing the course of events over possibly two generations, but that is how it occurred.

When the businessmen were successful and the town grew, families needed not only stores, but general services and every other known occupation. One person sent for another and Jews became settled in almost every nook and cranny of America. For example, one family had five children, each one adding their talent to the pool. One child became a teacher, one a lawyer, and three established businesses. The first opened a grocery store, the second, a hardware store and the third, a clothing store; thus did the small towns grow. This in a nutshell is the story of how Jews arrived in the small towns that dotted the American landscape.

Iowa, Wisconsin, Kentucky as well as every State in the Union had small pockets of Jews who endeavored to keep hold of their Jewish identity. There were hundreds of them, along with the organizations already mentioned who were faithful members of Jewish communal bodies and Synagogues. What happened to them and where are they now? Well, the truth is – they no longer exist. The youngsters grew to adulthood, left their communities to attend college and university, and never returned. In large part, they intermarried, finding non-Jewish partners. Even in places such as New York with its major Jewish population, the intermarriage rate is 57% of all couples. In Iowa, and the like, it is over 90% and climbing. These Vanished Communities once were the toe-hold of the immigrant Jews and transmitted American values to them. Perhaps their job is finished. The Jew has attained equality and all its perks and lives in today's America as an equal. But the memory of small town Jewish living and achievements has earned its place in history.

Ottumwa

One morning, walking past Rabbi Chaim David Regensberg's open office door, the Rabbi called to Jay and inquired if he would like to travel to Ottumwa, Iowa to officiate at a *Bar Mitzvah*. Students would commonly spend the *Shabbat* in small communities that did not have a resident Rabbi. Jay enthusiastically agreed as it sounded interesting. The remuneration was room and board, travel expenses and $100 for the weekend. In 1957, that was a lot of money. In that same year, Jay and I traveled in our not terribly roadworthy car to the wedding of friends Simi and Ben Shandalov, held in the Shaarei Shamayim Synagogue in Toronto. On the way, we received a $100 speeding ticket which I still possess. But, that's another story!

Jay officiated and was the "Rabbi." The congregation was indeed satisfied, and he was asked to return in a few months time as another *Bar Mitzvah* was in the offing. The first time I did not accompany him, but from the second visit and after, at their request, I did go and we both enjoyed the experience immensely.

As the Burlington Railway train meandered through the states of Illinois and Iowa, the Midwest of the USA was laid out before our eyes. Field after cultivated field with their precise rows of planted crops whizzed past and rural America was seen at its best. White farmhouses, barns and grazing cattle looked like picture postcards and the five hours travel time to our destination was a pleasant interlude.

In Ottumwa, we stayed at the Ballingall Hotel. It was built in the early part of the 19th century and it looked it. The hotel was dimly lit and the walls were papered in an old-fashioned pattern of velvet-flocked flowers with more giant flowers on the carpeting. The bedrooms were spacious, but the bathrooms were old-fashioned with leaky faucets, stained bathtubs and toilets. They were proud of the renovations which had taken place thirty-five years earlier. I think that the major updating was to remove the hitching post for horses from the front of the hotel; nothing else was visible to my eye.

One Friday evening, Jay had left word at the desk to be awakened at 7:00 a.m. but to be sure to knock on the door and not telephone. The Synagogue building was less than three blocks from the hotel and services began at 7:30 a.m., so that there was ample time scheduled. The next morning, a knock on the door awakened us. It was winter, the room was pitch dark and Jay stumbled around getting dressed and left.

He arrived at the Synagogue, the doors were locked, there were no visible lights, the area was deserted, and not a soul around. He glanced at his watch and noted that it was only 6:30 a.m. Returning to the hotel he asked at the desk why was he awakened an hour earlier than he requested. The sleepy clerk replied that he wanted to make sure that the Rabbi was on time as he knew how important it was to the Jewish folks to start precisely on time! Concerned citizen or busybody?

After the initial visits, the Congregation requested that Jay come on a monthly basis, and soon after, they asked that he consider becoming the Rabbi of Ottumwa once he received ordination.

Our First Congregation

It was a huge decision. Moving to Ottumwa would mean leaving family, friends and the comforts of an area with a large Jewish population. We were big city people in general ... Would we be happy in a small town? We discussed the situation at length, weighing the pros and cons. The truth is that we had never lived with such limited opportunities for education or shopping, for that matter. We decided that a Rabbi in a small place would have time to perfect his skills, rather than competing in the larger arena of a place with numerous colleagues. Also, Ottumwa was enthusiastic about the prospect of our coming and so, we decided to take the plunge. We were moving to the Southeast of Iowa and Jay became the Chief Rabbi of the area with the seat in Ottumwa.

THE FIRST TIME THAT JAY AND I drove into Ottumwa, we decided to drive around and get a bit acquainted with our new surroundings. The main street was four blocks long and four blocks deep – that's sixteen blocks of commercial activity including offices for the local doctors, dentists, lawyers and real estate people. Then there was the area of older homes and farther out were the newer homes. I wanted to keep driving around, being certain that there was more to the town ... there had to be ... but there wasn't ... That was it!

The Congregation rented a typical small townhouse for us. It was a white clapboard home with two stories and a porch in front, as well as an old-fashioned swing, which we found perfect for relaxation and sunning. The yard in back had flowering plants as well as rhubarb growing wild. On either side of us were houses; versions of the same style. But the view across the street was special. There were only two huge, elegant old-fashioned houses with wrap-around porches, circular driveways and carpets of green lawn that were well kept at all times. These were the two funeral homes in town; good neighbors and very quiet. The street with the house at 424 West 2nd Street where the "Jewish" Rabbi lived and the two upper-class undertakers was considered a most desirable address.

Going shopping had always been a pleasant pastime for me. Chicago's State Street with its many very large department stores was my turf. I knew it well. But, in Ottumwa, there was one department store and an assortment of other not too promising-looking shops. Then I saw the J.C. Penny Catalogue Store with a number of dowdy-dressed women mulling around. "Oy Vey!" This was a downer! How was I going to survive here in a place with seeming little chic or panache?

Ottumwa was the commercial center for the surrounding areas which consisted of 45,000 people. The 8th-graders from surrounding areas would come to town to visit as their graduation trip. You could see them walking down Main Street looking up at the tall four-story buildings! As Ames, Iowa was not far, a horse-drawn buggy would clip-clop down Main Street (that is actually what the main street of Ottumwa was called) bringing the Amish farmer, wife and family in their distinctive clothing to the big city to do errands. The gentlemen looked just like *Chassidic* Jews with their beards and black clothing. The irony is that except for the *Meshulachim* whom we frequently entertained, nobody dressed in that manner except for the Amish. It was an interesting facet of living there, part of our adventure, as we grew to calling our stay in Ottumwa.

Ottumwa's Synagogue was over 100 years old. A Centennial

Book had been published with pictures of its founders. Gentlemen with long, well-cut beards, dressed in the fashion of the day were pictured. Many had appeared at the train station, most notably in New York, with an amount of money in their hand. The money would take them as far as Ottumwa and there they remained, established families and businesses, lived and died. This was the story of so many of those featured. The Synagogue was a beautiful edifice with a balcony for the women's section.

The founders were Orthodox Jews in practice. One interesting fact is that there was a *Mikvah* in the Synagogue. There was also a complete, unopened set of the Talmud that was at Jay's disposal. He was the first to use it since it was purchased over sixty years previously. One fascinating fact was that these founders had made their children promise that one Sabbath a year all the Jewish business establishments would be closed in the town. Even while we were there, the wider community knew that *Shabbat Shuva*, the Sabbath between *Rosh Hashanah* and *Yom Kippur*, the Jews were not to be disturbed. It goes without saying that the stores were also closed on the High Holidays.

Jay became the Rabbi of the community. They adored him and his word became law. There was one elderly gentleman who corrected Jay while he was reading the Torah the first Sabbath morning. He was correct in doing so, but the other worshipers yelled out, "If the Rabbi says that's the word ... that's the word!" Amazingly so, Jay never made another mistake in reading the Torah in the three years that he served the community!

Ninety families were members of the Synagogue, which included folks from towns in the area such as Oskaloosa, Fairfield and Centerville. There were a few hundred of such small unknown towns such as these in the US. The Hebrew School functioned two afternoons per week and popular Sunday morning classes were also held for the children. Jay taught all the classes as well as functioning as Cantor and Torah reader. He was a *Kol Bo* Rabbi. On Sabbath mornings, services began at 7:30 and concluded at 8:55 a.m. so that the businesses could open at 9:00 a.m. sharp!

Being in an area far from the centers of Judaic knowledge

brought with it some strange practices. Soon after we arrived in the town, we decided to check out the cemetery, as much information and folklore can be learned from it. We were walking among the tombstones which dated back to the 1800s, fascinated with their inscriptions. We noticed that on many stones, the Hebrew names, dates and other words were spelled, shall we say "creatively." The name "Tzvi" was spelled with the letter *Vav* instead of *Bet*; and the female name "Esther" was spelled with a *Shin* instead of a *Samech*. There were many spelling errors. When we questioned the odd choice of Hebrew letters, they replied, "It's all right, we were told that names can be spelled a variety of ways!" Other than correcting more than a dozen gravestones, there was little that we could do. If it wasn't so sad, it would have been funny.

As well as the Women's Group who were in charge of maintaining and beautifying the Synagogue, there were also other Jewish groups such as Hadassah Women's Organization, and Bnai Brith for the men. Everyone belonged to all the organizations and the members, besides being related to one another, were also friends. It was a close-knit community, with all knowing everyone's business on the distaff side, but always there with a helping hand on the plus side.

WITHIN A FEW MONTHS AFTER OUR ARRIVAL, our first child, Tamar Minda Karzen was born on November 20, 1959, Friday in the wee hours of the morning. The first time that I held her was after lighting *Shabbat* candles, with her bright, dark, intelligent eyes wide open, staring intently at the flickering flames. This was her first Sabbath on earth and the spiritual feeling and thankfulness that I felt was overwhelming.

My mother's name had been Chana Mindel, a Yiddish name, but it didn't seem suitable for our little girl upon whom we chose to bestow a Hebrew name. The translation of Chana in Hebrew is grace. Tamar also is translated as grace in Hebrew. We tweaked Mindel a bit and it became Minda. However, there was a popular song at the time, "Tammy" sung by Debbie Reynolds; Tammy she became and is until today.

Tammy was less than two kilograms (four pounds, two ounces) at birth. We left the hospital empty-handed as a baby had to weigh five pounds before permission was obtained to take the newborn home. It was an anxious month as we returned to the hospital day after day to feed and hold our tiny infant until she reached the proper weight to bring her home.

I had little experience with babies and spent many anxious moments studying Dr. Spock's book on child care.

New mothers were hospitalized for a week in those days and when you left, you were so weak from staying in bed, you needed nursing care yourself. However, one time, I shuffled to the nursery in my "fashionable" hospital gown and robe. As usual, there were a variety of visitors, all making those silly sounds in front of the nursery window. There were sixteen male babies with blue blankets and, Tammy with her pink, was the lone girl. There was a familiar face clucking at our baby and upon closer scrutiny I saw that it was Johnny Cash, the pop singer. While on tour he was involved in a traffic accident and was being treated at the same hospital. He was not yet a superstar, but especially in our neck of the woods, he was a person of interest. He kept singing, trying to get Tammy's attention, but to no avail. She was so tiny, but seemed to be determined to grow as fast as she could. After three weeks of visiting the nursery every day, we brought our five pound baby home.

One time Tammy, aged approximately two months, was crying ... No, make that screaming and I had no idea what to do. I checked the obvious, such as an open diaper pin or some other mishap and couldn't figure out what was wrong. I had such guilt feelings ... I had received this perfect being and somehow, she appeared to be totally miserable. I cried along with her. Then I noticed that she was pulling her own hair. I pried her tiny fingers away and she stopped, as if by magic. There were a number of occasions that I was totally flummoxed, but good Doctor Spock and Molly Gendler helped get us through many tight spots.

Molly Gendler became our "Mom" while we lived in Ottumwa. She was a wonderful woman, with a large heart and helped us in every way. She was my confident and teacher; there was nothing that Molly would not do for us. Molly knew the ways of small town living and was friends and in some cases, also a relative of our members. She was the only Sabbath observant person in town and was the single house that we would eat in, or accept food. She gave me recipes and helped us live in a non-*Kosher* environment. Every few months we would order one-quarter of a cow from a butcher in Chicago. It would come packaged with names like *Brustdeckel* for *cholent*, pound packages of ground beef and steaks, two per package, roasts and other meats. They would then be deposited in our six-foot-long freezer to await the time to defrost, serve and eat. Whenever we received a shipment, we would eat all the steaks within the first two weeks and then slowly work our way through the rest of the order. No more calling the butcher every week or so; everything was a new way of living and an adventure.

A memorable event occurred when the time that we were expecting a delicatessen freezer order from 999 Delicatessen on Devon Avenue in Chicago. There were hot dogs and packages of corned beef, tongue and other delicacies. Unfortunately, it arrived on the Saturday morning before Labor Day aboard the train. So, it sat in the train station, not refrigerated, through Monday. Tuesday morning, we were called to inquire when we would pick up the smelly package that awaited us. Not only did we miss the wonderful food that could not be bought in town, but the contents had turned to an ugly shade of green and decorated with white mold and were consigned directly to the garbage. No Deli for the Karzen family for months after that catastrophe!

Tammy was so much fun and we spent hours just looking at her. On the Sabbath or even at Pesach *Sedorim*, she was in her small, daytime crib taking in all the activities. We would be sure to include her in all the singing and, by osmosis, it appeared that she did learn the old family melodies. We were a real family and it was a joyous time.

By the time Tammy was nine months old, there was a sibling on the horizon. On the morning of January 23, 1961, at my regular appointment with the obstetrician, he casually asked, "Would you like to have this baby now? I think that you are ready." Well, as you know, any pregnant woman in her ninth month is always ready and I said, "Sure, why not?"

Molly Gendler came to the rescue, as she would many times when we lived in Ottumwa. Tammy, aged fourteen months, had to be looked after and cared for while I did my stint in the hospital. Another week!

When I entered Ottumwa Hospital in my faux "fur coat," a photographer snapped a picture of me – the Rabbi's wife, entering the building in her "fur coat." I imagine that it looked out of place for the situation, but it was the only coat that I could firmly close against the wintry Iowa winds. That situation taught me one of my first *Rebbetzin* Rules, i.e. Rabbis and wives must do everything not to look out of place by looking "too rich." Even the presumption of wealth is bad. If one has a wealthy congregation, I imagine that is one thing ... but for the average group, never, never appear to "out-money" your members. On the other hand, the Rabbinic couple must appear well-dressed, well-groomed and drive a decent car. Leave the Cadillacs for others; rule #1 applies to cars, also. If you live in a warm climate where everyone's home sports a swimming pool, you also can have one. But, for example, when we lived in Park Ridge and there was room for a good-sized pool, we would never install one, even with a cover for winter. Rabbis endure enough talk without giving the gossip mongers extra fuel.

An interesting 60s idea was not to breast-feed babies; formula was the thing. In the hospital, on the lowest floor at the end of the corridor was an area for nursing mothers. The one room that was occupied at the time held a mother and daughter who were both new mothers. The elder woman had been Iowa Mother of the Year in 1958; she had more than twelve children. Her daughter was on her third child and was still a teenager. These people had "violated" two social mores. Firstly, no one, but no one, had so many children. Families had 2.4 children and that was considered proper. Secondly, in the entire maternity ward, they were the sole nursing mothers. The Similac Formula was king! Today, in Israel, these ideas may appear strange, but that was the conventional wisdom at that time.

Uri David Karzen was also born under the five pound mark. However, the burning question now was what about the *Brit Milah* on the eighth day, and what's to be done about Rabbi Benzion Well, the *Mohel* who had to travel from Chicago. We sweated these questions for almost the entire week and thanks to The One Above, Uri reached the magic weight number and all plans were on track.

Uri was the first baby boy for an Ottumwa Rabbi in years. The hospital offered us their facilities for the festivities as half the town wanted to attend. It was a rare occasion and as we were minor celebrities, the buzz was there. Frankly, there was so little going on in town that the newspaper, The Ottumwa Courier, which boasted ten pages, would cover many minor events from our Synagogue Women's meetings to The Hospital Report, where Mrs. Lila Lockly was treated for burns on her hand due to faulty wiring of the generator for the hen house. This was a newspaper with no Real Estate ads and no Help Wanted; they simply weren't needed. But we did become interested in Pottawatamie County business and names like Waterloo, Oskaloosa and Fairfield, Iowa entered our radar screen.

Everything has a story attached. For Uri's name there are two. Firstly, he was named Uri after Jay's grandfather, whose name was Shraga Feivel, Yiddish for light and Uri means "my light." But, the name David was accompanied by a dilemma.

Rabbi David Kaganoff was one of the signers of Jay's ordination certificate. He also had a favorite uncle, Dan (David) Karzen, who had recently passed away. He was a terrific person, but did not have the religiosity or Torah scholarship that we wanted for our Uri. So we opted to follow a popular bit of Rabbinic wisdom. He was officially named David and when in the future he developed, it would become clear which David he followed. As it is, he has the qualities of both, scholarship and is good natured. It was a win-win situation, and we did indeed hit the jackpot with our Uri David.

Yuri Gargarin, the Russian cosmonaut, had recently made news with the Sputnik space capsule that he had successfully flown. For the first years of his life, our Uri was known as Yuri, as few recognized or cared about Hebrew names. It wasn't until he began school in Skokie, Illinois, that he finally understood that he was Uri, not Yuri.

Brit Milah day finally came. The train arrived on time with the family and Rabbi Well with his giant smile, jokes and black bag in tow.

We decided to have the ceremony in our home so that it could be more private. Had it been in the hospital, it would have turned into a public event. Still, it was wall-to-wall people. Everyone seemed to be there, including our Synagogue members, Jay's clergy buddies, from Baptist Ministers to Catholic Priests, curious non-Jewish neighbors, the Society Page newspaper reporter, politicians, doctors, lawyers and there could have been even an Indian Chief considering where we were. Everyone was always interested in what the "Jewish" Rabbi was doing and this was a stellar occasion.

The *Simcha* was wonderful, but I must confess that from that day until probably three years later, I was tired. Having to take care of two babies under fourteen months was a challenge and there was no family around to help ... except Molly Gendler, and I still do bless her memory. I am not kidding when I say that I couldn't take a real bath in an actual bathtub until Tammy became four, and Uri, three years old. They were always into mischief. It's funny when I think of it now years later, but not at the time.

Sister Rozzie was engaged to be married and wished for us to meet her future husband, Howard Zuckerman. Traveling from New York, they dropped in to visit us for a few days. He was disappointed to see us in proper clothing; he had expected to find us in overalls, sitting on the swing on the front porch, chewing on a piece of straw. They gifted me with a bottle of French perfume. I was delighted, never having owned such a luxurious item.

What a treat! However, early one morning, it was too quiet in the house. My new mother's instinct forced me to get up and see what the kids were doing. Tammy was asleep in her bed, but Uri was nowhere to be found. Where was he? On the stairway ledge I had placed a pot of dried flowers. It seems that Uri knew that flowers were supposed to smell and wanted to help out, which he did by pouring my exotic bottle of French perfume all over the dried flowers. Not only did the flowers stink, but it was too much of a good thing and the entire hallway stank of an overdose of perfume. He was a *Shovav*, but we loved him anyway!

PEOPLE COMMENT ON THE NEATNESS of our home. At any hour of the day or night, our home is presentable. This is because of a lesson that I learned early on when the children were toddlers. In Ottumwa, being that there was no main floor den or area that the children could safely play, they were in the salon all day. The kitchen was in the adjoining room and I was able to keep an eye on them. At bedtime, they were put to bed in their rooms on the second floor, but their toys were scattered all over the salon. I didn't straighten up the room before retiring for the night, as it would only look like a hurricane hit it again the next day when they resumed their activities.

One night, at 2 a.m., we answered the door to find that a death had occurred in the community and the family wanted to discuss the details of the funeral. Jay was able to comfort them in their time of grief. That was one of the services for which he was hired and he was learning the ropes of a pulpit Rabbi little by little. When the mourners entered the salon, I was so embarrassed that I wanted to crawl into the proverbial hole and hide. The room looked like a tornado hit it, followed by a typhoon. Toys were everywhere – I had to clear off the chairs so that they would have a place to sit.

The next morning, I thought to myself that I must straighten up the salon before we go to bed, lest this happen again. However, I didn't do it, and it did happen. A few months later, the same scenario occurred. The door bell rang, the mourners entered, and the room was a mess. My embarrassment was palpable, but it never happened again. Before I go to bed, every night the room is presentable. The old maxim, "A place for everything and everything in its place," is a motto that I live by. We have been fortunate enough to have ample space for all our "stuff." Isn't that why the Lord created drawers and closets in the first place?

ONE OF THE PROBLEMS THAT OBSERVANT couples face in non-Jewish environments is the observance of *Taharat Hamishpacha* (family purity). There is a set of laws relating to marital intimacy of which at its core is entering the *Mikvah* at "clean times." For additional information on this practice of marriage renewal, consult the many books available on the subject.

To say that this was a challenge would be an understatement of great magnitude. There was a *Mikvah* in the Ottumwa Synagogue, but it probably had not been used for decades and it was difficult to know if it was *Kosher*. So, the choices were the following … take a dip in the lake or travel to Des Moines, Iowa, which was the closest community, 90 miles away. Then, the problem of how to get there: 1) drive by car; 2) take a Greyhound Bus; 3) fly in an Ozark Airline airplane, with a rubber band to start the propeller (not quite, but you get the idea). Well, I did all three depending on the season. In the summer, the lake was satisfactory. I wouldn't recommend it normally, but that was the situation. The airplane was okay, if there was fair weather. However, there was no airport, only a landing field. Seeing that small plane with a dozen seats standing there waiting for its few passengers was not confidence building, after being used to huge airports like in Chicago and New York. In my mind, the prayers for the *Mikvah* and for travel, *Tefilat Haderech* (Traveler's Prayer) became one. Those planes were scary! And then of course, there was Iowa weather to contend with, that's where the buses came in. When it snowed, and it snows in Iowa a lot, I would catch my friendly Greyhound Bus and "Leave the driving to them", as they claim. I would watch the miles and miles of snow-covered fields as the bus drove to its destination slowly, because of the patches of snow and ice on the roads. One time, I left home at 8 a.m. and arrived back at 4 a.m. because it had begun to snow heavily on the way home and we had to continually stop as the driver was driving blind. He simply couldn't see out the window. Jay was the Mommy that entire day caring for the two little ones. I'm not sure who was happier that I was finally home, him or me. It was probably equal!

TIME WAS PASSING and we enjoyed being part of the Ottumwa community. Once, one of the women insisted that I spend a few hours with her and some friends – it was a surprise and I did not know where they were taking me. When we entered this home, I saw that the "surprise" was to teach me how to play Mah Jong.

I confess. I am not into and have never been a card player. I politely learned how to play that afternoon, but to their dismay, I did not become hooked on "Cracks" and "Bams" and I never played again.

There were many memorable times in Ottumwa. The Ottumwa Hadassah Chapter was active and met for a bi-monthly meeting and lunch. The occasion was often covered by the town newspaper and at times they even reported on the meal. As it was usually a "Ladies Luncheon Meal" of cottage cheese served on a half canned peach and salad, I never could understand why readers would find it interesting – filling column space was the object, I imagine.

However, once a year the National Office of Hadassah would send a guest speaker – that was big news. She was always welcomed like royalty, as we inspected her hairdo, clothing, hat, and shoes, looking for clues why this visitor looked so posh and sophisticated, so "Big City." It was a breath of fresh air as we were so used to each other. Our wardrobes and hairstyles were as noticeable as the wallpaper. The visitor represented high style and excitement. In retrospect, she was probably just a nice lady who dressed attractively, with a husband and family who lived lives as mundane as we did. It was small town lack of confidence and I'm not sure if it was justified or not.

One time, our Hadassah visitor brought us the news that a new hospital in Jerusalem was to be built inside the city. This was a rebuttal to the murder of nurses and doctors who were en route to the facility in Har Hatzofim. It had been built in an area which overlooked Jerusalem with its spectacular views, but during the War of Independence, the location made it impossible to function and ultimately resulted in these martyred heroes.

We listened carefully to her words and being avid Zionists vowed to help the cause and raise money for the new building. We decided on the novel idea of cooking and baking food items and selling them to the wider community. The local manager of the A&P Supermarket was enthusiastic about the idea and donated freezer space so that cakes, cookies, brownies, blintzes, and the Jewish "K" Rations of *Kugels, Kreplach and Kneidelach* could be sold easily and professionally. Mr. Krieger, the manager, was so enthusiastic about his Jewish ladies and their frozen *Kosher* food sale that he printed signs, arranged additional advertising and the community awaited this unusual event. Needless to say, it was covered in the local newspaper – the sale was front page news.

Now, the work began. Two friends and I decided to make two kinds of *Blintzes,* notably potato and cheese. On my kitchen table we rolled, floured, cut and fried the leaves for a few hundred of the delicacies. We boiled the potatoes and mixed the cheese filling. We remarked how next time it was the baking of Brownies for us! We also promised never to make another *Blintze* again and I don't know about them, but I didn't. There is nothing wrong with professionally-made frozen blintzes – they're fine! However, the sale was a roaring success. Monies were forwarded to build the hospital that we use today. From time to time, when I am there, I think about the fun time we had raising a bit of money. *The Hadassah Ottumwa Chapter* name appears on one of the wall plaques. It's a bit of history and it's a good feeling to know that our efforts succeeded so well.

Another fundraiser was the rummage sale. The group would rent a vacant store for four days to sell the clothing that was collected from members. This sale was anticipated by the community and they looked forward to buying the "Jewish" ladies' fashionable items. The Synagogue women's members handled the sales. It was an event that was always a sure-fire winner. In whatever Synagogue that we served, I was always an integral part of the group and I was prepared to take my turn selling the chic castoffs.

Rebbetzin Ruby was awaiting customers when a woman with three children entered. I approached her and helped her with selections. When she sat her kids down and picked up Uri's worn shoes that I had donated, I couldn't take it anymore. I felt so bad for her that she and her family were forced to wear secondhand clothing, that I took all of the items that she intended to buy, put them in bags and paid for them myself. When my friends saw what I had done, they sent me home, telling me that this was one project that I needn't help. It had affected me terribly and tears were welling up in my eyes. I guess that I did not act professional and I was fired from the job. That was the first and last time that I was ever fired ... and it was a volunteer job!

JAY'S POSITION WAS A NATURAL for him and fit his persona perfectly. He was happy and satisfied with the Congregation and life in Ottumwa. The members loved us, and probably thought of us as their kids. We were barely in our mid-twenties and the members were more than twice our age.

They were thoughtful of our needs and after Tammy was born, everything was provided for her in pink, as well as a stroller, jumping chair, swing and all the baby paraphernalia that was required and then some. The same situation occurred on the birth of Uri. We received another entire wardrobe in shades of blue. For the two wedding anniversaries that we spent there, elegant gifts were given. A high style credenza with a marble top was given to us which stands in our home to this day. Another year, a silver Tea and Coffee set, which rests on a beautifully decorated silver tray was the congregation's gift to us. They sent us flowers for the holidays and were generous with gifts and praise – what more could we want?

The retailers of the better stores in town were our members and were exceptionally generous. Every month or so, Jeannette Mirson, who owned a fine ladies shop, would telephone me and ask me to stop by the store to inspect an item of clothing that was perfect for me and I must see it. I would kid her that she was my personal shopper at the wholesale-retail market. Not a holiday passed that Jeannette did not think of me and act as my clothing fairy godmother.

Jeannette had a brother, Herbert Brody, who was the proprietor of the finest men's store in town. Every *Yom Tov*, Jay would be the recipient of a new suit or some fashionable piece of clothing. Herb liked to give Jay an entire outfit at one time and it had to be perfectly matched. So Jay was decked out with a suit, shirt, tie – the works. He was a walking advertisement for Brody Mens Wear, Ottumwa's Finest.

Herb, inadvertently, taught Jay an invaluable Rabbinic lesson. One day, Jay was conducting a funeral for Herb's elderly uncle. He was delivering the eulogy and noticed Herb sitting in the first row. When he said the name of the deceased, he said Herb Brody instead of the correct name. The sound of "OOOOO" was heard from the audience, but Jay caught the mistake and the funeral proceeded without further incident. However, a month later Herb suffered a massive heart attack and passed away at a too young age. Never again did Jay ever officiate at any occasion without having the name of the person in large letters on a card which he would hold in front of him at all times!

Probably, because of my background and intimacy with death at an early age, I felt that I couldn't do a *Tahara* (preparation of a body for burial). I was concerned that should a woman pass away while we were living in Ottumwa, I would be called upon to participate in this important *Mitzvah*. As it happened, there were several men whom Jay helped prepare in the proper Jewish way, but not a single woman. Thank Heavens, all the women were healthy when we arrived and all survived our sojourn there. To this day I am grateful for that, and I'm certain that they are also!

SO, WHAT DID WE DO ALL DAY? I had two tots. I admire mothers with twins or triplets. I can't even visualize their mother's day without help ... lots of it. Similac Formula was the primary food of both children at one time. They were stored and dispensed in bottles. At that time, sterilizing the bottles and nipples was the order of the day and I sterilized and sterilized. Panic time happened when there was a three-day *Yom Tov* and the refrigerator was stuffed full of bottles with their formula. It was a full time job. Also, having two babies in diapers was a challenge. Pampers had just been invented and were too costly for everyday use. There was diaper service, but I constantly ran out and spent a lot of time with the washing machine doing loads of laundry and the never-ending washing of diapers.

Jay would take the children out for an hour by taking them to the local zoo. The zoo had four rabbits, chickens, a lonely fox and a few other unfortunate creatures. It didn't take him very long to "do" the zoo. There was always the playground and that was fun, but there were few children where we lived; it was dilapidated and sad looking. As a family, we would go to the "Dairy Queen." That was always an adventure and there was one medium size, modern drugstore and pharmacy where we would explore the aisles. On Saturday evening, if you were really bored, you could go to Main Street and watch the A&P Supermarket unload their large food truck.

There were afternoon strolls where we would take the kids for an airing. With the two children in the stroller we would visit our members in their places of business going from store to store and *shmuzing* with them. Some said that when they saw us coming they would reminisce about Rabbi Benzion Well and his family.

Our friend, Rabbi Well, had been Uri's *Mohel* and had been the Rabbi in Ottumwa in the early 40s. His son, Don, was a tot when his family served the same families. Rabbi Don Well has been a friend of ours for many years. People laughed as they remembered Don pushing his stroller into the same showcases that Uri was attempting to do. It was a stroll down memory lane for our members who became good friends.

Tuesday evening was the star attraction of the week. Tuesday was our "Date Night" and every Tuesday, we would go to the movies. There was one theater that showed a different "A" and "B" movie each week. The best fact is that it was free, as Joe Cohen, our member, owned the theater and we had passes.

One Tuesday evening, it had been snowing heavily since the morning and we wanted to go to the theater. It was Tuesday, after all! We called there and asked if it was open and received an affirmative answer. The snow made the streets impassable for the car, so we bundled up, put on snow boots and trudged by foot to the theater. The place was entirely empty, we were the only crazies who had ventured out in three feet of snow – and don't forget that we had free passes. So we bought lots of candy, popcorn and drinks so that it shouldn't be a total waste for our friend Joe Cohen. We sat and spent the evening and had the entire place to ourselves except for the guy who was running the projector.

Since we had come to town, the Synagogue flourished. A new Rabbi brought vitality and new ideas to the community which was over a hundred years old. The building was renovated and refurbished. It was a beautiful example of a small Synagogue and could hold its own anywhere in the world. Then, a social hall was added and it was bursting with activities from organizational meetings to an occasional Sabbath or Holiday dinner. The youngsters, teens and members of all ages, spent more of their time in the Synagogue environs with its numerous activities than they had in years. The monthly bulletin went from two to four pages as the members' creativity was rekindled and ideas for activities poured forth. We are speaking of a group of 200 people who had to rely on themselves for Jewish education and entertainment. It was quite remarkable how active the community became. It was an accolade to Jay for his enthusiastic leadership.

At this juncture, early in our marriage, the word TEAM became apparent.

T – **T**ogether   E – **E**ach   A – **A**ccomplishes   M – **M**ore

Jay coined this phrase, "Together Each Accomplishes More" and it has stayed with us and the thousand plus brides and grooms of whose weddings he has officiated.

What a powerful thought! Its meaning conveys more than just two individuals helping each other succeed. The meaning is that two strong individuals, both in their individual spheres, not only helping the other, but contributing their individual strengths and talents to accomplish the task.

I HAVE ALWAYS ENJOYED WRITING, whether it was in the classroom, or school newspapers. Any medium of the written word is my "Bag." I have written humorous birthday songs, parodies and poems and fooled around with words much to the enjoyment of family and friends. One *Purim*, the Women's

Ruby, first place in Hat Contest, Bnai Jacob Synagogue, Ottumwa, 1960

Synagogue Group decided to perform a special operetta. The original was written by *Rabbanit* Libby Klaperman. I used her material, updated and tailored it for our small community.

The production was accompanied by the music of "The Flower Drum Song," by Richard Rodgers and Oscar Hammerstein, written in 1957, on which the play was based. There were colorful stage sets, costumes, wigs and stage makeup. Of course, as with every amateur production there are unique problems. The music maestro who played the piano was expecting a child and had she delivered two weeks earlier, we would have been in trouble. One of the lead singers (me) developed a cold and by prayers alone, made it through the production.

We decided to order professionally-baked *Hamantaschen* and had them flown in from Chicago. They were probably the most expensive pastries in history, but we tried to make the evening as enjoyable as possible. It was a tremendous success and years later while reminiscing about our time in Ottumwa with Laurel and Arnie Siegel, friends who had lived there and were our age, remembered the play and how it was the talk of the town for a long time. Of course, it made the newspaper.

Decorating the Synagogue for the holidays was another project that the women undertook. Every holiday had its project which we tried to bring a feeling of Jewish joy to the community. We placed decorative flowers on the pulpit for the High Holidays and greenery in the Synagogue when *Shavuot* arrived. *Sukkot* was another important holiday project with the building of the Synagogue *Sukkah*. However, because we had the two babies and could not utilize the *Sukkah* in the Synagogue on the holiday, we built one privately. The joke was that we were the only house in town with a *Sukkah*, but also the only house in the neighborhood without a Christmas tree!

FROM TIME TO TIME, WOMEN WOULD DROP IN to our home for coffee and a chat. Their interests often opened up new horizons. Geri Brown owned an antique store and taught me the beauty of antiques, and how to appreciate their uniqueness through history. After I told her the incident about my returning my wedding present of antique cups for an electric frying pan, and after she ceased groaning, she decided that she had to take me in hand. I would go "antiquing" with her. We went to farms where genuine antiques were being offered for sale. Rummaging through the offerings we once found a *Chanukah Menorah* that was very old. A real antique menorah in Chillicothe, Iowa! There must be an interesting tale connected to that piece.

Once, a friend was speaking about her husband and family, relating the problems with her sister-in-law and other aspects of her life – *Oisreden De Hartz* as it is known in Yiddish. I was half her age, but I listened attentively and when she finally stopped, she exclaimed, "Ruby, you are as good as a psychiatrist, and much cheaper!" In my naiveté, I asked if she does indeed see a psychiatrist. She replied, "Oh, my dear, you are still so young. One of these days you'll see one also!" That is one of the pleasures in life that I have missed, but from experiences like that, a concept was born; I call it "The *Rebbetzin* Coat."

PEOPLE HAVE OFTEN SOUGHT ME OUT to share their problems. I don't give advice. These folks just need a sympathetic and non-judgmental ear.

Jay has found the same thing – the older he became, the more problem situations there appeared to be. His graying temples attracted a large number of people who requested counseling, and he was most obliging.

So many problems are centered around in-law children. One of the blessings that we have and appreciate are the spouses of our children.

My Shellie (Uri's wife) and my Morris (Tammy's husband) have been wonderful additions to our family. In fact, once we gave a birthday greeting card especially for a son-in-law to Morris and he was miffed. We treat them no differently than our own children and they respond in kind. After the initial awkwardness, they have always called us *Ima* and *Abba*. Jay and I have received the blessing of wonderful in-law children and I am eternally grateful.

A *Bar Mitzvah* was to be held on the Sabbath with out-of-town guests. There was a gentleman from Council Bluffs, Iowa who was very impressed with the service and the way in which Jay conducted the affairs of the Synagogue. Their Rabbi had just left the community and they were seeking to fill the Rabbinical position. He offered Jay $500 per year more than he was receiving in salary. The money was a consideration, but not the major one. Council Bluffs was close to Omaha, Nebraska which had a decent size Jewish population. A Jewish Day School had opened and *Kosher* food was much easier to obtain. We were sure that Ottumwa would match the increase … but they wouldn't! People make mistakes and groups of people make bigger mistakes, and this one was a whopper – the salary of the new Ottumwa Rabbi was twice what Jay was receiving, and they had to pay all his moving costs. He lasted barely a year and was fired.

We had a wonderful goodbye party and received farewell gifts when we packed up and moved. Ottumwa, being our first congregation, will always have a special place in our hearts. We visited there before we moved to Israel and are still in touch with the Siegels. But it was time to move on.

BEFORE WE LEAVE THE ENVIRONS of Ottumwa, a sidebar is necessary. When folks first hear the name of Ottumwa, Iowa, it sounds like a joke. But many of you have a connection to that place and don't even know it. In the 60s there was a popular TV series and movie entitled "Mash." There was a character named Radar whose job it was to forever carry the radio equipment. He was naïve and most charming. Radar is Ottumwa's Favorite Son! Now you know the answer to one of the questions in the board game of Trivial Pursuit!

Council Bluffs

Council Bluffs, Iowa, here we come! Jay went from being the Chief Rabbi of Southeast Iowa to the Chief Rabbi of Northwest Iowa. Council Bluffs was a very pretty town and it was treated as a suburb of Omaha, Nebraska. The Missouri River separates the two and it is easily crossed by bridge. Unfortunately it is a modern steel bridge, not a covered bridge for which Iowa is justly famous. However, Council Bluffs was visually lovely – it was built on the bluffs that surround the Missouri River. Spring and summer were verdant with greenery and we especially loved the streets that were canopied by the branches of huge trees. Autumn was a blaze of color as Maple trees were in abundance. The red and gold colors of the leaves against the blue skies were an example of the Lord's painting skills at their best. In winter, the snow-covered scenes could have been used by Christmas card photographers as they were perfect, even to the church steeples that dotted the town.

After we arrived there, the Synagogue, as in Ottumwa, was

revitalized. Activities were held and the congregants were receptive to the increased activities. Everyone appeared to be happy and satisfied with Rabbi Jay's leadership. Rabbi Oscar Fasman, the president of the Hebrew Theological College traveled to Jay's installation as the city Rabbi and praised the community for their good taste in obtaining their new leader. Within a year, the Synagogue was renovated and a social hall was added. There were more *minyanim*, a Hebrew School, Sunday School and adult education. The Synagogue was flourishing. The people were happy – what could be bad?

The house that we lived in was an excellent example of the architecture of the 18th century. It had been built for a general in the Union army in the War between the States, the Civil War. General Grenville M. Dodge was a friend of both Presidents Abraham Lincoln and Ulysses S. Grant. He was a respected American warrior as well as an entrepreneur in the important task of building the railway. The railway was the lynchpin that connected early America together. East, West, North and South were joined by the railway lines that crisscrossed the country. Details of this historic home, which is now a museum, can be found on Google among other details of this American hero.

The house itself was spacious and luxurious, reminiscent of an earlier era. As you entered the large hallway, there was a gracious curved stairway on the left. This was to be used for the "Gentle" folks. There was another back stairway that led to the servants' third floor and began opposite the Butler's Pantry. (I used it for my Passover kitchen). Elegantly carved fireplaces were in all the rooms, and a magnificent crystal chandelier hung in the dining room. The master bedroom was large and, as with all the bedrooms, there was an entrance to outside balconies. However, every door was nailed shut for the duration that we lived there, as with two small children we felt that it was dangerous. Especially with our little *Shovav* Uri, I could see him hanging from the balconies just for fun. As it was, we were awakened one morning by the ringing door bell with a neighbor complaining that our two "Darlings" were tossing their toys out of their bedroom window from the second floor. Looking out, I saw toys scattered all over the green, verdant lawn that surrounded the house.

Across the large lawn, in the back of the house, stood a little house that had once been a tool shed. It was a miniature house and we converted it into a playhouse for the kids. The children used it daily and enjoyed it, but we had to keep it well-tended, as ours were the only children around and it would have been an eyesore for it to be messy with bikes and toys scattered all over. So, as the house was large, I was constantly busy with its housekeeping tasks, but I had another chore, as well. The yards on all sides of the house had to be tended. It was a lot of work, but we did love that house.

One afternoon, I was busy in the kitchen and the door bell rang. Upon opening the door, standing there was a fireman in full regalia holding three-year-old Uri's hand. He explained that he was here to return our son. I didn't realize that he was missing! What had happened was that the fire station was across from the largest toy store in town. Uri had gone, by himself, across two busy streets to buy toys. He knew that he needed money, so he took discarded checkbook stubs out of the wastebasket, and he went shopping. Some "nice" lady helped him cross the two busy streets and he went into the shop to buy himself some new toys. This kid was an entrepreneur and shopper at a tender age! Uri was always constantly involved in one situation or another. It was hard to punish him, because he was so cute with his big brown eyes and the fact that his escapades were clever, found us reprimanding him, but laughing together privately over his antics. Tammy was his "straight man"; they were like Laurel and Hardy and together pulled off some wild, unforgettable schemes.

As in Ottumwa, there was one family that was Sabbath observant, Leah Krasne and her adult son, Leslie. They were our guides to living an observant life and adopted the Karzen family, making us feel appreciated and comfortable. They owned the largest department store and were leaders in the community.

The makeup of the seventy-five-member family Synagogue was mostly the business owners and there were members who were politically active. The Jewish community was affluent, but not showy. Many were second and even third generation Iowans.

The Synagogue was flourishing. As in Ottumwa, I was president of the Sisterhood, which is the Women's group connected with the Synagogue. Here, *Sukkot* became a big event with a large *Sukkah* constructed for the holidays. We had decorating parties and I learned how to string cranberries and popcorn to be hung in it. Jeannie Passer chuckled as she showed me the proper way to string them and said she had learned it in school. Of course, she had attended a public school with much attention on the Christmas holiday. She claimed that she was asked to go to her teachers' houses to string for them because she was known as an expert. I gingerly asked about her own home, anticipating the worst. But she laughed and said she was just an outsourcer and never had a tree in her childhood home. Whew!

ONE TIME A PROMINENT GENTLEMAN and his wife approached Jay with a request. They had not been blessed with children, but they had a pet dog that they loved and it had recently died. The husband wanted to say *Kaddish* for the dog. Jay hadn't had this ritual question in any of the classes in the Seminary! He thought fast and replied that this man had recently had *Yahrzeit* for his father and he had said *Kaddish* for him with a quorum of ten men, as is proper. How can he say the same prayer for his dog, no matter how much it was beloved, as his own father, especially within such a short time? The husband relented, but insisted that some words be said for the beloved pet. Now, there is no one more creative in that type of situation than Jay Karzen! He concocted some kind of prayer with comforting words for the gentleman who left the Synagogue a happy man, certain that his dog was now in "Doggie Heaven." Luckily, he didn't request a *minyan* for *Shiva!*

Another experience which truly baffled him was the woman who requested that Jay say a prayer for the strawberries. When he replied that to his knowledge that there is no such prayer, she was hard pressed to believe that he had a certified ordination diploma, with no knowledge of this important prayer. He replied with a straight face that he must have been absent from class the day that this prayer was discussed. However, after a few years of mulling this request, he finally figured out where she got this idea. The prayers of *Selichot* are recited prior to the *Rosh Hashanah* holiday. On the day prior to the holiday, there is a special prayer, known as *Zechor Bris* (Remember the Covenant). Her father would say to her upon leaving for the Synagogue, *Ich gay zogin* (I'm going to pray) *Zechor Bris*, in his heavy accented Yiddish. If you recite the words *Zechor Bris* quickly a few times in a row, it sounds like strawberries. Now, every day before the holiday, when Jay recites this special *Selicha*, he also adds a little prayer for the year's strawberry crop!

Omaha

A huge attraction to our moving to Council Bluffs was that Omaha was so close by. It was a city of a half-million people at the time, and the Jewish population was good-sized and affluent. There were three large Jewish houses of worship; Orthodox, Conservative and Reform. The Jews were friendly with one another and as is common in small communities, members overlapped, with people belonging to more than one congregation. The Rabbis had a Rabbinical group and Jay enjoyed having the comradeship of the Jewish clergy. Rabbis Groner, Kripke and Brooks welcomed him warmly and he was quickly involved in the affairs of The Omaha – Council Bluffs communities.

Omaha had Jewish amenities that we had missed while living in Ottumwa. The beautiful, immaculate *Mikvah* was situated in Rabbi Groner's Synagogue. Arduous traveling and uncertain weather were a thing of the past. A Community Center was the pride of the Jewish community. It was a beautiful building which sported an Olympic-sized pool, gym and activities for all ages from tots and teens to seniors. Uri attended the Pre-School program and Tammy was in the Kindergarten. There was a fledgling Jewish Day School that went through third grade, which the administration hoped to add a grade each year until the school contained a full eight-year program. However, maintaining a Jewish Day School is an olympic-sized job and it seemed that every other day, additional monies had to be collected to keep the doors open. It was a problem. The year that our children attended was the last year of operation until a number of years later, it was re-established with Rabbi Isaac Nadoff's initiative.

THERE WERE CULTURAL ASPECTS of Omaha that we appreciated, such as were featured at the Omaha Stadium. Theater productions and live shows that made us feel that we were more in the mode of Chicago and not in the boondocks, were regularly held. Of course, we never could forget which part of the country in which we were living. It was easy to remember when the most important event at the ultra-modern stadium was the National Cattle Show and County Fair. The doings of the 4H Youth Association were broadcast weekly and when on the radio, you heard reports from The Option Exchange in Chicago announcing the prices on pork bellies and soybeans – this was the place that they were speaking about. It was ranch and farm country and you couldn't forget it for a minute!

At that time, Omaha had the largest and most extensive *Kosher* slaughtering facilities in America. *Shochtim* would come and live for a few weeks, and then others would take their place. The families didn't move to the city, and it was a constant changeover of personnel. There were no *Kosher* restaurants anywhere in the area, but there was Johnnie's Steak House. Catering to the *Shochtim*, they laid in a supply of prepared airline meals and a separate warming oven.

When it was time to celebrate our birthdays or anniversaries, we would dress up and go to Johnnie's to celebrate. It was an elegantly designed eatery and we would sit there in our Sabbath "best" clothing and eat our dinner from an aluminum tray with plastic silverware. The cost was $25 per meal! This was the only game in town and we celebrated every occasion in this manner. You must take what you can get, when you can get it and as we say, *Zeh mah sheyesh!* (This is what there is!)

We were no longer dependant on the Burlington train to keep a *Kosher* home and thrilled to have a bakery and butcher within a short driving distance. No more *Brustdeckel* and frozen *Challah* ... Halleluyah!

But, of course, nothing is ever perfect and one Friday as Jay was buying *Challot*, he casually stepped into the kitchen to check on the ingredients that were being used. Rabbi Ben Groner and he shared the *Kashrut* supervision as they were the two Orthodox Rabbis in the area. He saw a product that was suspicious and questioned the baker about it. The baker hemmed and hawed and realized that he was in trouble. Jay called Rabbi Groner to report the incident and by the time the Rabbi went to do a personal inspection, the product had been removed. It took a while for the situation to resolve itself, but it proved once again that the best supervision is one where the owner is an observant Jew and is interested in doing the *Mitzvah* properly.

One early morning at 4 a.m. the telephone rang and the desperate voice on the other end requested the Rabbi come immediately. It seems that a truckload of meat on its way from Denver to Chicago had arrived and he needed a Rabbi to "Bless" (wash) the meat as it was the end of three days. Should another twenty-four hours pass without properly watering the meat, it would no longer be *Kosher*. So Jay hurriedly dressed, complete with galoshes, as there was five inches of snow on the ground, and drove off to "Bless" the meat. He was dressed as usual in a suit and tie, not knowing that he would be expected to climb into the huge semi-trailer truck, and pressure wash the racks of meat with a lengthy monster of a hose. He climbed down from the truck soaking wet, both inside and out. No big city Rabbi would ever encounter a situation like this! After that incident, he was able to add "Blessing Meat" to his resume.

I WANT TO SHARE A FASCINATING TIDBIT about Dorothy Kripke, who was the wife of the Conservative Rabbi, Meyer Kripke. Every Monday, Dorothy would play a friendly game of bridge with her neighbors. Once in a while Susan, one of the foursome, would relate some aspect of her husband's work and his business, which was on the move and growing steadily. Dorothy gave her some money from time to time to invest, in the beginning as a courtesy to help out a neighbor. This practice continued for years. In her 90s, Dorothy Kripke passed away and left one million dollars to The Jewish Theological Seminary (Conservative) in her will. The money had been invested wisely, thanks to Susan and her husband – Warren Buffett!

America in the 60s

Camelot arrived in America in the year 1960, with the election of the 35th president of The United States of America, John F. Kennedy. His administration was akin to a breath of fresh air swooshing into the White House. A young man in his 40s, who was charismatic, vibrant, energetic, intelligent and not to mention handsome, was at the helm of the USS AMERICA, along with his glamorous wife, Jackie. It was believed in many circles that a Kennedy dynasty was being created that, along with his illustrious politically-active family, would "rule" the country for years to come.

Jackie was a fashion setter, her clothing style, especially the pill box hat which was known as the "Jackie" hat, her long flyaway hair, the oversize sunglasses and the elegant clothing that she wore became instant hits. We all wore, the "Jackie" which was a simple chemise dress and the dress and coat set that she favored became America's style. Everyone wanted to look like her. It was the first time in memory that there were small children in the White House and the famous picture of John-John, aged three, playing under the desk of his father became a classic. The family, with their triumphs and tragedies was played out before America's eyes as they were constantly being featured in the media, and became much like the royal family in England.

Kennedy's term of office lasted only 1,000 days; it was filled with drama and had a roller coaster quality. The highs couldn't go higher and the lows reached lower than rock bottom. Kennedy was the youngest person ever to achieve that office and the newspapers were filled with the boisterous activities such as benefit parties and high jinks. Popular music was played at State dinners and the stars of the Silver Screen and Pop Stars were welcomed to the White House for the first time. The government was conducted with a youthful attitude such as the creation of the Peace Corps and other unique ideas. We felt that all was OK with the country; it was being governed properly. It was the best country in the world and we, the citizens, were the luckiest people on earth.

But, and isn't there always a "but." It was a time of the Cold War with Russia. Cuba, which is 90 miles from the state of Florida's shores was a Russian protectorate and ally. The Russians wanted to establish an air base there, which would mean that America would be in close firing range of their deadly missiles.

When Kennedy learned that there was a flotilla of ships en route to Cuba from Russia, he told Khrushchev, the country's president, that if the ships attempt to land in Cuba, it would mean war and America would not hesitate to fire at the ships, blowing them out of the water. The journey from Russia was three days sailing, and America held its breath for the entire time. It was not certain if Russia would believe Kennedy, and the hourly radio and television news gave updates on how far the ships had sailed – knot by knot. Finally, on the third day, just a few miles from Cuba, the ships turned around and war was averted. We all heaved a collective sigh of relief.

In November 1963, Kennedy made the fatal decision to visit Dallas, Texas, to politic a bit and soothe troubled feathers as many Texas voters, with deep pockets, were unhappy with his policies. Although Jackie had recently suffered a miscarriage, he urged her to accompany him on the trip. As the presidential motorcade rode slowly along its path, shots rang out, hitting Kennedy, and John Connolly, the Texas governor. The car sped to a nearby hospital where the President was declared dead. The country was in shock. President William McKinley was the last president to be assassinated in 1901. All over the country, people stood outside in groups and wept openly. How could this happen? America was an open democracy and it was totally unbelievable. This type of thing happened in other countries, but not America!

It was just before noon on a beautiful Friday morning in November, the sun was shining and the weather was mild. I was just leaving the beauty shop, when the radio beeped for a special message: "The President has been shot!"

We stared at each other, but the words would not sink in. The President? Shot? What is he saying? Which president? What? How? Where? Never imagining that it was OUR President. As we listened to the announcement saying that the President was dead, a few more details emerged. The announcers choked up, voices broke into the sound of tears. We were all in shock and we joined him in a cacophony of crying, some silently and others openly. How could this happen?

On the way home, Jay and I stopped into a grocery store to pick up some last minute items for the Sabbath. The proprietor glared at us with our red, swollen eyes and said, "He had it coming, he was no good." My second shock in one short hour. How could an American feel that way? He was satisfied and smug about Kennedy's death. Was our country becoming like a South American Banana Republic? We drove home in a daze.

The following hours with the capture of Lee Harvey Oswald, the killer, who was then shot and killed by Jack Ruby, a small time gangster from Chicago, made it seem like the entire country was part of a police detective television serial, but this was real-life! The TV was on and not turned off for days. We were mesmerized by the sorrowful images of the funeral cortège and the images of Jackie Kennedy and her two children watching, as their lives were being turned upside-down. The picture of three-year-old John-John saluting the bier as it passed the White House or the Commander's horse with the empty stirrups, was heartbreaking and we didn't want to, we COULDN'T, miss a moment of this high drama. The American people's collective heart was broken.

As luck would have it, there was a 40th Wedding Anniversary weekend being held in the Synagogue for a wonderful couple who were celebrating that memorable occasion. Even though we all tried to make it a cheerful affair, at 10 p.m. Sunday evening, the hostess said, "Let's all go home, G-D willing, we'll plan it all again for our 50th." I remember wearing a burgundy-colored suit that evening in the hopes that my red, blotchy nose and eyes would not stand out as much, even if they matched my clothing. I'm sure that I didn't succeed in camouflaging the sadness that we felt one bit.

After the assassination there were roads, highways, music centers and at least one airport that was named in honor of the slain president. Jay and I decided to change the name of our small street to Kennedy Way. It was Uri's birthday and my in-laws sent the gift of a bicycle to him for the occasion. We gave them the new address and expected the US mail service to do its job. One morning, soon after, we received a telephone call from the post office, inquiring where our street, Kennedy Way, was located. The man had been born and bred in Council Bluffs and was totally confused, saying that he knew every inch of the town, and there was no such place. I told him that the City Council was considering the street name change and that as far as we knew, it had been officially changed. He muttered, "Those Goons at City Hall think they can do anything" and went on and on. I felt bad for the fellow, but we knew that there SHOULD be a street named after John F. Kennedy, and we were glad to have thought of it, even if the city fathers hadn't. Uri received his bicycle and the guy is probably still scratching his head.

A FASCINATING SIDEBAR to the Kennedy story relates to the Jewish People as a whole. The fact that the generation of John Kennedy and his siblings have never been accused of anti-Semitism or any unfavorable acts against Jews is truly remarkable.

In the 20s and 30s, the Kennedy family was among the elite of America. His father, Joe Kennedy, was a member of the upper class, wealthy, and a well-known anti-Semite. He was the Ambassador to the Court of St. James in Britain and was an admirer and friend of Hitler. His views were well advertised and helped in the process of turning the Jews into Non-People and the results of his venality were what took place in Europe.

The Satmer Rebbe cursed Joe Kennedy saying that his children and grandchildren should experience every tragedy possible to be brought upon them. And the curse was effective: Joe Kennedy, Jr. was a pilot in the air force and lost his life in action. John F. and Robert were assassinated. A daughter, Rosemary, was mentally retarded. Ted Kennedy had his "Chappaquiddick" and never made it further in his quest to be president. They suffered divorces, suicides, health issues, drownings and many types of bizarre, deadly situations, from John, Jr., the president's son, killed in an airplane crash to another family member fatally slamming into a tree while skiing. Caroline Kennedy, John and Jackie's daughter, married a man born Jewish, but converted to Catholicism. Even so, Old Joe Kennedy must still be spinning in his grave.

Council Bluffs Memories – Rabbinic Style

Living in Council Bluffs was pleasant. Jay was immersed in his work, loving every minute of the Rabbinate. He had his duties, as well as was the liaison to the wider community. At times he would invite various church groups to visit the Synagogue and explain aspects of our colorful religion, which the audience would find fascinating.

AMONG THE HUMOROUS INCIDENTS during the question and answer period which followed these presentations, a woman asked if it is true that at the end of a Jewish wedding ceremony, the men in the audience must remove their glasses and break them. Or why do the Jewish People celebrate a major holiday in honor of Russia (Obviously referring to *Rosh* "Russia" *Hashanah*.)

Once a gentleman telephoned and requested that Jay marry him and his fiancé. Meeting with the couple, Jay was assured that there was no *Halachic* reason why he could not perform the ceremony, and set the date of the wedding. The next morning, he received a call from the Omaha Rabbinic Association relating the rules of that body which indicated strongly that he could not officiate at the event. The reasons given were that all Jewish weddings must take place in an area Synagogue and that the couple must be members of a congregation and could not just engage a Rabbi to officiate. This ruling ensured that all Jews were married in a House of Worship, which was a beautiful practice. The strength of the organization was so that the Rabbis complied. The bad news was that Jay lost a wedding. The good news was the knowledge that all the marriages were conducted properly in Omaha.

Some of our most interesting guests were emissaries from organizations to collect funds. In Ottumwa, we entertained many of them and they amused us. Often, they were personable with a gift of gab and related to us what was happening in the Jewish world. These were men who traveled the world collecting monies for every organization and fund under the sun, from New York to Israel and many places in between. They wore *Chassidic* garb and it was easy to spot them on the street. We were the only place in town for them to eat a *Kosher* meal and it was a treat for them, as their normal substance was rye bread and hard boiled eggs.

One Thanksgiving afternoon, a *Meshulach* came to the door and we invited him to join us in our traditional holiday meal of turkey, stuffing, cranberry sauce and all of the regular goodies for that meal. He looked askance at our celebrating Thanksgiving and I reiterated that Thanksgiving is a legal holiday with no Christian overtones at all. As a matter of fact, it mostly resembles our Jewish holiday of *Sukkot* in spirit. He was a bit mollified and sat down at the table. He then requested cottage cheese or dairy as he didn't know us or our level of *Kashrut*, but Jay told him that we are eating a meat meal and wouldn't serve dairy products at the same table. He was a bit dismayed, but when we told him that the turkey was from Empire Kosher Poultry, he decided that the turkey was fit enough for him to eat. We showed him the containers of all the food on the table and he was satisfied. He ended up not only eating everything, but enjoying his first Thanksgiving dinner.

There is a story of an emissary who would go once a year to collect from the donors. He had been returning to the same people for years. One day, he entered an office and found that his friend, the donor, had passed on. He requested to see the son, and when he entered the tastefully furnished and spacious office was told by the son that since his father had died, he decided not to give to this charity any longer. Whereupon, the *Meshulach* approached the son with his notebook in hand and said, "Very well, then you erase your father's name from the list." He received a donation! That was a perfect example of a clever and caring gentleman.

Another memorable incident worth relating, concerning an emissary occurred once when we were visiting Chicago. As is regular practice, a *Meshulach* hired a local man to drive him from house to house to collect funds. They arrived at the first wealthy gentleman and was told that he was not home now, but was at a Mourner's Prayer Group reciting the Afternoon prayers. The driver inquired if the emissary would like to *"Chop A Mincha,"* (Yiddish slang to pray the Afternoon service) and received a negative answer, saying that he was too busy and did not have the time to stop. They arrived at a second donor's house and received the same reply; "Not home" and *Davening Mincha* at a house of mourning." After the third prospect was again not at home, *"Davening Mincha* at a *Shiva* house," the driver asked again and received the same negative answer. Well, the emissary's mission was a total flop. Had he stopped to pray and gone to the Mourner's house where all the wealthy benefactors were helping their friend with a *Minyan* in order to say *Kaddish* (Prayer for the Dead) he would have had all his clients in one place and no doubt would have collected a tidy sum. This is true example of "No *Mitzvah*, No Money." The fellow is probably still mourning his bad luck that day is Chicago!

It was Passover 1965, and I was reading the Hadassah Magazine, marveling at the changes in the State of Israel that were reported in that issue. I said to Jay, "If we don't go soon, Israel will change so much and I want to experience it now."

When we were the elder members of our youth group, a ruling had been issued that whoever did not plan to go to Israel and be a part of *Hachshara* in the near future, was not welcome anymore, so we regretfully left the organization that had been so much a part of our lives. However, we were at a life crossroads at the time; some with college plans, some with serious boy or girlfriends. It wasn't the right time for us to think about *Aliyah*. When I told my father that I would like to go to Israel on *Hachshara*, his answer was not, "No," it was "Don't even think about it," and he was a Zionist, 1950s style. In his defense, it must be stated that the country was in its infancy. It was a time of serious food shortages, no, correct that, "of everything shortage." It was a hard life and I was proposing to live on a *Kibbutz*, when my father reminded me of the school advisor saying, "Marry anyone, but not a Farmer." He was right, of course. Living on a farm or *Kibbutz* was my nemesis; it wouldn't have worked, I'm sure. However, as some of our friends sailed on the "The Shalom," the flagship of the Zim shipping company, I was disappointed to miss such an experience and adventure, but I was busy with Jay Karzen at the time and he did his best to console me.

SO, NOW WE FAST FORWARD ten years. We are living in Iowa, with two small children and the call of Israel beckons to us. We decided to ask my in-laws to care for the little ones for three weeks in Chicago. They would attend Arie Crown Day Camp and we would take our first trip out of the country to Israel and on the way, see a bit of Europe. The situation with the children was settled, but the second consideration was money for the tour. A trend was appearing, in that congregations would send their Rabbi and wife to Israel. Sounded like a good idea and we felt that if we suggested it, they would contribute or even fund the trip. I had Thank You notes printed, to send out after we returned extolling the places that we had seen and thanking the various donors. Well, they never agreed and we went to the bank, took out a loan and paid for it for the next three years. As far as the cards, we printed three hundred and it took over twenty years to use them up. They were useful all of that time, but I chuckle at our naiveté that the Synagogue would underwrite the trip.

I know now that unless there is a "Cheerleader" for the Rabbi on the Board of Directors, any perk for him is a non-starter. That goes for any congregation, not only in Council Bluffs.

Our First Trip To Israel

Travel! Those have always been magic words for us. To see Israel was a dream come true. Since I was a youngster engrossed in reading every book that I could get my hands on, especially those set in exciting places such London, Paris, and other venues of European culture, I was ecstatic. Everything was exciting including the entire passport process, the planning of a trip on foreign shores, the unfamiliar money, and the anticipated lengthy airplane ride.

When the airplane taxied on the runway toward Ben Gurion Airport, I thought that my heart would burst from happiness. The song, Halleluyah, was played over the loudspeaker and between the tears that flowed and the shouts of joy, it was easily seen that we were not jaded travelers. After alighting from the El Al airplane with the magnificent flag of Israel etched on its tail, we knelt down and kissed the ground as is the custom. I was so moved that I was speechless.

We could hardly understand anything, especially the advertising signs in Hebrew. Our Biblical Hebrew language skills didn't go far and we mumbled *Mah?* so many times and realized that in the true Hebrew-speaking world, we absolutely didn't know the language. The expressions and street language were foreign to us and we ended up speaking "Hebrish." Of course, when an Israeli spoke to us, they wanted to practice their English, so it was a stand off of who wouldn't understand each other first! I totally gave up trying to speak when we saw dogs obeying and answering their owners. Even the dogs understood Hebrew better than we did, and we never saw a doggy *Ulpan.* How humiliating!

Israel was the place where we saw the Bible come alive. Visiting areas where Abraham, Isaac, Jacob and other biblical figures walked and lived was a constant source of amazement. Actually experiencing and visiting Mother Rachel's tomb, the Tomb of Samuel the Prophet and the walls of the Old City was beyond belief. We could only speak in superlatives. The Old City was in Jordanian hands and we stood afar and saw the guard posts of the Israeli and Jordanian guards who, according to our guide, spoke to each with a *Boker Tov* and the Arabic equivalent and were friendly. But the same guide urged me to put a large hat on my blonde hair. Because, as he warned, the Arabs like "Blondies." To this day, I have no idea what he meant, but I quickly did as told because Yosef instructed me to do so. Tour guides are, by and large, an engaging, informative group. We all loved Yosef. Every guide had a personal story of what activity they were engaged in on the battle field. To Americans not having ever engaged in wars on their soil, each soldier was seen as an Ari Ben Canan, the hero of the book and movie "Exodus."

The guides were exotic beings; brave, knowledgeable and had access to a gun under the driver's seat, which made the bus trips an everyday adventure with a possible hint of danger along for the ride. The weapons were never needed, but there was a bit of anticipation as these were not the safe highways of Illinois, Indiana or Wisconsin, but prone to incidents of enemy activities.

The Traveler's Prayer was said every day to nudge The Almighty to keep us in mind and safe on these journeys. In the twenty-some trips that we made bringing tourists from all over the US to Israel, I cannot recall even one incident that was in any way frightening. Yosef was our guide on the majority of tours and when we informed him of our decision to join him and our People, he wasn't surprised, but commented that perhaps we should remain in America – "Look at all the good we were doing for Israel by bringing folks here." That was probably his only statement that we could not agree with in all the years that we spent time with him. As we've heard from *Olim* over and over again, saying, "We should have made *Aliyah* years ago! Amen!

The list of wonderful surprises that awaited us in Israel was lengthy. The fact that the streets had names that honored Biblical personalities, modern Israeli heroes or Jewish events such *as Kaf Tet B'November,* which is the day when the UN voted in favor of the nascent country of Israel was a source of delight to us.

From Thursday on, everyone with whom one interacted, wished you *Shabbat Shalom,* or afterwards, *Shavua Tov.*

The guard, usually a little old man, at the department store didn't check to see if you stole anything walking out, but rather if you brought in weapons. When you left, he would often offer a blessing to enjoy your purchases.

On public transportation a sign was posted among the ads which read, *Mipneh Seva Takum,* a phrase taken from the Torah meaning "Rise before your elders," or in plain language, "Give an elderly person your seat." This is taken literally and I have often been the willing recipient of this good deed.

A friend had asked us to call her relative who lived in a small place in Israel. The telephone, with its *Asimonim,* was a challenge, but I was lucky and contacted an operator who spoke a "little" English (Very little!). When my operator spoke with the one in the requested town, she inquired who was it that we wished to speak with. Upon learning the name, she told us that the relative was not home, but she was at a friend's home playing Bridge and that she would ring her at the friends place. I successfully sent the regards from her niece in Chicago. But I will never get over the amazement of everyone knowing everyone, which is a constant aspect of Israeli life. Of course, Israel is five times its size of those times, but Jewish geography is still a favorite pastime. It is said that there are six degrees of separation of people in the world. For Jews, it is two and for Observant Jews, just one. The reality is that if two religiously Observant Jews meet anywhere in the world, after speaking with each other for a few minutes, one is sure to know a cousin, neighbor, or friend. The game of Jewish Geography is a winner every time.

There is a charming story that so illustrates this point. Two men were traveling on a train.

One man whispers to the other, "What time is it?"

No answer. Again, he asks the time. Once more, no answer.

Then a third time, and no reply.

While walking toward the station, the fellow says to the inquirer. The time is 3:20.

"Why didn't you tell me when I asked you on the train?"

"You see, it's like this. I tell you the time and we start to talk about where we live, families who we know in common and the fact that I have a marriageable daughter – you seem to be a nice enough guy. But, to tell you the truth I don't want anyone in the family that doesn't own a watch!"

From the bus windows, we saw the fertile fields with sunflowers, fruits and vegetables. Yosef waxed ecstatic over every tomato hot house and wheat field. By the end of the trip we began to appreciate the miraculous feats of farming that had been accomplished. Even though we lived in the Midwest, which boasts much of America's most fertile land and there are countless acres of farmland, I had always ignored them. They were boring and fields were just fields. Fruits and vegetables came in the packages from the supermarket and remember what I felt about farmers, in general. But Yosef filled us with pride on that trip. And he was certainly correct about the taste of peaches and tomatoes – they were the tastiest that we had ever eaten.

There were so many memorable moments on our first trip to Israel. We were privileged to be part of the first audience after the reconstruction of the Caeserea Amphitheater where Isaac Stern, the violinist, gave a performance for the first time in 2,000 years!

Another historic happening was the reburial of hero patriot Zev Jabotinsky. He had died many years previously and was buried in New York. He and Ben Gurion, the former Prime Minister were bitter, lifetime enemies. After many years of internment on foreign soil, Jabotinsky's coffin was brought to Israel and we attended his State Funeral in Tel Aviv.

In Beer Sheva, there were two actual buildings, the five star Desert Inn Hotel and the two and one-half star Zohar Hotel where we were guests. When we arrived and were awaiting room assignments, the manager inquired as to who were the youngest in the group. We raised our hands and then were told that our room is on the top floor and that the elevator was not yet in service. Being good sports, we lugged our four suitcases up the stairs to the fifth floor, but other surprises were in store. There was no closet, no air conditioning and no telephone, but standing in the room was a small bathtub. So Jay walked down the stairs and wrangled a deal for a closet, which was two chairs with rung backs and four hangers, but they disconnected the portable, tin bathtub and carried it out. We couldn't have both. We felt hot, tired and dispirited, but then we heard a knock on the door and it was the manager paying us a courtesy call. He strode to the window, encouraged us to look with him out of the window and we saw a lot of sand, sand and more sand. He saw an entire city, laid it out for us, and he made us see it, as well. Every Israeli was a visionary and we loved them for it.

I had wanted to see Israel before it became a metropolis and I did. On that trip, being a visionary and an idealist was a part of the landscape. We saw what they said would be the largest port one day; that a facility would rise here and large ships from all over the world would arrive and the cranes would work daily. However, in Ashdod at that time, we saw lots of sand and water, but we faithfully took movies of the future port. Of course, that is exactly what happened.

We were taken to Eilat, which again turned out to be a handful of hotels with miles of sand everywhere you looked. We stayed at the Queen of Sheba Hotel with exotic fur rugs covering the cool, tile floors. There was a nightclub called, "The End of The World", complete with a woman chanteuse singing Blues in English and Hebrew. I decided that when we make *Aliyah*, if employment would be a problem, that I would go to Eilat and become a Chanteuse a la Hildegarde, complete with white, long gloves. Thankfully, that never occurred, but it was a thought and I delighted in it.

One evening we stopped at one of the northern religiously

observant *kibbutzim*. We were to have dinner and sleep there. The dinner was simple and extremely modest. It featured yogurt and vegetables. Jay thought that it was the first course and decided to wait for the actual meal and did not partake. To his consternation, that was the meal, and he was hungry until breakfast was served. Frankly, food was hardly a preoccupation in those years. Israel was past the *Tzena* and hunger was not a problem, however the idea of eating food as one of life's pleasures was far in the future. Food was a necessity and there was nothing frivolous or luxurious in any aspect of it. Between the modest meals and the hiking for three weeks, I actually lost weight. It was a marvelous, eye-opening trip and it sowed the seeds of our future life in Israel.

Being our first trip outside the borders of North America, we decided to take an extra week and travel to Europe. We traveled Italy, Switzerland and France, and spent the Sabbath in Belgium. I'm certain that I stared open-mouthed and gawked like a genuine tourist in every place that we went. In Italy, we were fortunate enough to go to Verona, the romantic, legendary city of Romeo and Juliet, where we saw the opera Aida, complete with live elephants, and piles of poo! We strolled down the *Banhofstrasse,* which was a main street of Zurich, where I have never seen so many watch stores. I bought a lovely timepiece with a graceful butterfly that covered the glass face. Unfortunately, at a later date, it was stolen. Somewhere in Heaven there is an entire room with the jewelry pieces that I have lost or have been stolen from me from my home, airports, hotels and ships. I figured out that I am ordained to enjoy the piece for X amount of years and then it is time for someone else to own it. I have no other explanation!

Our Sabbath in Antwerp was most enjoyable and part of the experience was my going to a beauty shop on Friday. It looked normal, but as the operator worked on my hair, I began to suspect that perhaps it was a beauty shop in front, but a bookie joint in the rear. I had an odd feeling.

Travel is broadening is the expression, and one new fact that we learned was that the language of the Belgian people is Flemish … we didn't understand a word!

Paris, France: A friend and his charming Music Maker Monkey!

Paris was … well Paris! The City of Lights was true to its name. It charmed us. From Montmarte, the Eifel Tower, the boat trip down the Seine River, the European architecture – we loved it all. The only big problem was, not anti-Semitism – it was anti-American. They disliked us; wouldn't speak English to the point that because of my terrible one-year college French, we made reservations in a restaurant for twelve persons instead of two. *C'est La Vie!*

On our return flight, we arrived in New York where Roz and Howard met us at the airport. We had fifty cents between us and they gave us ten dollars for pocket money to return to Chicago. Come to think of it … we probably never paid it back … note that on my to-do list!

RABBI BEN GRONER ACCEPTED a new position in New Orleans, Louisiana and the large, wonderful Orthodox Synagogue was to be without a Rabbi. Jay was interested in moving across the river and filling that prestigious pulpit. He contacted the placement office, headed by Rabbi Isaac Nadoff of the Hebrew Theological School with the hopes that they would help him to obtain the position. Rabbi Nadoff came to Omaha, met with the committee and they offered him the job! In truth, he was a terrific choice; scholarly, Orthodox in belief and practice with an open, inquiring mind, as well as tall, dark and handsome. It was a sure bet that he would be a perfect fit for the pulpit.

We had known Isaac and his wife, Jeanette, for many years as he was the brother of my childhood friend, Shoshana Nadoff, (z'l). We were disappointed, but not angry, as we realized that he and the congregation were meant for each other. Rabbi Nadoff spent the rest of his life in Omaha. After his death, Jeanette remained there – living her life among people who had grown to love and admire the Nadoffs. I do love to hear stories about congregations and Rabbis who have spent years together and the impact that the right Rabbi can have on the lives of congregants. It is a reflection of our own lives in the Rabbinate and the *Tikun Olam* that Rabbinic couples can accomplish during their tenure among the people.

THE LORD WORKS IN MYSTERIOUS WAYS is a phrase that has always been part of our credo. Had Jay been offered the Omaha pulpit, he would have readily accepted it. Tammy and Uri would have been sent to high school and *Yeshiva* in Chicago, and would have been "Out of Towners." They would have had a foot in two cities, and while numberless Orthodox families have lived that way for years, there is a better way ... that of living in a community of like-minded people.

While the Nadoff's were anticipating their move to Omaha, the placement office at the Skokie Yeshiva, Jay's Alma Mater, telephoned with the news that a new Synagogue was being organized in Des Plaines, Illinois, which is a twenty-minute drive from Skokie. Would he be interested? "Yes, we sure were interested!" We would be returning home to our families, friends and be ascertained of a good Jewish education for the kids.

Jay returned from the interview with the offer in his hand – Des Plaines, Illinois would be our future home. We once again packed our belongings, said Goodbye at the parties that were hosted in our behalf and tearfully left Council Bluffs, Iowa.

Des Plaines

We exited Highway 294, at the Des Plaines exit and were faced with *corn fields*! Everywhere we looked there were stalks of corn waving in the breeze. We had just come from farmland country and thought that we were going to be city folks once again, and here were more fields. I rubbed my eyes in disbelief. Where was the city that we anticipated? And then it dawned on us, when the committee had said a new Synagogue was forming, they forgot to mention that a new *community* was forming. We were once again pioneers.

There was no Synagogue building. Services were held in the gymnasium of the local grammar school. In the ensuing years MAINE TOWNSHIP JEWISH CONGREGATION would be housed in the following venues such as various members' family rooms, a model home, a trailer, an old house lovingly dubbed as The Haunted House, The Dolphin Motel meeting rooms and The Greek Orthodox Community Center, etc. etc. etc. The Rabbi's office was in one of our upstairs bedrooms, which made it impossible to conduct matters in privacy.

The privacy matter came to a head when a woman required counseling and coming to his home office for the meeting was not feasible. So she suggested that he visit her at her home. When she opened the door for him, he noticed that she was dressed in a negligee – he sensed that he was in trouble. When they were seated in front of her salon picture window, he breathed a small sigh of relief in the fact that, at least in appearance, it was semi-public. But then she related to him that one big problem for her was the fact that her husband was insanely jealous of her relationship with any other man, regardless of how innocent it was. "In fact," she said, "if my husband sees us sitting together like this, he is likely to blow our heads off with a gun."

With profuse apologies Jay quickly left this quirky situation – getting killed for his counseling services was definitely not in his contract!

After World War II, the suburbs were created and especially

families with young children flocked to new areas. The novelty of living in rural areas, with nature, the newness of the dwellings, the quiet, as well as the cleanliness of the surroundings were a magnet. The Suburban Way of Life was created and envied. Every state, as well as Illinois, expanded its area and dozens of new communities were built.

The same idea applied after the Korean War. Illinois expanded westward from Chicago and with $600 for the down payment and Honorable Discharge papers from the U.S. Army, the veteran was entitled to a home in the new area of Des Plaines. The existing City of Des Plaines was a community which was over 100 years old and was created originally to take advantage of the waters of the Des Plaines River. This is the narrative of communities as far back as ancient times. A water source was the magnet that drew people, as humanity cannot exist without a constant supply of water. The primary reason is for consumption, of course. However, rivers and streams were also used for transportation of people and goods, sports and other activities.

Our brand new suburb of Des Plaines was in its infancy when we arrived. It was a place of duplexes i.e. two homes separated by a common wall. The homes were attractive. We had a main floor den, a sunken salon, four bedrooms and 2½ baths. The Master Bedroom was en suite and it was the first and last time that we ever had our very own private bath. It was a one-time luxury for us. Each home sported a back lawn and a postage stamp-size front lawn. One morning, I left the house and saw a gardening supplies truck on the street. When I returned in the afternoon, each home was fronted by a small, skinny sapling neatly planted in the front yard. We had a leafy street created in a few hours. Well, not so leafy, as most of the trees died within a few months!

In a short while, many of the residents had poured concrete for patios which were an important addition to the property. The Synagogue owned the house for the resident Rabbi and family, and any additions or improvements were the responsibility of the Board of Directors. Funds for the house must have been the last budget item on the Board's list and the patio was not built via the Board. Finally, we scraped together the few hundred dollars to add the patio and thus increase the value of the Synagogue's property. We were very proud of it and it was a valuable addition in terms of the children's space to play safely outside.

One morning, a woman member dropped by and noticed the new patio. She became incensed that the Rabbi had a patio and she didn't. She left in a huff and was even angrier when she found out that we had paid for it with our money.

The rule that I have formulated over the years follows: I reiterate once again … The Rabbi cannot live or dress better or drive a fancier car than the members. Period … no exceptions, except for clergy who are fortunate to possess independent funds. This *Rule* was poured in concrete with this instance and has stood the test of time.

From the early days in Des Plaines, I have always advocated that clergy not be at the mercy of the congregation. I wanted to be my own *Baal HaBayit*, to own my home; not be at the mercy of a Board of Directors, no matter how caring they appeared.

Even though we were in our twenties, very young for sure, I maintained that if something should befall Jay, G-D Forbid, I would return from the funeral and a sign would be hung on the door: "Dear Ruby, So sorry for your loss, but please vacate the house in 30 days." Sounds ugly, but unfortunately, I have learned that this type of response from a congregation is not all that rare.

Over the years, I have singly advocated home ownership and there are Rabbinic colleagues and friends who listened and they praise me and remind me constantly how delighted they are with their home ownership. Unfortunately, there are two who come to mind that I literally got down on my hands and knees to beg them to purchase their own home and they refused … it is a scary proposition owing a large sum of money and being responsible for a property … but they are now filled with remorse after losing out, big time, but you cannot put your head on someone else's shoulders.

AS PEOPLE BEGAN MOVING INTO the neighborhood, Jay would go door-to-door, introduce himself and invite them to the new local Synagogue. When the prospective members would inquire what denomination of Rabbi he professed, first he would tell them that he is a combination of Orthodox, Conservative and Reform and then he would explain. He is Orthodox, as the word Orthodox comes from Latin, *Orthos Doxo*, meaning "the correct way." He is Conservative, because he is endeavoring to "Conserve" the Jewish faith in our generation and he is Reform, because he is trying to "Reform" Jews who have yet to see the beauty of Judaism. The truth of the matter is that none of those three terms appear in the Torah. Secondly, he is a "Joyous Jew" and he preaches "Joyous Judaism," based on Psalm 100 which states "Serve the Lord with Joy."

Everyone in our newly established neighborhood was young, 20s and 30s were the normative ages. Families generally had one or two children and were new to the challenges of parenthood. They were at the beginning of their work lives; some with careers and corporate ladders to climb and others going from job to job trying to find their niche. There was one constant. We were all without money. There were twelve houses on our block and we became good buddies. There is an expression that "A good neighbor is better than a distant brother."

That axiom was proven true by the block of homes on West Oaks Avenue. There was a knock on our door and standing there was a neighbor with tears in her eyes. She was going door to door collecting money for a loan to pay her gas bill or the utility company would immediately shut off her supply. The bill was $18 and each neighbor went to their lean wallets and donated one or two dollars or whatever they could spare to help her out. The neighbors eked out the cash willingly, but that was reality.

We were living in a brand new neighborhood, with new appliances, washers, dryers, dishwashers, refrigerator-freezers, central air conditioners and the like, but we were not only cash poor, but without any savings or families that could help financially.

One time I was at Dominicks, the local supermarket, and when the cashier totaled the bill, I was 29 cents short to pay the bill. I returned the tube of lipstick which cost the extra sum. But, I was so embarrassed and vowed at that moment that, G-D Willing, that would never happen again. There were credit cards, but due to our financial situation, I used it sparingly and furthermore, the State of Illinois did not allow the use of cards to buy food. So we were stuck ... it was cash or nothing so I returned that tube of lipstick with a red face and the determination to find a job to help supplement the meager salary that my hard-working spouse was earning.

Besides the situation of a lack of funds that we all shared, we enjoyed good times. One evening we set up a movie theater on our back lawns – they were small and we utilized three adjacent lawns. There were no fences, as no one could afford them, but it was more than adequate. We pooled our wedding movies and howled as we saw our "Young" selves in the formal settings.

In 1956, the home movie business was in its infancy. Jay's uncle, Hy Stick (*z'l*), was the Videographer at our wedding. Jay and I had to laugh as we watched the antics of second cousins enjoying our wedding, yet few shots of the groom and the bride. I was seen but once, standing at the head of the aisle waiting for the procession to begin. We always quipped that we were the hidden stars of our wedding!

Winter 1967 brought severe weather to Illinois. Beginning Wednesday evening, it snowed and snowed, covering the entire state, rendering life as we knew it impossible. The roads were impassable, the sidewalks were not usable and everything stood at a standstill. Friday morning, our doorbell rang. Upon opening the door, there stood a neighbor, the one non-Jewish woman on the block. She had bundled herself up against the inclement weather and took her son's sled to the supermarket for food supplies. She handed me an Empire Kosher Chicken and said that she thought that I might be able to use it for the Sabbath. I kissed her and thanked her profusely. How thoughtful she was to think of us at that time. I was planning on salami, but thanks to her, we celebrated the Sabbath as it should be.

That day there was a *Bar Mitzvah* scheduled at the Synagogue, which was cancelled. A wedding on Sunday had the Grandmother being carried to Golf Road, the nearest major street, to find a taxicab. But the major drama point was the helicopter that airlifted a pregnant neighbor to a hospital. Because of the inability of the state government to deal with this major weather situation, Mayor Jane Byrne, of Chicago, was defeated in her bid for a second term. One could say that she was "snowed under!"

Within a few years, we all began to find our financial footing. One neighbor had an ingenious idea for a trucking company and it proved to be a lucrative one. Another became the legal representative for one of the "Banana Republic" countries. He traveled a lot, but we knew when he was home, as there were bodyguards sitting on his roof.

While Jay was building the Synagogue, physically and spiritually, I returned to school and the course that beckoned to me was Interior Design. Except for the math that was required, I loved every aspect of it. After finishing the first semester, I took an extensive course from Parson's School of Design, as well as The Design Art School of Chicago. However, when I graduated I faced a major problem. I had mastered theory but needed practical experience.

Interior Design is a Sabbath business in the entire world except for Israel. There was not one Interior Designer in the Chicago area that was a Sabbath observer that I could shadow and observe. My brand new AIDA card (Association of Interior Designers of America) was burning a hole in my wallet. I wanted to use it, but even the bi-monthly meetings of the Interior Design Society of Illinois were held at a downtown hotel on Friday night. Here I was, an Orthodox Jew, not to mention a Rabbi's wife, with small children – to attend even one meeting with my colleagues was impossible.

I did have a few, very few, clients. There were friends who did seek my services. Joan and Bernie Revsine, residents of Peterson Park, a neighborhood in Chicago, have not changed the rooms that I decorated in their home, over thirty years ago. They still love them and mention it whenever we are together – they're waiting for me to return and update their rooms one day.

Harold Rublin (*z'l*) hired me to do a few model apartments in his project.

Rabbi Ben Shandalov, of The Hebrew Theological College, requested that I try to spruce up the dormitories. The upshot is that the doors of the students' rooms are painted one of four colors. It is most attractive and the boys love it. However as much as I enjoyed the clients that I had, I wasn't setting the world on fire, so I decided to pursue another career that was more lucrative. Perhaps my youth was another handicap to success, as designers handle large sums of money and one must prove to be trustworthy. Obviously, youngsters in their 20s have a short record.

MAINE TOWNSHIP JEWISH CONGREGATION (MTJC) was an unqualified success. After being a group of wandering Jews, praying in different locations, we finally purchased land, hired architects and were off and running. The day of the ground-breaking was emotional in the realization that the untold hours of meetings of the Building Committee had finally come to fruition. Upon completion of the building, a parade with flags, music and dancing in the streets was held, bringing the Torahs into the new Sanctuary.

The Synagogue grew quickly and soon there were three hundred, then four hundred and at five hundred family units, the membership leveled off. The architects maintained that the small sanctuary used for prayers during the week, classrooms, offices and rest rooms be placed on the first floor. The second story housed the very large Sanctuary that was used for services on the Sabbath and holidays. It also was used as a social hall with weddings, *Bar* and *Bat Mitzvah* celebrations and events of all types. The afternoon Hebrew School boasted hundreds of students which meant that we were in *Bar / Bat Mitzvah* heaven.

Every Sabbath, at least two youngsters celebrated their events. There were weeks that there were four celebrations in one day. Friday night a *Bat Mitzvah,* a double *Bar Mitzvah* in the morning and one at the Afternoon service. It is estimated that over 1,200 youngsters celebrated their special occasions under the auspices of the Synagogue.

Creative happenings at MTJC were a given. Every *Simchat Torah* eve the congregation would parade to a nearby nursing home facility with Torah Scrolls, happily accompanied by the local police with red lights flashing, to bring some holiday spirit and joy to the residents. Hundreds participated in this annual *Hakafot* celebration. To see the tears of joy, smiles and clapping of the Golden Agers was an emotional experience for all.

The Synagogue was the recipient of numerous special commendations. One was for the above nursing home event, as well as the *Purim* Feed-A-Family Project, The *Selichot* Night Social *Shiduch* Evening for singles; the Passover Seder and *Shavuot* Blintzes luncheon. The Sisterhood (Women's Auxiliary) sponsored a Bagel / Lox Gourmet breakfast each Mother's Day and the Men's Club a spaghetti dinner each Wednesday pre-Thanksgiving to give the ladies a break from dinner chores, while preparing for the next day's turkey feast. The *Torathon* was an educational tool that brought other area Synagogues to our building to learn and be inspired by Judaism.

It was an exciting time in the history of MTJC. We were leaders in the community. Even folks who attended our weekly Bingo Game for fundraising purposes were proud to say that they were members of MTJC. The joke was that many of these proud members' names never appeared on the membership list. They figured that they paid for their Bingo games and that was all the money that the Synagogue would ever see from them. These people were neither "pray-ors" nor "pay-ors," but the Sunday evening Bingo Game was like the eleventh commandment to them: *You Shall Play Bingo At MTJC On Sunday Evening.*

The Synagogue loved us and we gave our all for the members.

Over the years, Jay, who morphed into *Saba*, became a fixture in countless lives. Whether it was to conduct a wedding, funeral, or other family event; to visit a member that was ill in hospital or to counsel on subjects both common and bizarre – *Saba* was there.

MANY INCIDENTS HAVE BECOME LEGENDARY. There was the wedding, held in the Sanctuary, where the families came to blows, knocking over the partitions and the rolling bar. Another affair was held under the stormiest of skies. From the car to the hotel, *Saba* became drenched. His pants, shoes and socks were sopping wet and when he walked down the aisle to the bridal canopy to await the couple, his shoes audibly squished with every step that he took, leaving footprints on the white bridal runner.

Funerals also were replete with quirky behavior. There was a father and son who were unfortunately gunned down in their place of business. The funeral was unbearably sad with the two caskets side by side. Unfortunately, family relations before this unhappy event were low. The mother-in-law started to scream to the hated daughter-in-law, "You should be in the box, not my beloved son!" and the woman started to scream epithets at her mother-in-law. All of a sudden, the caskets were shoved; people were yelling and a melee ensued. Whereupon someone shouted: "Rabbi, do something!" *Saba* started to intone the Twenty-third Psalm. He figured that these words were as good as any others. He couldn't remember learning any prayer in the *Yeshiva* that covered this bizarre situation!

One time, after the cemetery service, we went directly to the mourner's house in order for them to begin their mourning period in proper fashion. We waited a half-hour, and then an hour, finally leaving. We found out later that the children had gone to the lawyer's office to read the will. The father had been a wealthy man and they wanted to make sure that no one sibling arrived at the attorney by himself. They didn't trust the other sisters to have a fair session without all of them there at once. "True *Nachas* from children," as they say. It was appalling. The gentleman didn't deserve such callous behavior.

There was one time that we went to a house early in the evening following the morning funeral service. We rang and rang the bell, but there was no answer. This was strange as they should have been home beginning *Shiva*, the observance of the seven days of mourning. Finally, someone came to the door and partially opened it. We could see suitcases seemingly ready to be carried out. What happened was that the couple had tickets to go on a cruise. They were certain that Mother would have wanted them to go and not lose the fares that had been prepaid. So they went and I imagine had a wonderful time.

But that was one step up from the couple who told *Saba* that they held cruise tickets for a dream vacation. Their mother was ill and in the hospital in the final stages of her life. Their plan was that if she passed away while they were at sea, the funeral home would freeze the body and there would be a service when they returned!

Believe me, these situations truly did occur; who could make them up! Of course there were hundreds of events that we attended where the people behaved properly. In the main, people are good and want to do the right thing. And they want to love and respect their Rabbi. A Rabbinic couple can and should hold a special place in the members' hearts.

We attended countless *Smachot*, joyous events. However, we did draw the line at attending Sabbath parties with members. Sabbath was the time that we spent with the children as a family. Over the years, there were youngsters that spent their Sabbaths and Holidays with our family. Larry Krule, Jeffrey Schoenberg, and Douglas Zelden all became *Bnai Bayit* at one time or another. We were their spiritual parents. They all became adults to be proud of and credits to *Am Yisrael*.

The Rabbi / *Rebbetzin* is often a lonely existence, in many aspects. They must be on a slightly different plane as they should be the moral and spiritual guides to their community. The distance between those two planes is a delicate balancing act and must be monitored constantly.

Dedication of a Magen David Adom Ambulance to the People of Israel, donated by the members of the Maine Township Jewish Congregation, Des Plaines, Illinois, after the Yom Kippur War, 1973

THE SYNAGOGUE WAS A BUSTLING BUILDING. There were services daily, of course, and meetings of the various groups mornings, afternoons and evening. The Sisterhood was my baby from its beginning. As in Iowa, I advised and mentored the groups for programming, both educational and social.

In our young community, we all grew up and matured and there were life-long friendships formed. One of our points of pride is that with all the many presidents of the Synagogue, Women's group, Men's Group, Boards of Directors, as well as staff, we were friends, even good friends, with so many members. Sherwin Pomerantz and Barbara (*z'l*) and Myrna and Jeffrey Buckman became our lifelong best friends, and we have shared every type of experience with these, our dearest buddies.

Of course, friendship is a two-way street. To have a friend, one must be a friend and that is not always the easiest of situations. At times, it is hard to maintain good relations, but very rewarding. After an incident occurred with the normal political overtones that occur from time to time, Myrna would look at me, wrinkle her brow and said, "Y' know Ruby, sometimes its hard to be your friend!" I know, Myrna, I know!

ONCE THE CHILDREN WERE IN SCHOOL full time, I decided to find employment. The only disagreement that I ever had with my wonderful father-in-law was on this point. In his generation, if a wife worked, it was felt that it showed the world that the husband was not a good provider. This was a throwback to early times in history, when men were the hunters and women would guard the fire in the cave and raise the children. I wasn't as concerned about the fire going out in our cave as much as I was unhappy with our financial plight. Besides, I was never content to go to lunch with the "girls" and do a bit of volunteer work. That simply wasn't my style in my 20s and it never was after.

I became a Weight Watchers lecturer after losing weight on their program. It was a fascinating and interesting time, but the program was a strict diet and impossible to maintain for a long stretch of time. Unfortunately, I never attained my goal weight and my career as a representative for the organization was ended. Unfortunately, the weight crept back and I was where I started. There are two other women who were lecturers and now live in Israel. We're all still fighting the life-long battle against unhealthy fat. I also tried consumer marketing and a number of other possible jobs, but they were unsatisfactory.

A New Career

One day I saw an ad for Real Estate Salesmen. It seemed ideal for me as I would be my own boss and could set my own hours. Sabbath observance is a challenge outside of Israel and as happened, I was the first registered observant salesperson on the Chicago Board of Realtors and the North Shore Board of Realtors organizations.

I made an appointment with the Kruger Realty office located on Main Street in Skokie whose Broker was Harry Rabin. We hit it off immediately. Harry had grown up in a typical Jewish-

American home, where *Kashrut* was observed as far as the purchase of meat and the separation of meat and milk products. But the industry, i.e. the OU organization, was in its infancy and there was little interest in the general community of a high standard of observance. Harry believed in the tenets of Orthodox Judaism. He was a member of an Orthodox Synagogue and when he said *Kaddish* for his parents, he would only attend an Orthodox service. He was delighted to have an observant person in his office and always treated me with the utmost respect. He would make certain when the office schedule was made up and a salesperson was obligated to man the office, that I was never scheduled for the Sabbath or Jewish Holidays. Of course, I reciprocated by working on the Christian holidays. It worked out well. But the best part of Harry was his Zionism. He was the most dedicated right-wing Israel lover that I had ever met up to that time!

Years later, when I had already been living in Israel for a few years, I became interested in how the various Jewish-American communities had helped in the establishment of the State of Israel. Friends, former New Yorkers, related how in the middle of the night, they had snuck down to the docks to help load cargo destined for the nascent state. Another related that his father had been with a representative of Ben Gurion at a secret meeting where famous gangsters raised millions of dollars to buy arms.

After hearing these stories, I began to inquire … and what about Chicago? I was very young at the time and I couldn't remember any nefarious goings on at all.

In a trip back to Chicago, I began to research the subject and my findings led me back to my friend Harry Rabin. It seems that when Harry was back after serving in the US Army, he began collecting guns, ammunition, grenades, and any souvenirs that the soldiers brought back from their stint fighting in WWII. He placed the weapons in barrels and hid them behind the Torah Ark in his Synagogue, which was located on the South Side of Chicago. The barrels were filled with his and friends "collections" on the bottom and on top were toys for the children.

The first two shipments arrived in Israel, and one can imagine the delight on the faces of the defenders of the State, as well as the children when the barrels were opened.

But then the Synagogue was sold and the "Closing" was to be on the following afternoon. That night Harry and his crew called the Rabbi requesting the keys, so that they could remove the barrels before they could be denied entry. The Rabbi was astonished, having no previous knowledge of this situation. Harry laughed when he related this story to me and said that the group was late even for *Selichot*, as the action was named.

Harry's wife, Lee, told me of the times that she would find weapons that he collected in between the clean diapers for her babies. She related that one time the family was at a neighborhood carnival and a man approached Harry and gave him two guns, and Harry, not having anywhere else to carry them, put them in the toy bags that they were carrying. Harry was a wonderful person and I admired him for his creativity and honesty. Unfortunately, he was hit by a city bus, injured badly, and spent the end of his life in a nursing care facility where he never recovered.

Selling Real Estate can be a difficult and heartbreaking job. It is possible to work for weeks or even months with a client and then they will see a sign advertising a house to be sold by the owner and within an hour, the deal is finished. The salesman is out not only many hours of his time, as well as the funds that were expended for auto fuel and other expenses, but the disappointment can be intolerable, and this can happen time after time. Or, as I have said, that selling houses is an educational process for the client. The salesman can spend months teaching clients the ins and outs of the market; which neighborhoods are suitable for the family and other numerous details – and the client will walk into an OPEN HOUSE one Sunday and all of the salesperson's efforts go down the drain. This was the down side of the business, but I had many successes, which is what keeps you going.

I often do my most creative thinking when lying in bed at 3 or 4 a.m.; this is one such instance. There is a neighborhood called Timber Ridge. It is a small idyllic, leafy green, quiet enclave in Skokie, with four and five bedroom homes and it was becoming increasingly difficult to sell the well designed, large, interesting homes. The problem was that the area's local school district bordered Evanston, which has a substantial Black African-American population and the White residents didn't want their children to attend racially-mixed schools. I knew that there were many young Orthodox families who would be ecstatic to live in this verdant area with these impressive houses, and the best part was that schools were not an impediment to purchasing in this area, as the children all attended Jewish Day Schools. With that argument, I sold the first Timber Ridge home to Dr. Naftali and Judy Gutstein. They lived there for many years, raising their family, and just recently sold their beloved house and moved to smaller quarters. The area is now 100% Orthodox and the Synagogue that was established to serve these residents has been enlarged many times over. Timber Ridge I count as one of my successes. However, I would have enjoyed more of them.

The Million Dollar Round Table Salesman plaque was awarded each year. I was always a part of that distinguished group. In today's prices, on the face of it ... what is a million dollars? Every decent home in Jerusalem costs that; here, we speak in telephone numbers. But remember that in the 70s, the average price of a home that was sold in our area was $30-45,000. We sold a lot of houses, year after year. One year, our office had the most salespeople represented in the Round Table and Jim Kruger, the CEO of the firm, decided on a special treat for the winners. We were picked up by a limousine, corsages or boutonnières of flowers pinned on us and driven to a very special restaurant for a sumptuous, gourmet meal and luxurious evening where I enjoyed my regular fruit plate!

In the office, we became like a family. After a while, we knew who could be trusted not to steal away clients, who was likeable and who should be avoided.

There were times that we would return to the office at 10 p.m. carrying "Earnest Money" (money to assure the sale of a building). Harry was gone for the day and the safe was locked. We would divide the cash between the salespeople in the office to take home overnight and return it, to be placed in the safe in the morning. There were numerous times that I came home carrying $20,000 or more – it was all in a day's work. The odd fact was that whenever we were "overnight bankers," it was money that came from a client that was a Greek restaurant owner. They always had large amounts in their pockets. It was probably "tax exempt" money from their establishments. At least that's what we were told and nobody asked any questions.

One Sunday morning I was to show a large home in Des Plaines. This area was a ten-block radius which housed a number of Mafia types; at least that was the rumor. Ringing the bell produced no response and for some unfathomable reason I went around to the rear of the house where the kitchen was located. Again, no response to the bell. Turning the door handle the door opened. The kitchen table was set for breakfast with eggs congealing in plates, coffee in cups, the TV playing and no one there! It appeared that they had fled, just leaving everything behind. I quickly left and thought better of calling the police. This was Chicago-style Mafia tactics at work and I didn't want to end up in Lake Michigan wearing cement shoes!

Every Friday morning the salespeople of the office were required to visit all the new listings and evaluate the properties. We would pile into three cars and it was a festive feeling – we generally had a good time. One Friday, returning to the office, we reported our findings on a lovely home in Wilmette.

"That's very interesting and I'm glad that you all liked the house ... but it was the wrong one!" Harry exclaimed and added that the owner wanted to know why we didn't show up, she had even prepared coffee for us and was disappointed.

Odd circumstances brought us to this not-so-funny point. Looking at the appointment list, it appeared that the address numbers were switched. We had found the number printed on our list, the door was unlocked and we figured that the lady of the house was at a neighbor for a few minutes and would soon return. In the meantime we did our usual inspection, walking from room to room and making notes on the property. She never did return, so we returned to the cars and went to the next house. Lucky we didn't put up a FOR SALE sign!

I was working with a couple for months and we finally found their dream house. They signed the contract on a Thursday evening, deposited Earnest Money and I figured that it was a done deal. Early Sunday morning I received the dreaded "Morning After" telephone call. It seemed that in the Synagogue on that Sabbath, the Torah reading was the portion in the Book of Leviticus, *Shemini*, where it describes *Tzoraat*, impurities that can appear on skin, fabric or leather items. The couple decided that there was *Tzoraat* in the walls of their to-be-new house and decided to call off the deal. Can you imagine me explaining this situation to the Broker, who possibly had not stepped into a Synagogue in over fifty years?

As I wrote previously, there were heavy times, disappointments and heartbreak. In truth, a salesman needs skin as thick as an elephant to be a successful Real Estate agent. There was a young man who had been at the job for a few months. One day, we learned that he had committed suicide at home. I was elected to clean out his desk and return his personal effects. Betty, the office wag, remarked: "We all know that this is a difficult, demanding job, but he took it a bit too far." Very tragic situation and as I said previously, a skin of thick elephant hide is a must for a career in Real Estate.

Jay and I decided that it was time to leave the Duplex, which was owned by the Synagogue, and purchase our own home. I found the perfect house, one block from the Synagogue. Our address, 1515 West Davis, Park Ridge, Illinois, was part of a ten-block radius which was attached to the suburb of Park Ridge. At the end of the block stood the Synagogue building, whose address was Des Plaines. The reason given was that Park Ridge would not issue a liquor license to a House of G-D. What the Catholic Churches did in Park Ridge, who knows? But it was known that the good folks of Park Ridge were not happy to have even one Synagogue listed under their name in the telephone book.

Hillary Clinton's family were residents of that suburb and she attended Park Ridge West High School. Once, while she was visiting Israel, I managed to approach her and gave her regards from her old home town. Her face broke out in a wide smile – I'm glad that she has fond memories of the place. It could pose for a picture postcard of an ideal spot of an upscale small town. It was and is a good place to live – Jerusalem, however, is better.

There were only two houses on each of the blocks and they were surrounded by green, well-kept lawns. Ours was a Ranch home, which meant that the living room, dining room, kitchen, three bedrooms and baths were on the main floor. There was a full basement with fireplace, walls of books, loads of storage and a Ping-Pong table. There was a large laundry room and enough room for Uri to set up his drum set and his other projects. We tried to place him as far away as possible from other family activities, trying to save our ears and sanity. I'm not sure that we succeeded.

Each of the children had their own room. Tammy's room was pink with touches of lavender. She had one wallpapered wall which sported ballerinas in graceful Degas poses. Uri's room was wallpapered in a novel pattern of traffic signs with the STOP sign printed in vivid red. Not that it ever stopped him from doing what he wanted, but it was attractive. Outside of Uri's window there stood a Maple tree which showed us by its Autumn colors when Fall arrived. I have a picture of that tree with its hues of flaming reds and golds. It was a masterpiece and a true representation of The Lord's heavenly color palette.

One time we were having trouble with the telephone lines. The repairman arrived and asked, after checking the numerous phones, if there were any others. We answered in the negative. Then he noticed an errant wire and started following it, which led to Uri's room. It seems that there were two illegal phones in the house – all in Uri's room!

Uri loved to browse in Radio Shack, which was one of the first stores devoted entirely to electronics and a magnet for gadget devotees. Uri had set himself up with a phone at his desk and one by the side of his bed. Did we have egg on our faces! I apologized profusely to the phone company representative for the illegal installations. He left the house muttering something about dishonest kids and what's worse is that parents don't even know what the kids are up to!

While engaged in writing this episode, Uri confessed to another prank which we never knew about. Uri's bedroom had a connecting wall to the salon. He cut a hole in the wall and placed a microphone in it. Then he found a piece of the wallpaper and covered it with only the wire sticking out. He never used it, only wanted to discover if he could do it. Maybe he was too influenced by James Bond movies!

The irony is that Tammy had requested a phone for her room and we had refused, as we felt it was too indulgent for a teenager to have her very own telephone. We tried to raise the children to follow modest ways, and in a world that was materialistic as well as increasingly affluent, it was not easy. Tammy did have our old television in her room and being a year older than Uri, she was the sole driver of the third car that we owned, at least for the time until he earned his driving license. However, in truth, life became a lot simpler when they became drivers. Previous to that, we were always hauling them someplace. The transit system in the suburbs was a joke and it was drive them or they would have to remain at home.

The paneled Family Room on the lower level was the perfect place for parties and gatherings of every kind.

The Sweet Sixteen parties of our nieces, Terri, Michelle and Davi, the daughters of Chay and Sandy Karzen (*Saba's* brother and his ex-wife) were held there. Also, Sherri's (*z'l,*) daughter of Sherwin and Barbara (*z'l*) Pomerantz, was celebrated there.

Parlor meetings for organizations and every type of happy event saw our home as its venue. From Israel, Rabbis Eliezer Waldman and Avinoam Horwitz from the reestablished city of Hebron in Israel utilized our home. It was a pleasure and privilege to try to aid whoever requested this suitable large area, for numerous worthy causes.

Sometimes the cause was not exactly friendly. There was a gentleman who aspired to a position in the Illinois Statehouse; he was known to be hostile to Jews. We organized Parlor Meetings in the area, the largest held in our home and he was soundly defeated. This was grass roots politics at its finest.

I volunteered every year to be a collector for The United Way, going from house to house collecting funds for charity. I felt that it was important. Chuckling to myself, I would collect the quarters that my neighbors would donate. The residents in the area surrounding our house were not Jewish and they were very fine people, but the value of *Tzedakah* was not generally understood. When I contrasted the quarters and the five dollars which I donated, as opposed to the substantial funds that the Jewish community generates yearly, it was laughable. These were upper middle class folks and the manner in which they offered that quarter was certainly not the Jewish way.

Uri was an adorable, darling child with large dark brown eyes who was growing to be a handsome young boy with those interesting eyes. I think that some of his teachers were not as strict as they should have been because of the remorse that appeared in those peepers when Uri was caught doing something that he shouldn't have been.

Sam Cohen was his second grade Hebrew studies teacher; he also taught in our Synagogue's afternoon Hebrew School. I would receive phone calls from Mr. Cohen profusely apologizing for bothering me, but Uri was not paying attention; not that he was unruly, but he was too quiet. Once, he requested a meeting and handed me a bag. When I opened it, I found over a dozen tiny figures of superheroes, cars, and animals which Uri would bring to school, line up at the end of his desk, play with them and just ignore what was going on in the front of the classroom for the next hour. Happily this phase did not last too long and he graduated from Hillel Torah with good marks. The thought was that he would attend the *Yeshiva* High School upon graduation. However, the school was in a management crisis and it was decided that he join Tammy at The Ida Crown Jewish Academy.

It was *Bar Mitzvah* time and as the only son of a Rabbi in a large congregation, it was a major event. *Rosh Chodesh Nisan* 1974 was the big day.

Uri had been studying to undertake the position of Cantor for the Morning service, as well as to read the entire portion of the Torah and offer his speech. It was a lot of work and tension for a thirteen-year-old boy. Unfortunately, the week before the event, he had one mishap after another. Returning home after his last lesson, he decided to inspect the window wells of our neighbors. When he walked in, with scratches on his face and hands and trouser knees torn, I told him that I was going to wrap him in cotton (bubble wrap had as yet to be invented) and only then would he survive until his *Bar Mitzvah* Day in one piece!

The service was held on Sunday Morning, *Rosh Chodesh*, so that family and friends could attend without any Sabbath desecration. There was a luncheon after the service for hundreds of guests, which included the Synagogue members. The same evening a dinner was held at the North Shore Hotel in Evanston for family and close friends.

We were overjoyed that there were family members who flew in from New York. My mother, Rose and her husband, Max Glass, Aunt Rozzie and Uncle Howard, as well as my Aunt Gussie and Uncle Max all honored us with their presence. Aunt Gussie was a sister of both my and Rozzie's mother and it was the first and last time they were in Chicago, probably one of the few times in their lives that they had left New York. The joke was that it is the exact distance from Chicago to New York, as it is from New York to Chicago, but it seemed that New Yorkers never figured that out. It was rare to see our extensive family members in Chicago. We were thrilled that they made that journey for the happy occasion.

Laurel and Arnie Siegel of Ottumwa, Iowa were old friends from that community and brought greetings from our former parishioners. When Arnie arose to speak, he brought down the house. Coming from the small Jewish community in Ottumwa and seeing so many Jews in one place, he remarked that he didn't know that there were that many Jews in the world!

When I think back now, the event was a little "over the top." The meals were as gourmet as the caterer could deliver. After the salad course and before the entrée, sorbet was served to "cleanse the palate." Folks were unaccustomed to this dish and some thought that we were hosting a very strange dinner. The thought was that the sorbet was dessert and that there was no main dish! However, the dessert was a chocolate-covered pear in wine, especially flown in from the *Kosher* Gourmet Mecca of New York. (Where else?)

Uri wore a fancy suit with a distinctive black velvet bow tie for the service and both he and *Saba* wore matching tuxedo outfits for the dinner. Tammy looked adorable in her long dress, but to this day she tells me how she hated her hairdo. You can't win them all! And I, I blush to think of this, but here it is! At Marshall Fields Department Store, I found what I thought was the most elegant of evening dresses. It was a bright red sheath with rhinestone shoulder straps and a matching cape that swirled as I danced. My outfit was complete with a rhinestone tiara. I felt like a queen and hoped to look like one. It was a typical bash, a la the 70s, way overdone, but it was a marvelous event and we had a wonderful time; a family event to remember.

Tammy once remarked to me that she was sometimes appalled at the sassy way in which some of her friends spoke with their parents. *Saba* and I always spoke respectfully with our parents and we expected the same of our children. They complied and thinking of our family situation, I realize now how relatively peaceful it was in the house. I am hard pressed to remember knock down drag out fights between the kids. Of course, they argued, but it wasn't verbally vicious and not speaking to each other was absolutely verboten in our home.

ON BOTH SIDES OF OUR FAMILY, there were aunts, uncles and cousins that didn't speak to each other for years. The reasons were lost in the mists of time. It didn't even matter what the root of the disagreement was, because nobody could remember it. There are many examples of this familial hostility, but the following are two real beauties.

Ten minutes before we were to leave for Uri's wedding, the telephone rang and my mother-in-law informed me that the previous evening, her two sisters had an argument and that they would not sit at the same table at the wedding; I must change the seating. I told her that to change the seating was impossible now and they would have to endure each other's company for the two hours of the meal. I hope that they did enjoy the wedding in spite of sitting together. One of the problems in changing the seating was that two other sisters hadn't spoken to each other for years and when originally doing the seating, that situation had to be dealt with.

The second example is truly tragic. As already recorded, my father was stricken by a heart attack and passed away within a matter of minutes. Unfortunately, my Aunt Zira and Uncle Manny were not on speaking terms with him at the time. Years later, they admitted that one of their deepest regrets was that they had not spoken with my dad before it was too late. We never know when the "too late" comes. I have told my sisters that no matter what they do or say to me, or not say to me, I will NEVER stop speaking with them. We are all guilty of acts of thoughtlessness in what we have done or said to each other, but not communicating is below the red line – it simply cannot be!

Holding grudges and not speaking is another human condition which one must avoid. There were two instances which friends had felt that *Saba* and I had impinged on their *Kavod* (honor). The acts had not been interpreted correctly by them. We had done nothing, but nevertheless, felt their coldness toward us. These are friends that we see every Sabbath and it was uncomfortable. I approached both women and expressed our unhappiness at their attitude toward us. I simply would not be in a situation and be ignored when standing around *kibbitzing* with friends due to a grudge on another person's part. They were accepting of my apology, even though I knew in my heart that it was unwarranted, but *Shalom* is the ultimate goal. In the future, if we will not be good friends at least we can be pleasant to each other. This is *Sinat Chinam* at work, and one must make every effort to avoid it.

IT WAS FASCINATING TO WATCH the children grow up. They were alike in ways, but so different in others. On one side, Tammy, a darling child, was always a little lady, but on the other, could be named the "Keeper of the Flame." She found a path and stuck by it. Her nature is one of calm and steadfastness, traits that are helpful to the position of leader. Wherever Tammy found herself, her personality, aptitude and attitude propelled her to the top. Even when she was a youngster enrolled in Modern Dance classes, it was no surprise to us that she was the lead dancer in the line dance. As a member of the National Council of Synagogue Youth, (NCSY) she attained the position of Secretary on the National level. She was popular, had many friends and was a good student.

Because Tammy was an excellent pupil all of her school years, attending Parent-Teacher conferences was always a pleasure since her reports were usually outstanding. That's why the following incident stands out in sharp relief.

With Tammy, Jay, and Uri, 1978

One day, when Tammy was in fourth or fifth grade, Rabbi Abraham (Duni) Bruckenstein, principal of Hillel Torah Day School, called and asked for us to come in for an appointment. We simply couldn't imagine what it could be. After hearing the source of the problem, we all chuckled as the situation was almost laughable. What happened is that there were four students in the class who were seriously behind in the study of Bible and not only were the kids good students, but they were all the children of Rabbis! The situation was remedied by special tutoring given to Tammy and her classmates. But it was kept a bit quiet as it was not good publicity for the school which was, in fact, an excellent institution.

Uri had another personality altogether. As you know, as a tot, he was a *Shovav*, "Dennis The Menace" type. As he matured he showed an aptitude for business in interesting ways. *Saba* and I could never figure this one out. Tammy always had her possessions such as pencil box, or whatever, in excellent condition. Uri would borrow pencils from his sister, use them for a while and SELL them back to her with the points whittled down and the erasers half used! He was good at persuasion and ended up as the President of his Senior Class at the Academy as well as President of the Chicago Youth Council. At one time, we had the honor of three presidents including Jeffrey Schoenberg, president of United Synagogue Youth at our Sabbath table.

Uri was a member of *Bnei Akiva* and spent much of his time with others in the group. There were both fellows and girls in involved in all types of the organization's activities. Since Uri and Shellie Weiss were fourteen years old, they had gravitated to each other; Shellie appeared to be a lovely girl, intelligent, popular and we knew that they were a quasi-couple. When Uri was sixteen years old, I casually mentioned to him that Shelli is a sweet girl, but at his young age perhaps he should not be so exclusive – that there are other nice girls in the group. He quickly remarked, "But, *Ima*, I like her face!" and that was the end of that. What more could I say?

There was the mother of a friend of mine whose son was an

important doctor, with every plus … position, health, wealth and handsome, no less, but, no nice Jewish girl to share his blessed life. She would call me every few months to see if I had a woman with whom to introduce him. He was already in his early forties and she was concerned about his situation and wanted not only his happiness, but grandchildren. He did marry eventually to a fine woman and I can happily report that she got her grandchildren. But this friend and others who married later or never did find their *Bashert* taught me a life lesson.

Yes, Uri and Shelli were childhood sweethearts and they did marry young. I was eighteen and a half when I married, but as I tell my shocked grandchildren, I was in my second year of college. That seems to soften the fact for them. Some people mature early and some never mature and are never ready for marriage. Each case must be judged independently on an individual basis.

Before we knew it, Tammy was graduating from The Ida Crown Academy. She wanted to spend the following year in Israel and we knew deep down that it was no gap year, but that she would make her life there.

Rabbi Reuven Aberman came from Michlala Seminary in Jerusalem to recruit students. This was the same Ruby Aberman who had been *Saba's* counselor in *Bnei Akiva* and Camp *Moshava*. But, as he sat in our home extolling the virtues of a year in Israel, I had mixed feelings. I didn't want her to leave. I resented Rabbi Ruby and even Israel. I truly fought with myself, with the truths that we had brought the children up with the virtue of *Aliyah* and I couldn't be a hypocrite just because it made me unhappy. They had listened to *Saba's* sermons all their life, and now it was the time to face this fact. I have always worn my emotions on my sleeve, but this situation was the worst I had ever experienced in my life.

Tammy, very excited, flew off on an El Al airplane, and I wore sunglasses for months. It was weird sitting in the Synagogue in the winter wearing dark glasses. Myrna Buckman would sit with me and hold my hand as I sobbed. She once said to me that if I thought I was fooling anyone, I wasn't. I didn't care.

With my own amateur physiological analysis, I realize that I am probably in that mold because of my background and many personal losses. However, know that I am tearful at happy occasions, too. I am easily moved and my eyes well up and the tears flow. Even when I would be a spectator at the children's plays and events during my time as the Administrator at the school, I would sit in the rear. I would be so thrilled at the accomplishments of the pupils, that I would sneak out the back. I didn't want anyone to notice the inevitable red eyes.

It may be strange when at an event, such as a concert or a pleasurable time where there are Israelis enjoying themselves, the thought comes to me that I am so glad that we, Israelis, are having a good time – because we deserve it!

There are enough, more than enough, times that are sad and we communally overcome them. We must appreciate the good times, live in the moment and take pleasure in even the small, happy moments of life.

One year later, it was Uri's turn. He graduated, was a member of The National Honor Society, as was his mother and sister. *Saba* and I knew that he, also, would not be coming back except for a special occasion from time to time. As he himself has told me, how could he not want to live in Israel? We had done an excellent job of influencing our children. As an example, even when he was a baby, his high chair tray had paper covers to keep it clean and on them were pictures of the Aleph-Bet and Israel. What more could we say? They were both eight thousand miles away in Israel, happy with their lives. Tammy did attend Michlala Seminary and Uri in Kiryat Arba, a student at the Nir Yeshiva and *Saba* and I, home alone in our empty nest. It wasn't easy.

Administrator of Hillel Torah

I had been working in Real Estate for a number of years when I received an invitation to a meeting with Rabbi Abraham "Duni" Bruckenstein, my friend Rachel's husband and the principal of the children's grammar school. I had no idea why he suggested this meeting, and I attended quite reluctantly. When he suggested that I take over the position of Administrator of Hillel Torah, I was flummoxed. After speaking with *Saba*, I decided to lay it all out physically, and think about the offer seriously. How did I do that? I took a yellow legal pad and jotted on the top: Pros and Cons. I then simply listed all the points that I could think of why I should accept the offer and why I should, perhaps, give it a pass. Both sides had numerous items listed, and it took a few days until I felt that I was excited at the prospect. I can't think of anything worse than waking up each morning dreading to go to work.

Well, I decided to give it a whirl and I spent eight years at the school, which were filled with much accomplishment.

It is written *"Ain Kemach, Ain Torah!"* – "Where there is no bread, there is no Torah learning!" and as each monthly payroll had to be met, those words became my mantra – keeping the coffers filled was a tremendous responsibility. My job was so varied. There were aspects that I loved and some which I loved less, but the goal of educating the future Jewish Community was worthwhile and I never forgot it. Even today, when I am about and I hear the words, "Mrs. Karzen," you can bet that it is one of the "GrandStudents" that are calling to me.

Duni Bruckenstein was a creative genius and he loved children – it was evident in every decision that he made. What was good for the students, was what had to be done or acquired for their development. In the early 80s, when he decided that the students had to learn how to use the new-fangled gadget called a computer, the money had to be found. We attended the Education Committee meeting of the Jewish Federation of Chicago to request Seed Money for the project. There were probably twenty men in the room and when we presented our proposal, one fellow arrogantly exclaimed: "I live in Wilmette and the students there have no computer courses, so why should your school offer them?" Wilmette is a wealthy suburb of Chicago, which pays school taxes that are among the highest in Illinois. Of course, our arguments went nowhere after his opening statement as everyone in the room came from an affluent suburb and computers were in no one's curriculum. I could almost feel the sneering as we left that august gathering. They were probably thinking … "Who do they think they are? Are their children more important than ours?"

Of course, everyone knows what happened to the future of computers. As it was, Harold Rublin, one of the most interested and important benefactors of the school passed away and funds were willed to the school. We set up The Harold Rublin Center for Computer Science and it was a tremendous success. Initially it was the 7th and 8th grades who were the recipients of Harold's generosity. Then, evening courses for the staff and parents who were interested. Within a year, the program was extended to the entire student population and the first and second graders became computer savvy, which was a novelty at the time, but as we know today is commonplace.

The anecdote is told that when a five-year-old saw her grandfather struggling to send an e-mail, she inquired, "Didn't you ever go to Kindergarten, *Saba*?" Such is our world today! As it was, I personally never found the time to attend the classes. The statement "shoulda"… "coulda" truly describes this situation … but I didn't and I "shoulda" and "coulda".

Having funds to run the school was not simply an everyday problem, it was a 24-hour-a-day problem. Sherwin Pomerantz, our good buddy, was the owner of the firm who printed the school's paychecks as well as stood behind them. There were many times that "Robbing Peter to pay Paul" was the order of the day and Sherwin was a brick for me. He never let me down.

In September, the school was flush with cash as tuition money was collected. By April, our cash flow was always critical and I spent sleepless nights tossing and turning trying to figure out what would be my next move. At the March board meeting, I announced that I needed a special volunteer, who would go to his bank and take out a "Balloon Loan" to cover the April 1st payroll. The thought that the staff would be unpaid before Pesach was unacceptable. The staff was owed the money and should not feel like slaves! (A Passover pun!) Their dignity and the appreciative gestures of being paid on time by the school was a prime concern. So, Board Member Shimon, (name changed), picked me up in his Jaguar (a first for me) and spoke on his car phone (another first for me, never saw one before). We entered and he led me to the special VIP section of his bank, where coffee was served in china cups with petit fours (*Kosher* on an antique plate with linen napkins, no less). I enjoyed the elegant service and sophisticated repartee, but I loved the fact that I left the bank with the precious check in my hand. We were saved for another paycheck period!

I had a special secret "Angel" list consisting of ten fellows who were caring and generous with extra funds, as well as discreet. For example, when the annual 8th grade class trip was announced, it was a problem. There were always a few pupils whose parents simply couldn't afford the extra expense of a trip to Washington D.C. or Springfield, Illinois with their classmates. By calling these friends, a collection would be made and it was never mentioned to the parents or students.

Every year, the school would have *Shlichim* from Israel engaged to hopefully enhance the students' Hebrew language skills. Before they arrived, Rabbi B. and I would drive around finding apartments for the educators and their families in West Rodgers Park, close to Synagogues and facilities where they could be at home for their stint in the US. After locating the places, we would then furnish the rooms, trying to make them as homelike as possible. On my Angel list, there were a number of nursing home facilities owners. After a phone call, a truck would deliver all the linens that were needed. All the new towels, sheets, pillowcases came from local nursing facilities. I was thankful that they weren't monogrammed! There were other situations that called for monies that never showed in the budget and these Angels always came through with graciousness. It was always a pleasure to deal with them.

The best day and most fun of the year was *Rosh Chodesh Adar* AKA *Mi' Shanichnas Adar.* That day, the large gymnasium became a carnival site with music, booths with games of chance, skill, prizes, clowns and of course, costumes. It was inevitable that every little girl came as Queen Esther, one cuter than the next. One morning the The Stilt Walker knocked on my office door with a most trying problem. He couldn't enter the gym because he was too tall with the stilts on. I looked at this young man with his forlorn face and suggested that he put the stilts on inside the gym doors. His face immediately lit up and he left. Problem solved … if only they were all that easy!

Having grown up with Chicago winters, I am used to them, but I don't have to like them. When the weather bottomed out at 50 degrees below zero, the door locks of cars were frozen solid. The garage door automatic openers wouldn't work either, so it was impossible to travel in any case. The snow made life impossible and frankly, I hated inclement weather. My mother claimed that I was phobic about the awful weather that Chicago experiences constantly.

Having my position at the school brought my hatred of snow to the fore. One of my responsibilities was the running of the school buses. In inclement weather Maierhofer Bus Company would cheerfully awaken me at 4 a.m. (Why so early?) to inform me that it would be a Snow Day and that there would be no bus transportation. I would wait until 6 a.m. and then telephone Rabbi B. when the mechanics of informing parents via radio announcements would begin. It was a regular routine and that was winter life in Chi town. But the real hazards of a Snow Day began the day after. Of the seven hundred students in the five buildings, eighty-five percent rode the thirteen yellow buses back and forth each day. The city would clear the streets by piling the snow on both sides of the roads. During the Snow of '67, there were areas where the piled snow reached the second floor of buildings. I had real nightmares of my little ones waiting on the corner for their transportation and getting lost in giant snowdrifts. It never happened, but I heaved a giant size sigh of relief as each time the children assembled safely in the hallway upon arrival.

Do you remember reading the following anecdote in a copy of The Reader's Digest? I was the contributor. It was a bright, sun-drenched winter day and the teachers decided to take the children outside to play in the playground for recess. Each teacher had an aide and it was a real job to dress twenty kids warmly for their excursion. They pulled on sweaters, jackets, leggings, hats, gloves and galoshes and were almost finished, when a five-year boy said that the galoshes that the teacher had just spent five minutes trying to stuff the shoes into the too tight boots, remarked that they were not his boots. The teacher then spent another few minutes tugging at the boots to remove them, whereupon the tot exclaimed, "They are my brother's. I couldn't find my own this morning!"

The Early Childhood wing of the building housed the three classes of Kindergartners. It was a bright, light-filled area decorated in primary colors which the children enjoyed. My Interior Design skills came in handy there as well as the locker area. Instead of rows of drab Khaki-colored metal units, they were painted in pastels; light blue, yellow, light green and pink. The youngsters loved them and at my last visit, the lockers appear to have kept their designer colors giving the dim school hallways a festive air.

Speaking of lockers ... dealing with hundreds of kids anything could happen ... and often did. Twice a year, during *Chanukah* and Passover vacation, Bob and his maintenance crew would clean out the lockers.

Once Bob came to me and said that I had to come with him and see his latest find. While cleaning out lockers he came upon this study in childhood behavior. Opening the door, we saw an incredible sight. There were dozens of neatly folded and closed brown lunch bags which had been dutifully brought to school, stashed and quickly forgotten. What had this kid been eating for three months? He probably shared his friend's food which was the same peanut butter and jelly sandwiches that he had brought to school. So many kids brought peanut butter to school every day that I couldn't help but wonder why they hadn't turned yellow by now.

While my own children were students at the school, there was no formal lunch program. But twice a month there were offerings. Once a week was Hot Dog Day and the other special day was Hamburger Day. We, the mothers, would bring the food, cook and serve it and have a fun time in the bargain. I can still recall Eva Weiss wearing a big white apron, stirring a huge cauldron of boiling hot dogs while Elaine Wolinitz (*z'l*) would smear mustard on the buns after I cut them in two. Sandy Rublin would arrange the plates artistically with potato chips. We had an organized assembly line going there. When the US Department of Agriculture decreed that ketchup was a vegetable, being made from tomatoes, we felt that we were giving the students a real meal. The most important fact was that the kids enjoyed it. Also, it was the one day that the smell of peanut butter did not pervade the school.

The PTA voted to establish a lunch program. Two cooks were hired and it was a worthwhile experiment. But some of the children were picky and nothing pleased them. Some wouldn't eat yellow food or anything that wasn't solid – mushy mashed potatoes were out! However, on the whole it was successful, but it did not last long. We could never find cooks that were reliable. I spent too much of my time searching for people and unless I wanted to go into the kitchen and do it myself, the project was doomed. It folded and the Planter's and Jiffy's companies must have been ecstatic, because we were back to you-know-what!

One day I was giving a tour of the school to a representative of an organization that shall remain anonymous. He was delighted at our spotless, well-equipped kitchen and lamented as to the lack of a lunch program. After I explained the problem, he indicated that not actually running the program did not mean that the State of Illinois should not fund a phantom lunch program. He mumbled to himself that six hundred children times $2.10 each day adds up to a goodly sum of money and as we were not being subsidized, we were missing out on those government funds. I was so angry at his suggestion which, of course, was totally immoral as well as illegal. I reiterated that this was a Jewish Day School and that our integrity was worth more than $2.10 per child. I resented his despicable suggestion and showed him the door. I was seething and I'm sure it didn't sit well to be berated and tossed out by a woman. We never heard from that organization again. The group was supposed to teach us how to live within our budget, as well as show us how to raise additional funds. That they did. They surely did, but in the morals department, they had a lot to learn.

Two days in a row were never the same. There were so many interesting incidents. I received a call from the Kashrus Division of the Chicago Rabbinical Council to advise us that the product V8 Vegetable Drink was being dropped from the *Kosher* products lists. On the following Friday, I inserted the notice in the Friday Newsletter that the drink is under question and to refrain from sending it with the children for lunch.

On Monday morning, when I arrived and opened the office door, there was a couple sitting there, who were long-time parents in the school and they didn't look happy. As a matter of fact, I'm sure that there was steam coming from the father's ears; they were furious. They yelled as to how the school was becoming a bunch of religious fanatics and how could I dare say that V8 is not *Kosher*; what could be wrong with it and on and on. They were so incensed that they removed their son from the school where he was in seventh grade. I have always regretted that time. Perhaps I should have tried harder, as now the family who was marginally observant, is not at all involved in the Jewish community. I hope that one day one of those people who call out to me on the streets of Jerusalem will be that boy, now man, hopefully still attached and interested in Judaism and Israel.

Communities all over the world had been demonstrating on behalf of Russian Jewry and lo and behold, they came … slowly, a trickle at first and then, there were entire organizations formed to welcome and provide for the immigrants. We, at Hillel Torah, were moved by the parents that shyly brought their children to the "Jewish" school. Judaism was an unknown entity for them and we were thrilled to be able to provide schooling for them. Rabbi B. and the staff immediately set up special classes and began to mainstream the pupils. Pedagogically, it isn't correct to have fifth grade students in secular subjects learning in a first grade Hebrew class, so tutoring for the Russians was instituted. As they lived in Chicago proper, school bus routes had to be set up with Chicago routes as opposed to the buses that operated in the suburbs. There were times that I would look at our normal deficit and wonder where the extra funds would come from. However, the school stinted with nothing. Whatever was needed was provided. Top enrollment for the Russian program was no more than fifteen students and we endeavored to make knowledgeable Jews of these youngsters.

However, by the third year of this special program, despite all the directed attention, enrollment began to slip. The maxim that "If one pays nothing, it is worth nothing" was the guideline to tuition and other expenses. The charge was $2 per month, per child, which covered tuition, bus transportation, lunches when served, and any other expenses. My Angel list came in most handy for the Russian students. The problem was that they began to feel entitled to everything without cost, and their parents went along, by and large.

We had maintained extraordinarily good relations with our neighbors on the block. However one morning, a woman called to report that she had caught a boy cutting flowers from her front yard garden. In her shock, she blurted out that he should pay for them. "Ve don't pay nothing!" When I called the boy to report to my office, he insisted over and over again that "Ve don't pay no money … Ve don't pay no money!" The following week, as I lifted the cover to the copy machine, I saw a bill from a computer store covering the expenses of a computer, desk, chair and even a desk light. It was a significant amount – marked paid and the customer was one of our "poor" Russian families. We won't even mention the *Chutzpah* of the youngster who used the school's copy machine for personal use. And what was a pupil doing in the school's office machine room anyway?

As the year rolled on, there were fewer and fewer Russian students enrolled in the school. When I inquired why they were leaving, the inevitable answer was that they were moving. I was very happy that they were doing better financially and could afford to live in a more desirable neighborhood. But when I casually asked one child if there was an attached two-car garage on his new house, he replied, "No, a three-car garage. It's a really a big house!"

The Russians had become "Yankee Doodles," as I called them and wanted their children to attend REAL AMERICAN PUBLIC SCHOOLS. We were sidelined. I don't know if there was anything that we could have done, but it should be known that Hillel Torah School made every effort to educate these children in Judaism. I sometimes wonder what happened to them or maybe its better that I don't know.

After six years, there were only three students who graduated and with honors at the end of that experiment. As I handed them their diplomas, I saw three youngsters who now possessed the correct tools and were on the way to living Jewish lives.

THE YEARS ROLLED ON AND WE were to celebrate our 25th wedding anniversary. Sister Judy and her hubby Aryeh (*z'l*) had a spacious family room in their home and it was decided to hold the festivities there. It was sponsored by all of our siblings and, I believe that it was the last family *Simcha* where all of our aunts, uncles and cousins attended in Chicago. It was a warm, homey atmosphere and a wonderful time was had by all. The traditional family jokes were hauled out and related and it did not matter that we had heard them many times before. The laughter rang out. The Ray family was together. I remember that celebration and think about it every once in a while. It was a special slice of time for the family and to mark it, we were presented with a brass chime clock. The clock has been present in our living room ever since and not only does it represent love from the family, but it has marked our lives as the years have marched forward with a gentle chime on the quarter hour.

Speaking about clocks, in our living room we always had a clock set to Israel time, so that we could know where and what our Israeli children were doing. A woman visitor spied the clock, whereupon she informed us that our clock was set at the wrong time. When we told her that it reflected Israel time, she exclaimed, "What a wonderful idea, where can I buy a clock like that?"

Time … We all have the exact amount and what we do with it describes our lives. One of the ugliest phrases in the English language is "To Kill Time." Mindless activities such as endlessly surfing the Net, or the indiscriminate watching of TV, hour after hour, is a waste of the precious hours that have been allotted to us. I am not bashing either the Net or TV. Both are important elements of our lives today, but moderation in all things is the key to a happy and fulfilling existence.

RECENTLY, I HAD OCCASION TO MEET a classmate after sixty years of no communication. It is always exciting to see what has occurred in the lives of friends, now that we are in our senior years. This was a woman with whom I had shared a desk, lunch, homework, teachers and recess in our early school years, but her family moved from Chicago in third grade. We began to "catch up" on each other activities and I was nonplussed by what I heard. She graduated from high school, began college, but attended only one semester. She was never employed, but dilly-dallied for a few years until she met her husband. They married, two children were born, and they grew to adulthood.

In all the years my friend was happy to remain at home and was not even interested in volunteer work. I admit that I must have stared at her open-mouthed by her recitation. I asked her what occupied her time all those years and she could not give me an answer. "Time just goes – one day is much like the other." What a poor, poor soul. I was most unhappy when we parted. What a waste of a life! This was a friend that I thought had everything going for her; two parents, (which to me was no small thing!) bright, intelligent (we were the two best readers in first grade) nice clothes, toys and games and everyone liked her.

US Supreme Court Chief Justice William O. Douglas, Steven Patt, President of Chicago Decalogue Society (R) With You Know Who! 1974

It was difficult not to compare her with all the other girls with whom I had grown up. Every one of my class went on to higher education. There are teachers, psychologists, businesswomen, doctors, an author and even one Interior Designer; good women who have multi-tasked with family and employment all of their lives adding not only Years to their Life, but, Life to their Years. (Thanks to *Saba* for that phrase!)

My friend was clueless as to volunteering; had never experienced the joy of giving, which is indeed far superior to receiving, as the saying goes. The world is a better place because men and women volunteer. Every organization on earth depends on the inspiring volunteer who wants to better the lives of people by their activities.

There is an apocryphal story concerning the energetic women of the Hadassah Organization. It seems that a man dies and, because of his nefarious activities, is sentenced to spend eternity in Hell. Upon his arrival, instead of blazing fires and unbearable temperatures, it is amazingly cool and pleasant. "What's going on here? I expected to find the fires of Hell blazing as a punishment?" "Oh, some Hadassah women came down and installed Air Conditioning," was the reply.

Because of our volunteer activities, organizations honored us at breakfasts, luncheons and dinners; Israel Bonds, Jewish National Fund, Israel Tourism Association, and a few others. Jay was honored by the Hebrew Theological College and I by the Jewish Federation. We were "draws" and the affairs were successful and raised funds for the various causes. We were the honorees for our Synagogue when it celebrated ten years and when Jay celebrated twenty years in the Rabbinate. The effort of being an honoree is unknown by the general public, but it is hard work to insure the success of the affair. We undertook it time after time because of the worthiness of the cause.

Getting Closer to Israel

Once the children had made *Aliyah*, we began to make frequent trips to Israel. Besides the private excursions that we made as often as possible, Marc Sommer of Ideal Tours requested that we become the hosts for his sponsored tours. The groups consisted of Americans from country-wide. There were folks from California, Florida, as well as Chicagoans and other Mid-Westerners. By actual count, we flew over the Atlantic Ocean on that seemingly interminable trip, twenty-eight times before our *Aliyah*! Upon hearing that enormous number of crossings, Rabbi Meyer Kahana (*z'l*) quipped that the Israeli government should give us a special *Teudat Zehut* for our steadfastness and Zionism. He also thought that we were *Meshuga* and adjured us to make *Aliyah* as fast as we could so as to avoid eating anymore of El Al's rubber eggs for breakfast!

Like all of life's experiences, those accompanying tourists were both exhilarating, maddening and at times sad. In the 70s and 80s, it was not common for the average middle class American to hop on a plane. The word, Jet-setter, indicated individuals who had the initiative, time and money; it was mostly reserved for the famous among us. Movie and singing stars, royalty and the fabulously wealthy vacationed and traveled to exotic places, not Mr. and Mrs. Average – they only read about these junkets in the newspapers. The passport was not a common possession and it was part of the adventure to apply and receive one.

On one trip flying to Israel, there was a woman who refused to drink or eat in flight – she didn't want to have to use the restroom. The upshot was that she fainted when we changed planes in London. Here I am, in a strange country with an unconscious woman at my feet. The only good thing was that English was the spoken language. It could have happened in Belgium and my Flemish is terrible!

There was an elderly gentleman who came with us and purchased costly jewelry as a gift for his daughter. His memory was spotty and I took it from him for safekeeping. One of the iron clad rules of traveling is to refrain from taking jewelry, as it is difficult to insure its return; either by robbery or loss. Of course, what happened when we landed back home is that he had forgotten all about it and I *shlepped* it for three weeks, worrying about the contents of the velvet case and its safety. As I handed it to the daughter, she was delighted and Joe said to me, "My, that was nice of you to buy my daughter a gift!"

Unlike today, when there is almost nothing that cannot be found in Israel, some items were scarce or even unknown in Israel. Our luggage always included for our children or friends items that were hard to come by. Uri requested that I bring cans of pineapple as a treat. For years, no trip was complete unless we brought three or four cans of the fruit. Canned fruit is heavy, but no matter, we dutifully carried them making our already heavy suitcases almost immovable. One time, the group was staying at a luxury Jerusalem hotel. At breakfast, I noticed that there were slices of pineapple on the table, being used in a variety of ways. Uri was standing next to me and I queried, "You told me that there is a scarcity of pineapple here. Why is it on the table being used in all kinds of ways. It doesn't appear to be a scarce item?" Uri just looked at me and said, "Oh, there is plenty of pineapple here, but it's so much cheaper if you bring it from the States." We never *Shlepped* those heavy cans again. We were paying for them in any case. His logic totally eluded me.

Speaking of hotels, we opened and closed many hotels and restaurants in our time. But once, we were the first group registered to stay at a luxurious Jerusalem hotel. It was beautiful, brand new, but unfortunately, a few kinks hadn't been ironed out as yet. As happened, on the first day of touring, we returned to our room and the room number sign had fallen off. We didn't think that we had been thrown out, but what had become of the room that was reserved for us? Also, one couple required a crib and was told that it would be there when they returned from their day trip. It was, but another family wanted to know why their crib was taken away as they also needed one. The workmen had taken it from another guest's room instead of the supply room. The mantra on that stay was, "The hotel had just opened, we must be understanding." But it's hard to be understanding when a family returns from a tour in the August heat with a crying little child and all you want is to put the tot to sleep.

People were talking about the Jewish Marriage Encounter experience with increasing frequency. We became interested in the project as we thought that it was an avenue to help people conduct their marriages in a more satisfying and fulfilling way. Jay, as part of his job as a community Rabbi, was involved in counseling couples and I thought that I would enjoy investigating more about the subject. We signed up and before we knew it were deeply involved in a form of *Tikun Olam* by becoming the "Rabbinic couple" on the team of presenters.

The format began on Saturday evening in a local hotel. The team in charge of the program consisted of four couples, one of them a Rabbi and his wife. The goal was not to repair broken marriages, but to teach the art of communication to couples who had good marriages, or how to improve their "Couplehood." This was accomplished by the participants writing to each other after listening to a presentation by the leaders. There were songs, poems, thoughtful ideas and surprises during the forty-eight hours of the conference. On Monday evening, the conclusion was a wedding ceremony where the couples re-consecrated their wedding vows to each other. In an atmosphere of truth and sincerity, hundreds of couples remembered why their husband / wife was the one soul that they had chosen to be a life partner.

After we finished our weekend which was presented in an excellent manner, Jay turned to his very emotionally-drained wife, and said those familiar words … "We can do that, maybe even better!" Soon after, we were asked to participate and the rest is history. We were dispatched all over the country: New Jersey, Florida, New York, California and of course, in our own back yard of Illinois.

There were memorable events, such as when a couple knocked on our door at 1:30 a.m. and begged to speak with us even at that ungodly hour. Their problem was infertility and they had traveled the medical route without success. *Saba* decided to play *Lubavitch Rebbe* and asked them if they have a *Kosher Mezuzah* on their bedroom door. They were astonished to hear that one was needed. Ten months after that night, he received a long distance telephone call from the new parents. It appears that upon returning home, they did affix a *Mezuzah* on their door and the new baby was a girl. They hesitantly inquired if he would mind if their new daughter would be named Jane, in honor of Rabbi Jay. He was indeed honored. Somewhere there is a woman, perhaps a grandmother by now, who is deeply indebted to Jewish Marriage Encounter.

Although I was busy from morning to night with the school, the Synagogue where I taught Adult Education Hebrew classes, the Sisterhood, being a wife, mother (absentee, but that job never ends) daughter, daughter-in-law, sister, sister-in law, niece, cousin and friend and all their accompanying activities, there was one goal that I hadn't fulfilled. I had never finished college and earned a B.A. I decided to return to school and finish what I lacked, which was one full year of thirty credit hours. The National College of Education offered a course which gave "Life Credits" towards a degree. I then spent two evenings per week on the school's campus in Arlington Heights, with loads of homework to finish for each class during the rest of the time.

There were times that I thought that I must be crazy to try to keep such a schedule, but the year passed and graduation loomed. Graduation exercises were set for Saturday afternoon, outside on the grounds of the Northwestern campus in Evanston.

Classmates approached the administration trying to have the ceremony changed because of the Sabbath, to no avail. However, on the appointed day, the heavens opened up and it was monsoon-like weather. My diploma was nice and dry when I received it in the mail. This was the second time that inclement weather impacted positively on my life!

Saba was proud of me and wanted to know what I wanted for a graduation gift. I replied that I wanted to go for a ride in a gondola. He said, "But that's in Venice, Italy!" and I quickly retorted, "Yup, that's it!"

Within a short while, we were flying en route to Italy. The water canals in place of streets enchanted us. Water taxis ferried us to the street where our hotel was situated, then porters lugged the suitcases up to the fourth floor. They were placed in the fantasy bedroom that looked like a palace royal apartment. The Sleigh bed had a mattress that was so high that there was a step-stool to enable us to climb into bed. I so enjoyed gazing at the antique furniture, the rich window hangings – the luxurious quality of the entire hotel was a gourmet feast for the eyes. The scene from our window reflected every movie that I had ever seen and every book that I had read about exciting Venice. It was a marvelous experience from start to finish.

In early morning after breakfasting in a charming flower-filled, small garden where the scent of roses immediately filled the nostrils as you stepped outdoors, we would head for the market to enjoy the activity of the marketplace. This was *Machne Yehuda* with the Grand Canal waterway as a backdrop.

Each day we explored the bridges, the museums with their magnificent paintings and spent a good portion of our time on the water. On Murano, the island where glass is blown, we bought gifts for the family and a glass bell which miraculously has survived all the years and sits today on our salon coffee table. The Gondola ride was a "kick", except that the Gondolier in his traditional outfit and straw hat insisted on singing the song "Chicago" instead of "O Solo Mio" which is what the atmosphere demanded. The price tag for that ride was $50 per head, an enormous amount of money in the 70s.

We have returned to that magical city a number of times with AACI cruises, and last year I heard the Gondolier quote a price of $100 per head. Will he now sing *Heveinu Shalom Aleichem* if he is engaged by us? Each time our ship enters the Grand Canal, it is impossible not to have a sense of awe at the magnificence of the structures, where it is still easy to imagine the fairy tale life that once was.

T.I. (Teacher's Institute) was a program under the auspices of the Associated Talmud Torahs and after I had obtained my long anticipated B.A. diploma in secular studies, I wanted to acquire a degree in Jewish Studies. Two years found me every Wednesday evening at the building where the Ida Crown Jewish Academy was located. Rabbi Gedaliah Rabinowitz and Rabbi Isaac Sender (a friend of long standing) were my *Rebbes* and it was a difficult, but worthwhile and inspiring experience. The course concluded with the studying and writing of a paper on Rabbi Moshe Chaim Luzzato, The *Ramkal*. I prize my degree in Jewish Thought very highly, but that was just the beginning of serious study and certainly not the conclusion. Learning something new every day is a valuable rule of thumb … No matter how old one is, there are always new horizons to conquer. Never stop learning … Never!

WITH BOTH CHILDREN LIVING IN ISRAEL, we became members of PNAI (Parents of North Americans In Israel). It was difficult to sit through a meeting without red eyes. Our glances would be met by other parents all having the same thoughts. Our children had rejected the way of life in which they were reared. It was a difficult thought with which to come to grips. Almost without exception, we had grown up in immigrant homes, our parents had struggled financially to raise their families. But most of us had attended college, had stable employment and in numerous cases became professionals. There were many Rabbis, doctors, dentists, lawyers and successful business people, all grateful to America for the opportunities that it had afforded Jews. No where in the world had the Jewish narrative been as successful, and now we were facing this conundrum. Our progeny preferred Israel and were not with us. We had friends whose grown children were now living with their own families within walking distance of the grandparents homes, accessible enough to spend the Sabbath together. What a seeming blessing. We had expensive phone calls where I steeled myself not to cry as the clock ticked away, wanting to share in the lives of Tammy and Uri for a precious few minutes. I recall the day that Tammy received her Israeli citizenship and was so excited that you could feel her exuberance those thousands of miles away. It was one of those "Eureka" experiences, where you realize that nothing will ever be the same and that change is on the way and it will come.

We, PNAI members, were dyed-in-the-wool Zionists. We were the heart and soul of every Chicago-Israel program, whether it was the annual March For Israel, buying Israel Bonds or raising funds for every Israel-based program, Hadassah, The Jewish National Fund (JNF) and schools. We couldn't resent Israel – we couldn't. It came to the point that I couldn't sing the words to *Hatikvah* or watch the blue and white flag flying proudly in front of Hillel Torah School. It was time to consider moving to Israel. At first it was a remote thought and it grew sharper over a short time.

There is a verse in the Torah, *Leviticus* Chapter 25:10, which states: "You shall sanctify the fiftieth year." We decided to adhere to that commandment. *Saba* was forty-eight and I was forty-five. We had two years to accomplish it. Of course there were obstacles and many hurdles.

First, we announced it to the Synagogue and to the school, but it seemed to be such a long time, and people though that we would come to our senses before then.

Uncle Manny was livid when he heard the news. I can still hear him shouting (as you already know this was his normal volume button!) "Are you crazy. You want to leave two *Meluchot?* (Kingdoms)." He was referring to our two careers which were indeed impressive i.e. *Saba* being the Rabbi of a large, important Synagogue in the North suburbs of Chicago, and I being the Executive Director of one of the largest Jewish day schools west of the Hudson River. We just smiled and I kissed him for being so concerned about our well-being.

When the telephone rang at 5:30 a.m., we knew in our bleary-eyed, not quite awake as yet state, that it was the children. Uri and Shelli were excitedly blurting out that they were formally engaged. Surprise, it wasn't ... as they had been "going together" since age fourteen, but when a child makes that kind of announcement your life status is raised a notch, especially the first one to be wed. The *Bnei Akiva* Organization, knowing of their interest in each other had sent Shelli to *Kibbutz Tira Tzvi,* and she was now a student in *Orot* Seminary. Uri was originally dispatched to *Kiryat Arba.* However, *Kibbutz Yavneh* was where his Sabbath family lived. It was the home of Knesset Member Sara Stern-Katan, who was an extraordinarily busy lady, but the feeling was that Uri did not need a great deal of mothering. However, currently he was an IDF soldier, and therein lies a marvelous story.

The wedding was to be in Chicago as both families resided there. It was an an especially poignant time as Shelli's father, Elimelech (King) Weiss passed away soon after the engagement. The affair was toned down, so as not to offend the sensibilities of Necchi, Shelli's mother and the family. For example, instead of a flower-bedecked *Chupah,* her father's *Talit* was used, but it was, nevertheless, an elegant affair. There were two parts to the festivities; the wedding which was held in a large hotel with the dinner closed to all but family and close friends. Then, the following day *Sheva Brachot* with hundreds of friends and Synagogue members. He was, after all, the Rabbi's son. *Saba* had been the Rabbi of this congregation for twenty years and no matter what, this group had been our friends and supporters since the very beginning. There was no other way. Even though the bride and groom preferred a smaller affair, the reality was that there was no choice ... we had to live there in peace and harmony with these people after the festivities were concluded.

But there was one very large obstacle – *Tzahal* (The Israeli Army). Uri could not get a straight answer whether he would be allowed to have official leave to return for the wedding. He had to be present at the *Ufruf,* the wedding and hopefully for at least a week after to celebrate the *Sheva Brachot.* It was also to be a few days before Passover and week after week passed and no ... "Yes, you can leave and be in the USA for your own wedding!"

Panic was beginning to set in and I asked anyone and everyone how to solve this problem. There were a number of Israelis who were teachers at school and I set the problem before them. One suggested that I write directly to *Rav Aluf Raful Eitan,* the Chief of Staff of the Israeli Army. I thought, why not and I quickly composed a letter to Rabbi Eitan, not knowing that *Rav Aluf* means TOP GENERAL and has nothing to do with the word Rabbi, which connotes a clergyman. Whoever heard that I had addressed this letter to Rabbi Eitan laughed uproariously. It seems that he is totally secular and I had given him ordination! The important fact was that Uri showed up on time, had colored marshmallows wrapped in gauze material thrown at him for his *Ufruf* as a hope for a sweet life with his bride and the wedding was a wonderful family affair. Years later, Uri told me that the famous letter that I wrote was still in his military file. It's great to give someone a chuckle once in a while and that letter did it!

It was 1982, Menachem Begin was the Prime Minister of Israel and politics, as usual in Israel, was in high gear and created disheartening headlines every day. Mr. Begin was sandbagged by President Jimmy Carter of America and was forced to return the city of Yamit, which had been built from the sand of the Sinai desert. It was a lovely area with well built, large homes and a thriving shopping center. When one approached the city, it was easy to rub your eyes believing it to be a mirage. It was a true oasis in the desert.

For weeks, activists would protest the removal of Israeli citizens, due to political expediency. Buses of students were brought in to "man the trenches" and join demonstrations. Uri was a student in the Nir Yeshiva and one night, in the pre-dawn hours, the buses arrived in the area of Yamit. The students were told to walk in the direction of the doomed city and should the soldiers stop them, they would don their *Tefilin* and begin praying the Morning service.

Well, the soldiers stopped them and arrested the students for praying in an unauthorized place. (Of course, this was garbage talk, but we're not discussing politics now.) They spent three days in a brand new jail which contained a library of Biblical study books and the students passed their jail sentence most pleasantly. They were released and trials were set for four months, hence. At that time, Uri was in the Army / Yeshiva and within a week after his arrest, he was back in his army uniform.

In the meantime, Tammy and Morris had become engaged, with Shelli as their matchmaker. I boarded the airplane with two tasks to accomplish. First, to help with the wedding plans and second to attend Uri's trial. Trying to help Tammy purchase her wedding gown, I requested a *Simla im Rakevet* (a dress with a train!) I had not yet grasped the idea that not every phrase has a direct translation from English to Hebrew.

The wedding celebration was held in two parts. The ceremony and party took place on the rooftop of the Shalom Hotel in Bayit V'Gan, with a most entertaining choir consisting of friends of Morris. It was a happy occasion, but there was one disconcerting note. The wedding took place during the First Lebanon War. Many of the invited guests were in uniform and would enter the hall, find their seat and put their rifle under the seat. To Americans, it was unsettling, but other guests seemed to take this in stride and so did we. The second half was a large celebration in Chicago. When the celebrant is the child of a pulpit Rabbi, that is the norm. Tammy had spent her childhood with these friends and members of the Synagogue. They were all invited to share in our happiness and why not? A caring congregation becomes family and belongs at peak family occasions!

My adventure with Uri's trial began as Uri, Shelli and I squeezed in the back of a taxi on the way to Gaza. Uri, in uniform, had his gun at the ready. The driver was an Arab, as was the passenger that sat next to him. The man was dressed in beige traditional robe and headdress trimmed in gold. At his waist was a knife with a handle that made him look like a bit player in the Peter O'Toole movie, "Lawrence of Arabia." We were driving along and in the middle of nowhere, the passenger alights and begins walking. There was nothing but sand and more sand, as far as the eye could see. There was no civilization and we saw no traces of human habitation all the way there.

The whole experience would have made at least a four-star movie script. The court in Gaza was housed in a grey stone building surrounded by a courtyard, which most probably was built in the 1800s. Originally it appeared to be a fortress turned into a government court house, when the British ruled Palestine. I could easily imagine Errol Flynn or Douglas Fairbanks Jr., (1940s movie stars) being involved in a sword fight on the irregular stone steps of the primitive staircase leading to the upper story.

The courtroom was square with sawdust on the floor. In the front were three military judges dressed in Khaki sweaters. The prosecutor and the defense attorney faced each other, with the witness chair behind a small table between them.

As the twenty-plus defendants arrived, they each stood their army-issued rifles in a row along the wall. They seemed to be sentinels witnessing the proceedings.

The defendants were young, in their early twenties. There were three women among them. I stared at their small gold earrings glinting in the dim light. To my American mind, the defendant youngsters with rifles and jewelry made a bizarre combination.

Of course, I couldn't comprehend any of the proceedings as my understanding of Hebrew was poor, but I listened attentively. I must have stood out like a sore thumb against this backdrop with all hardened Israeli soldiers and one blonde, middle-aged woman from the United States.

The afternoon wore on and all of a sudden, the defense attorney shouts out *"Mincha"* and the witness table is conscripted to be used as a *Bima* for the Afternoon service. Later when the proceedings were ended for the day, the principles were trying to set the upcoming sessions to complete the trial. But one day was *Purim* and another was too close to *Pesach* and then *Yom Hashoah* and *Yom Hazikaron* and so on. That exchange strengthened my resolve to make *Aliyah* and become an integral part of the Zionist experience. All my life, the considerations of public discourse was Xmas, Easter and all dates of the non-Jewish world. This is where we belonged, where our Jewish spirit belonged, not in Park Ridge, Illinois.

THE YEARS WERE PASSING and there were many life changes in both our families. Judy and Aryeh and their son, Tzvi, after his first pulpit in Manitowoc, Wisconsin moved to Memphis, Tennessee to occupy his second position there. They then returned to Chicago – we were so happy to have them nearby. Sandy and Chay lived in Skokie, Illinois with their family. It was nice having their three daughters enrolled in Hillel Torah when I held my position there. Ilene divorced her first husband, Irwin Gordon, and moved with her three children to the Golf Mill area. She then married Gary Fierstein, who was a wonderful human being; a real *Mentsh* as we say. Unfortunately he passed away at an early age.

Roz and Howard built a true *Bayit Neeman B'Yisroel*. It is a pleasure being with them when we visit New York for occasions. They live in Brooklyn, New York and have a Sabbath / Holiday home in Monsey, New York. Their two sons, Jonathan and Michael married two true *Neshey Chayil* and with their families are a source of Jewish *Nachas*. The Monsey house is on the edge of a forest preserve and has a glass-enclosed indoor pool with a roof that opens up for fresh-air swimming. Once, I was in the pool alone and looking up, I saw a deer watching me intently.

We stared at each other for a few minutes, but when I gave a friendly wave of greetings, it bounded off most gracefully. My Bambi left me alone to enjoy the water by myself. I adore swimming, and I have a wonderful time pretending that I am Esther Williams, singing to myself and dancing in the water. She was a movie star in the 40s and 50s whose films always featured her in the water with a chorus of guys and gals all swimming acrobatically together in graceful formations in a pool that was meant to resemble a flower-filled garden. One of my favorite activities is enjoying a pool, but having never lived in a climate that was suitable, I enjoy what I can, when the occasion arises.

Speaking of Esther Williams brings up the subject of Jewish pride. Prior to the establishment of the State of Israel, Jewish pride was a negligible commodity. There were dozens, if not hundreds, of famous folks who had changed their name so as not to bring attention to their Jewishness. Hollywood did it as a matter of policy. Not only was Esther Williams Jewish, but Tony Curtis, nee Bernie Schwartz and a host of others. We never dreamt that so many of our matinee idols and people in the news were of our faith.

In the 60s, the situation slowly changed with stars such as Barbra Streisand retaining their names. Unfortunately, she is a product of *Bais Yaakov* School system in New York and has been married to two non-Jewish men; but that's another problem.

As Israel took its place among the family of nations, people gave it moral support and funds. Today, as G-D has blessed us and we are strong and flourishing, detractors have come out of the woodwork. Traditionally, people love the underdog, and we have serious political problems. Since this is not a treatise on diplomacy, let me just say that the political situation is another problem, but when has it been any different?

Gary, Ilene's second husband, was an engineer at the Motorola

Three Sisters, Judy Levin (R), Roz Zuckerman (L) and me – the "Filling" of the sandwich, 1996

Corporation and an unforgettable incident occurred one day at a family get-together. Gary had brought with him a gadget that he was working on in conjunction with the employees of Motorola Corporation in Tel Aviv. It was a black hunk of plastic and it looked like a telephone receiver. It was approximately 12 cm. long (8 inches) and must have weighed 2 kilos (5 lbs.) He explained that this was a telephone that we would carry with us – we would not be attached to any permanent installation. Initially we thought that he was mad. Secondly we thought that he was just plain crazy! How could it possibly be ... to carry a telephone with you and besides that, the object that he had was heavy and ugly. No way! Of course, the rest is history and we never did have the opportunity to apologize to Gary, as he was deceased before the revolution of mobile telephones occurred. If one day there is a museum with the story of the mobile phone, our Gary's name should be on the top of the list!

During the course of time, my mother, Rose Ray, married a fine gentleman, Max Glass. They lived in New York and from time to time I would fly there to visit with them. However, she began to suffer from Dementia. One morning, as we were to leave to go shopping at a Waldbaum's Food Store, her favorite, I noticed that she had her shoes on the wrong feet. This was the beginning of a slide into the illness, which ended in her death. Every succeeding visit, her illness would manifest itself worse. Once before leaving for the airport, she insisted that I have coffee with them. She brought me a dinner plate and while holding the jar of instant coffee realized that this was wrong, but couldn't figure out that coffee requires a cup. Then she would forget the names of *Saba* and the children and finally, one trip when she totally didn't recognize me, I realized that my visiting was futile. I would call from Chicago and Max or the caregiver would give me an update, but in reality, my mother was gone.

Finally, during a stopover in New York back from Israel, I called and when my mother had the telephone in her hand, she miraculously was lucid for two minutes. She said, "I know that I am ill and I am so miserable that I would jump out of the window, if I could." But then, she was back in the grip of her illness. She passed away from a melanoma, two years later.

My mother and Max had a good life together. It wasn't too long after that, on the night that there was a historical electrical failure in New York, he was hit by a car, taken to the hospital, but because of that bizarre happening, passed away perhaps due to the lack of immediate emergency care, but perhaps not. Who knows?

After my mother's death, I wrote a long letter to him thanking him for giving my mother years of happiness and companionship. He was a gentleman to the end and I will forever be grateful to the gentle and unassuming Max Glass.

Living in Las Vegas, Nevada, Ilene is now married to Larry Pondel, another great guy who is a fine addition to the family. Sandy was divorced from Chay, is married to Linda and also lives in Las Vegas. Chay married Yoel Lustig and they continue to live in Skokie. Not having family close by, at the very least, on

Las Vegas, Nevada, $1,500 Richer, Brought Home Gifts and A Profit!

the same continent, is the worst thing about making *Aliyah*. Thanks to e-mail and low-cost telephone calls we keep in touch 'cause family is family; nothing is more important.

Sister Judy lives in Chicago, unfortunately, Aryeh, her mate for over fifty years passed away. She enjoys her son Tzvi, his wife Esther and their three children who live nearby.

A story concerning Howard was published in a book that spent a considerable amount of time on the Best Seller list. There was a man who flew to New York to present a business proposition to Howard. After arriving, he tried to telephone him, but met with no success. In frustration, he called a friend who told him that it was a Jewish holiday and when evening falls, he could then contact Howard. After speaking with him, it was arranged that Howard should come to the hotel room. After the discussion, Howard spied a Pizza Box. He tore off one end and wrote a check on it for one million dollars ... and it was properly cashed!

Another one of those very early in the morning calls from Kiryat Arba, Israel brought the report that Elimelech Tzvi was born to Shelli and Uri. The news that we were grandparents was unbelievable! Our joy at their announcement was boundless; what does one do when this happens? Well, what we did was celebrate. We made a grand affair *Kiddush* for the members of the Synagogue, hosted the Friday night services with an elegant Dessert Reception, as well as treated the Hillel Torah staff to lunch.

When we received the 6 a.m. call one year later from Tammy

and Morris that Elichai Aryeh was born, we did everything once again. Folks were enjoying all the partying and kept asking when the next one would be. They did not have long to wait until Rachel Galia became the first granddaughter to the Karzens, born to Tammy and Morris of Efrat.

We were the first of our friends to become honored members of The Grandparent World and everyone wanted to share in our happiness. A tradition was begun that for each birth, Barbara, Myrna and I would climb into Myrna's van, whose license plate reads CARPOOL MOM (you know what she has been doing all her adult life!) and we would take a trip to the Baby Village and buy complete layouts for each of the babies in their turn. We had as much fun as watching the funniest movie – the squeals and laughter made other shoppers stare at us, but, we didn't care. We always had a fun time together. It was like being back in high school and the honorary aunts had as good a time as the Grandmother who was happily shipping all these great items, but whose arms were empty. We have a friend who wrote a children's book for Israeli youngsters whose grandparents live in the Diaspora. The title is My Grandma Lives at The Airport – that became our motto and El Al became a shareholder in our finances.

I love adventures of every kind, whether those of travel, food or experiences – that is what keeps life exciting. When Racheli (as she is and will be forever known) was born, *Saba* and I flew once again to welcome the new arrival and visit our growing family. As my birthday occurred while we were there, we went to Eilat to celebrate and for a bit of R&R ... rest and relaxation. Noticing the parachutes hovering above, I decided that was what I would like for my birthday gift – I wanted to try Parasailing!

The young men proprietors looked skeptical as I approached them to order a session.

One said, "But, you'll have to run along the beach!"

"So I'll run along the beach," I replied.

"But, you'll have to wear a harness!"

"So, I'll wear a harness!"

They brought up a number of other pre-conditions, not believing that I was serious. Finally, they shrugged their shoulders, and put the harness on me. I ran alongside the boat into the water and was immediately swept up into the air and was flying without an airplane. It was a magnificent feeling and as I looked around at the scene of water, sky and white, puffy clouds as far as the eye could see, all the while thinking how an artist would have swooned at the beauty. It was a most heavenly experience!

When I returned to earth, *Saba* felt that he had to try it also, so he was harnessed in and swooped into the sky. Unfortunately the motor on the boat to which he was tethered, died and I saw him suspended in midair and dropping like a stone into the water. Newspaper headlines flashed through my mind... RABBI DROWNS IN RED SEA and it was just after the holiday of Passover! To his credit, he insisted on going again and this time he flew through the air like a graceful bird.

On another birthday, Tammy was taken aback when, at her request on the suggestion of a gift, I replied that I would like the experience of swimming with the dolphins in Eilat. She didn't bat an eye, but made the reservation. By this time, I was almost twenty years older than the Parasailing experience and it showed on the operators faces when I came to the reef.

There were a trio of divers who were on duty together; one Pro and two assistants. The young, handsome fellow who was my Pro, held my hand so tightly the entire time. I was sure that he was afraid that he would lose this old lady and probably his job because of it. Nevertheless, I suited up in the wet suit and fins and then flipped and flopped to the waters end, where we walked and then swam into the deeper waters, all the time being held by the hand by my guardian. I felt that he would have liked to use a metal chain to keep me by his side, but he was most pleasant, probably wondering what he did to deserve being my babysitter. He could have been snorkeling with the others who were gorgeous twenty-year-old beauties in bikinis, but he was mine and I went along with the others and we swam together.

Eilat, Always a Skipper!

I have been asked to describe the experience many times. What did it feel like? It was unnaturally quiet. The beauty of the corals dazzled the eye and we were told that we must be quiet. How you could speak while wearing a snorkeling mask and trying not to suffocate was beyond me, but, I went along. Then the dolphins spotted us and swam so close that you could feel them brushing your arm. They were smooth and sleek, swimming swiftly and just ignoring us. I think that I also heard them speak. It was a kind of whistle and they were probably laughing to themselves looking at the nutty humans dressed in outfits pretending to be fish.

As we emerged from the water, there was *Saba* eating an ice cream cone, sitting on the beach with the other "Fraidy Cats." This time, however, he didn't try to match this adventure. It was a singular experience and I wouldn't have missed it for anything.

My father-in-law suffered from heart disease. The first serious operation was on the experimental side and he was told that this repair should last about eight years; it lasted eight years. He had purchased a tuxedo for Uri's *Bar Mitzvah* bash, but never wore it as he was in the hospital at the time; the same was true of another formal occasion. We told him only half-kidding that he was to buy no more tuxedoes; whatever he would wear would be fine. At Ilene's wedding to Gary, Dad was again hospitalized, but at a doctor's conference prior to the affair, it was declared that he could attend the wedding, which was to take place in our Synagogue, MTJC, just a short distance away. Ilene's parents walked her down the aisle and all appeared to be as normal. However, at the dinner, Dad became ill and was rushed back to the hospital where he died later that night. We had a close connection and I loved him dearly and respected him highly.

One time, sitting at his hospital bedside, he told me an amazing story. He related that two nights before, he dreamt that he was going through a dim tunnel and there was a bright light at the end. When he started to emerge from the tunnel, his mother appeared to be waiting for him and waved him back; she indicated that he was to go no further. That was the end of the dream and he awoke.

Now, today, we have heard this narration numerous times, but this was before Dr. Elizabeth Kubler Ross published her studies on Death and Dying, the title of her well-known book, which publicized this same occurrence in many instances. However, it was an unknown finding at the time that my father-in-law related it to me. I was astonished and don't know why he chose to share it with me alone, and not to any other members of the family. To this day, I am perplexed.

THERE WERE SOME TRYING TIMES at this juncture of our lives. *Saba* was hospitalized with a Hiatal Hernia that the doctors suggested be taken care of before our moving to Israel. Having a family member or friend in the hospital, even for a birth, but especially for an illness is a source of worry and lays a pall over the days until the patient is released. The Synagogue Board decided that as long as he was ill, perhaps he should leave the Synagogue before the High Holidays and not wait until the

December, as planned. Perhaps he would not be well enough to officiate and that they better have another Rabbi on hand.

A Synagogue in Colorado called *Saba* and offered him the position as Rabbi for the High Holiday period. Hearing what MTJC was planning, he accepted the offer. Needless to say, our Synagogue straightened out their thinking in a hurry and *Saba* called Colorado and declined their generous offer.

There is an apocryphal story told that a Rabbi was ill and the Synagogue Board voted him a *Refuah Shlayma* – the vote was 10 to 4 in favor!

The Pomerantz family, our dear friends, were struck by catastrophic situations one after the other. Barbara was stricken with Cancer and was fighting the disease valiantly. Their daughter, Sherri, after spending a year in seminary in Israel, was accompanying me home from services. They were to lunch with us on *Rosh Hashanah* and we were looking forward to enjoying the *Yom Tov* meal together. On the way home, Sherri requested an aspirin, as she had been suffering from headaches the last few weeks. Three months later, after it was revealed that Sherri had a benign brain tumor, she was operated upon, however, she never awoke from the operation. Her death left the community reeling. At the same time Sherwin's computer business was compromised and brought untold hardship to the family.

Sherwin and Barbara made the decision to make *Aliyah* and set February 1982, just a few months away, as their target date. They decided that Debbie, seventeen years old and a senior at the Ida Crown Jewish Academy, would accompany them. We pleaded with them to allow Debbie to live with us and graduate with her class friends. There were our children's empty bedrooms and a car for her personal use; it would have been our honor to have her live with us. But after having lost their child so soon, it apparently was too emotionally difficult to have her remain in Des Plaines and she accompanied them.

Aliyah

August 1985, we began to seriously plan our *Aliyah* for the following December. We excitingly visited the Midwest *Aliyah* office and he confirmed that we knew as much about the process as he did. We didn't want to take anything from Israel. We were entitled to one-way tickets, as well as money towards the moving fee for our lift, but we refused all monetary help from the country. We did accept living arrangements where we were scheduled to go to Beit Canada, the *Merkaz Klitah* located in Talpiyot, a neighborhood in Jerusalem. We interviewed moving companies, put our house up for sale and tried to prepare ourselves psychologically for the biggest step that we had ever taken outside of our marriage. Was it scary? You bet. Our knowledge of Hebrew was biblical and we couldn't communicate at all. Like everyone else, we were afraid of making mistakes and looking foolish. It took a while to overcome that fear and while we now can speak and even orate publicly, if necessary, there is a huge difference between our communication skills in English and Hebrew. Also, my Hebrew is skewed. I know decorating terms that Hebrew scholars are unaware of, simply because I need and use them.

For the majority of Anglo *Olim*, there were two sources of income, the first is Social Security which began for women at age sixty-two and for men at sixty five. The second are pensions again directed to the senior population. Well, we had a huge problem, we were too young to receive Social Security and neither of us had pensions from the workplace. There is also a small amount of money from *Bituach Leumi*, but again because of our youth, we paid into the system for years, not benefited. We had to work, but what or how ... that was the big question. However, we had faith that it would work out and we forged ahead.

We had led numerous trips to Israel, very often with a family that was celebrating a *Bar* or *Bat Mitzvah*. Seeing the *Balagan* at the *Kotel*, with no direction or formal instructions on how to manage a celebration of a youngster in this religious rite of passage, in this holiest of places in Jerusalem was most disturbing. To top off this situation was the fact that there were just a few elderly Rabbis on site, who spoke little English and had zero understanding of how to make the occasion meaningful. So we decided to start a *Bar* and *Bat Mitzvah* Service. We sent out a brochure to every English-speaking Rabbi in the world, on every continent from Australia and New Zealand to Britain and North America. I'm certain that an overwhelming amount of Rabbis threw the brochure in the circular file (the wastebasket), but between the brochures and networking, Rituals Unlimited was created.

What I was going to do for work was a giant question mark? I had no idea, but complete faith that the Lord would not lead us to Israel and just let me dangle with no meaningful activity prevailed. Besides, it was a MUST that we obtain employment as there were no funds to be had, without working for them. The only hand that we would receive was the ones at the ends of our arms! Looking back, I realize how frivolous it was to take this giant leap without a financial safety net, and it took a lot of guts and faith in the Lord's goodness. We may not have had money, but we had that faith and boundless enthusiasm and knew that it would all work out.

By September, Dov Shandalov, who was the son of our good friends, Simmie and Ben, was appointed as the new Executive Director of Hillel Torah. He was a young man, known to us since he was born and had always impressed us with his numerous abilities. Dov has been in that position for over twenty-seven years and has been an asset to the organization since Day #1, so that vacuum was ably filled.

At the Annual Dinner, I was recognized for my achievements and presented with an antique mirror which I cherish and reminds me constantly of the exciting and meaningful years that I spent at the school, as well as the friendships that were formed; it was a part of my life, where I gave as well as received.

Pleasant memories of the school will always be part of my soul. The Synagogue was a different story.

When our impending *Aliyah* was first announced, there were a few members who were envious, wishing that they could come with us. The majority were apathetic, being ordinary American Jews, they were ensconced in their busy lives, enjoying that which was afforded by America. Receiving a good education was the means to superior employment which meant a top salary in any field. In the 50s and 60s, one knew that with an education they would rise higher than their parents and would be more affluent; and this happened. Since the financial meltdown of 2008, the situation has changed and many students graduating from universities are jobless and return to live with parents. This was virtually unknown in our time.

The third group of members were angry at us for leaving, and we understood this, also. For over twenty years, *Saba* had been there to minister to them in every situation, happy or sad. Now, to whom would they turn? It's hard to find and relate to new individuals ... it was a change and change is difficult.

At *Yom Kippur* services, as Jay finished his sermon, one man arose and exclaimed, "You'll be back, Rabbi. You'll be back!" Others asked us to reconsider, as they wondered how will they get along without *Saba's* familiar face at Synagogue services, not to mention weddings and funerals. There were people who had come to counseling sessions for years ... what would they do?

As we looked into their eyes, we saw their pain, their confusion, but we clung to the folks who were proud that their Rabbi and *Rebbetzin* were fulfilling the destiny of the Jewish people by actually living in Israel, which is the only commandment that you can do with one's entire body. We were ready for the challenge.

We were feted and feted. There were parties and get-togethers wishing us well from friends and family. The Sisterhood of our Synagogue gave a luncheon in my honor with the theme of "RUBY BROKE THE MOLD!" emblazoned on a banner that was hung across the stage. My sisters, aunts and cousins mixed with Synagogue members of long standing, as well as women who had recently joined, all honored me with their presence. Friends from long ago, and from every stage in my life, even those that had a connection with the day school, as well as *Rebbetzins* from sister Synagogues, all gathered to wish us *Hatzlacha* in our new life.

There were original songs performed, as well as a skit written with vignettes from the stages which we had all lived through during the period of our being the leaders of the Synagogue. There was much laughter and a few tears as we looked forward to the challenges that were to come.

The house was sold and the moving company spent three days packing our belongings, which filled a fifteen-foot container. There were fifty cartons of books, and this was after *Saba* had given away two hundred books from his personal library.

We spent weeks sorting out and giving away items that went back to our wedding day. My wedding gown was given to a *Gemach* for Russian brides. We had a yard sale which is an experience all its own. Aunt Judy, Aunt Chay, and Aunt Myrna (honorary) helped us with it, but they couldn't meet our eyes without welling up. We were the first ones to break the circle of the family of the Karzen, Rays and our dear friends. It wasn't easy, but we soldiered on.

Our key rings became the symbol of our *Aliyah*. First, we returned our safe deposit and office keys, then the cars were sold and the car keys were absent and then the day finally came when our house keys were in the hands of new owners. As we took a last walk around the house, a home that we had loved, *Saba*, who never cried, was sobbing. I, who cry at supermarket openings, was teary-eyed. I felt that *Haya Tov, Tov Shahaya* ("It was good, but it is good that it was") and it was time to move on.

December 15, 1985, we climbed aboard the El Al airplane, with eight suitcases, the Torah which we had bought in honor of Tammy and Uri decades ago and an electric typewriter. Helping us carry all of our belongings were a group of twenty-three people that we were leading to tour Israel, some to celebrate a *Bat Mitzvah*. *Saba's* Rituals Unlimited service had its first clients and we were on our way!

CHERRY ON THE TOP

Part Three

Living The Good Life

ALIYAH! WHAT A MAGIC WORD. As the El Al airplane landed, the music played *Halleluyah,* and we felt that it was for us alone. In a way it was, as we were the only *Olim* on the plane – in 1985, a mere 1,100 people came to Israel to live permanently. A representative of AACI was there to greet us and to shepherd us to the office of the Interior Ministry where we were made officially *Olim.* We exited with our brand new Identity cards in the ubiquitous blue vinyl cover. I had requested that they officially register me as *Rivka,* but the clerk refused and so to this day, I am Ruby – (*Resh-vav-bet-yud*). It is a unique name. I have never run into an Israeli with the name, except for those fellows named Reuven, who use "Ruby" as a nickname. It was also rare in the US. Most of the "Rubys" are found in the Southern states where it was a popular name for African-American women.

Saba, on the other hand, had a different problem. He wanted his Hebrew name recorded, as Jay would have come out spelled as Gay, and who needed that? He was successful in getting his way, and on all of his documents, he is known as *Yaakov.*

A cab ferried us to Jerusalem, where we were expected at the Bet Canada *Merkaz Klitah* (absorption center) in the neighborhood of Talpiyot. At that time, it was a rural area, and the view from our window was that of verdant hills, many trees and the occasional shepherd leading his flock of sheep along our street.

I was ecstatic at the wonderment of actually being here without a return ticket tucked into my purse. I awoke each morning, with the December sun shining through the window pane and simply couldn't believe that we had accomplished this life change – a smile never left my face. I walked around on air and I must confess that my rose-colored glasses are still operational. Of course, I realize and know for a fact that there are many problems with living in Israel, but I have always tried to heed the Torah's command to find the good in Israel and not focus on the bad. But, at this time everything was good and we had one funny experience after another.

Our apartment comprised of the entrance hall, which had a small dining table two chairs and our "closet." There was a niche where a pole hung between the walls creating the closet. Hey, there was no door ... but it was a closet and we placed the cartons that we brought with everything that we thought that we would need until we bought an apartment and received our lift with everything that we owned in this world.

The bathroom was small, sporting a shower, sans curtain, but it had a *sponga* mop which got a lot of use as the water from each shower inevitably spilled out into our "dining room."

The kitchen was so tiny; no oven, but two burners and one cabinet. That was OK, as we had no kitchenware, save what we were given when we first arrived at the Center. Each *Oleh* was given six pots and pans of various sizes and a few plates, cups and flatware. I laughed when I thought about all the dishes, cutlery and kitchenware that was floating on the Atlantic Ocean wending its way toward us. But this was fine. I wasn't cooking, at any rate. *Saba* and I ate out just about every meal, while we explored the city seeking *Kosher* restaurants. It was a dream come true. Chicago had *Kosher* restaurants that frequently opened, but closed within a short time. That happened in Jerusalem also, but there were so many of them. At this point, we have opened so many hotels and restaurants in Jerusalem that we have truly lost count ... but there are always more on the horizon.

There was a nice size bedroom with a desk, additional hooks for clothing and more cartons that seemed to stare at us constantly. There were cartons everywhere and it was hard finding anything, but we knew that it was temporary and one can manage anything if it is temporary.

I loved the tiny space. There was nothing to clean and cooking was rare. I felt like we were living in a college dormitory and thought it was fun. At the end of the eight months, *Saba* was delighted to move into our new home. I was excited, but having been responsible for a large home for so many years, this was like a vacation to me and I enjoyed it tremendously.

The first Friday morning, upon opening the door, I found a smiling face with a tiny lady bearing a bottle of wine and two *Challot* for our Shabbat table. Donna Grushka, representing AACI, was doing her weekly *Mitzvah* work – helping new Olim. As we welcomed Donna into our chaotic apartment, we never dreamed how intertwined our lives would become with AACI. Donna, Evie Weidenbaum, David London, Don Edelstein, Bernie Barnett, Judy Cohen and a host of others would become not only friends, but partners in making Israel a welcoming place for thousands of Anglo *Olim* in the years to come.

The rules of the place were that it was only for singles and couples without children. There were two other older couples, Charlotte and Charlie Gogek, and Ruth and Sidney Feibus. We became good friends, whose friendships has lasted until today. Unfortunately, the Gogeks have both passed away, but the Feibus' and we maintain a cherished relationship. Naturally, there were some babies born and they belonged to everybody. It became a community and we were like grandparents to the youngsters who lived with us.

Among the rules, which only the Anglos took seriously, was that no one was allowed to be accompanied by pets of any kind. We had given our wonderful kitty, known as Tiffany, to a farm where we hoped that she would live out her life contentedly. However, she was hit by a car and died of her wounds within six months of our *Aliyah*. The Russians, however, had brought their pets, both dogs and cats with them. I was amazed that they had ignored the supposedly strict rules. They shrugged their shoulders in a "So What!" manner when I inquired of their *Chutzpah*. That was the first time that I realized that we Anglos generally follow the rules; the Russians probably laughed at us and called us *Frierim* or whatever the equivalent word is in their language. One family had an upright piano in their small living quarters. How they managed to put that in their four allowed suitcases, I'll never fathom!

We had a strict schedule. We were students once again. From Sunday to Thursday we attended *Ulpan* for five hours each day that lasted for five months. We attended faithfully and spent at least a full hour every evening on homework. They had placed us in *Kita* 17, which was the highest level. It was easier for *Saba* than I, but I hung on with my fingernails and did okay. The teacher was Chana Horwitz, a Master teacher who exuded Zionism. She was marvelous and taught us old songs and all the cultural aspects of Israeli life. I realize after so many years here, that there is a body of knowledge that we will never acquire. Old time folk songs and Kindergarten ditties, names of flowers and diseases, expressions that once were popular relating to Israeli life years ago and other subjects will never be part of our lexicon. We came armed with Biblical Hebrew and have been perfecting our language skills ever since. To this day, there are two subjects that must be discussed with us in English, one is medical and the second is banking. As the irreplaceable Jerusalem Post columnist Sam Orbaum (*z'l*) would opine, he never knew if he owed the bank money, or the bank owed him, because of his difficulties with the nuances of the Hebrew language!

There were two activities that stand out in my memory. One was doing my homework in the laundry room waiting for the washer or dryer to be available. We were serious students. Being the eldest in the class, we feared that the youngsters, our fellow pupils, would show us up ... so we studied. The male / female versions of the language are difficult for an English speaker to master. Frankly, I'm delighted that many of the Israelis that I casually speak to appear to ignore those rules anyway.

The second important activity was the fact that Nechama Leibowitz, the renowned Torah scholar, would come once a week to give a lesson – in Hebrew. I told her that the longer she was gracious enough to give of her time to us, the easier her Hebrew became! She thought that was a good joke. We never realized the fine opportunity we enjoyed with being taught by one of the finest scholars in Jerusalem. But, that's Israel, I thought ... one never knew what would happen next!

The MAJOR activity of every evening was THE TELEPHONE! Whole evenings were spent sitting on the steps and waiting for your turn at the telephone. This was the time before mobile phones were on the market to the general public. In fact, a number of years later, when they became available, but costly, my friend, Avi Kara, who is my *Kablan-* partner bought one of the early Pelephones, but had no one to call! The problem was that no one else that he knew owned one and it never rang. Once the Cellcom Company entered the Israeli scene, that made the portable phones affordable ... the race was on. I read a recent article that claimed that there are more cellphones in the world than toilets. Even children possess them for safety issues and to tiny tots, a toy mobile phone is their favorite plaything.

Recently, we were lunching with the family and our three-year-old great-grandchild, Tzofia, asked if she could see my cellphone. I handed it to her, whereupon she immediately asked, *Savta*, where is the camera?" The telephone was seven years old; it was a "Dumb" Phone" as opposed to the "Smart" phones that were the rage at the time. I said that it was an old phone and there was no camera. She looked at me rather pityingly and said to her *Ima*, "*Savta* doesn't even have a camera on her phone!", and returned it with a look of disdain on her small face.

A few weeks later, we were telling this story to some friends and one fellow asked if he could see the phone. "You have a camera. It must have been one of the first telephones that had one." But it was so hard to see, I had completely missed it. Soon after, I was forced to buy a more up-to-date phone with e-mail and Facebook and other applications including an easily visible camera. It is still a "Dumb" phone, but at least my little Tzofia is once again proud of her *Savta* who has a REAL telephone!

Also amusing was when I bought my first phone, Neriyah, our grandchild who was then ten years old, was appalled that I had no score on the phone's games application. He then played all of the games and registered a respectable score. His *Savta* wasn't going to have a loser phone, no sir!

Back to the *Merkaz Klitah* in Talpiyot and the one telephone for the entire building of over fifty residents. The rule was that each person was allowed five minutes per phone call. The first problem was that there was always a queue. I can never remember being first, second or even third, never less than fifth or more. The second problem is that coins were not accepted; an *Asimon* (slug) was required. But the third problem was the worst. When you dialed, and the number was busy, it was back to the end of the line to try again. It was easy to spend two hours just chatting with fellow residents mostly about the unusual situations that we found ourselves in, being brand new *Olim*.

There was no such thing as being called to the phone to receive a call, as the telephone was constantly busy. It was an impossible situation. Being that *Saba's* service business, Rituals Unlimited, was in its infancy and it was a must that he receive calls, he rented a beeper. The calls were directed to Uri who would then beep *Saba*. *Saba* would call Uri to find out who called and then telephone the client. However, it still entailed waiting for the telephone. At times, we would go to the nearest public phone which was located in a nearby supermarket which closed at 6:30 p.m. Being used to service businesses that were open to all hours of the night, I inquired why they closed so early in the work day. The indignant manager retorted that supermarket employees also have families and why should they work in the evening. Of course, she had a point then but within a short few years, the Supersol Supermarket on Agron Street would be open 24 hours a day. That experiment was short-lived, but today, even a 10 p.m. closing is not rare.

Speaking of food stores, I saw the letters, *Mem-Kuf-Lamed-Tof*, painted on many walls in bright red. They were not to be missed. I wondered where that famous *Makolet* (food store) was located. Until it was pointed out to me that the word was *MIKLAT* (shelter), I had been searching for that advertised store. Perhaps there were even some American products being sold. Subsequently, that same Supersol Supermarket, did feature an American products week once a year, and it became like old home week for us. Old friends like Heinz ketchup and Starkist tuna fish we bought in quantities, as one never knew when they would be available again.

The first Friday morning as an *Olah*, I took my plastic basket, like an typical Israeli housewife, and set out for my first foray into the supermarket. It was a nightmare. I couldn't recognize any of the products except for the colorful box of Tide washing powder and Windex, as the local product looked exactly like the American window cleaner sold in the familiar blue bottle. I was flummoxed. Even the bar of margarine, or the jar of gefilte fish, as well as all the foods that I had purchased all my life, were totally unrecognizable. I was standing there with what I thought was cottage cheese in my hands, but I simply wasn't sure and decided to ask an Anglo-appearing person for help. There was a gentleman standing next to me and when I asked if he spoke English, a smile came on his handsome face and he said, "Ruby, don't you recognize me?" His name was Paul Laderman and he had not only attended the Hebrew Theological College, but he was also one of the youngsters who had frequented my father's delicatessen on the West Side of Chicago. It was a wonderful reunion and Paul helped me shop that day, but it took a few years until I was comfortable with Hebrew shopping lingo.

Having few dishes, it seemed a good idea to have paper plates on hand. When I asked the store manager for them, he asked, "You want to eat on carton?" Turning to the next customer, I'm sure that I heard the phrase "Crazy American." That was the first time that I heard the phrase as it was definitely audible, but over the years, many folks would at least think it, when I requested something that hadn't become part of the Israeli scene, as yet.

Saba wanted ice cream and innocently went to the store to buy a pint. The pickings were slim and when he asked if that was all the variety available, the manager reminded him that it was January and all that was available was *winter ice cream* as ice cream was a summer product – to cool off. He received the same sociological lesson when he tried to buy potato chips; they were for the summer – for picnics. Foraging down the aisles of the mammoth supermarkets of today, where every product from all points of the globe is available year round, we still joke about the seasonal ice cream and potato chips of yesteryear. The world has been driving down the consumer turnpike at breakneck speed with Israel among the forefront. We have come a long way.

WITHIN A FEW WEEKS WE HAD PURCHASED our first car. It was a Subaru and the first non-American car that we had ever owned. To my delight, I didn't have to record all the niggling items that didn't work or required adjustment and return to the car dealer for small repairs. This had never happened before. We had owned many new cars, but there was always a service repair list that had to be seen to … except for this foreign car. Israelis have asked if I miss our large American cars and truly, we don't. At one time, we were the owners of a bright red Mazda Sportscar with headlights that electronically lifted up when in use. I loved that car; it was unusual to see one like it on the road in Jerusalem. It had to be sold after a few years, but it lives on fondly in my memory.

Also, within a short time, we purchased an apartment. The address was Herzog 9, located on the first floor with a small garden attached. I hated it so that I didn't want to even go to the closing. It was so small that the dining room was already too crowded for us, with Tammy, Morris and the two grandchildren, Elichai and Racheli who was a baby, as well as Uri, Shelli and Elimelech, their son. I had envisioned a living room where we could entertain a crowd, but this was impossible. However, it was a reasonable price. One of the reasons was that the owner had used the cheapest possible materials and labor, forcing us to redo all the electricity and other standard items to bring them to code. However, utilizing all of my decorating skills, it was nice enough by Israeli standards of the time, but I disliked it intensely. Even the garden was a hazard as whatever was placed on the patio was stolen and we were robbed twice via the garden door.

Interestingly enough, when it was sold to lovely newcomers, we had occasion to visit a number of years later. There was my carefully chosen wallpaper, mirrored closet doors and carpeting still very much in use. When we entered the room, the wife exclaimed, "Here comes my Interior Designer!" It's always pleasant to meet a satisfied client, even an inadvertent satisfied client!

We had lived for so many years in the suburbs of a metropolitan city that Jerusalem was small by comparison. For example, Barbara and Sherwin Pomerantz's home in Ramot "B" was considered a long distance and it was a "lengthy drive" of less than fifteen minutes. In today's traffic, a solid forty-five minutes must be allotted for the exact same trip.

We were excited about living in the city center as it has many advantages: being able to walk "Downtown" and stroll around Ben Yehudah Street with its many restaurants, a movie theater and stores that seem to fill our shopping needs. This was before the era of malls. It was small town stuff, but it was magical to us and we loved it.

LIVING NEAR THE PRIME MINISTER and the President gave us a kick. Also the fact that the best hotels were in walking distance and our American guests and *Saba's Bar Mitzvah* families were constantly coming and going. We had the best of both worlds by residing in Rechavia.

One Sabbath morning while praying in The Great Synagogue, *Saba* spied one of his *Bar Mitzvah* families. After services, he asked them if they would like to meet Yitzhak Shamir, the Prime Minister. They went along with what they thought was a terrific joke and agreed. *Saba* led the group to Aza Street and said, "Shamir will be passing by in a matter of minutes." Sure enough, they gaped in amazement as Shamir approached. *Saba* introduced them and he chatted with them for a few minutes. In his gentlemanly, cordial manner, he wished them an inspiring trip to Israel and to be sure to come again.

The story behind the story was this. Every Sabbath morning, the Prime Minister would walk to his office in the Knesset and at 12:30 p.m., practically on the dot, we would encounter him walking briskly, returning home to the Prime Minister's residence on Balfour Street, followed by two Secret Service agents driving slowly next to him. We received letters from the family, noting that this encounter was the highlight of the group's trip and they dined out on this story for years to come. "This would never happen in Cleveland, Ohio," they penned. No, I'm sure it wouldn't!

On one side of Balfour Street is the Prime Minister's residence, while the other side are apartment buildings, where regular folk, Jerusalemites reside. I was engaged to remodel one of the apartments, which looked straight into a bedroom. For all I know, it could have been Shamir's own bedroom.

The times were so innocent and so different. We, my crew, including Arab workers, worked there for three months. Our cars were parked directly in front of the building; the trunks were not searched and no questions asked. There were two guards with no weapons in view, who stood in front of the PM's house. We became so friendly that when we brought drinks for our crew, we were sure to include the guards. Those times are gone forever, I guess.

TWO YEARS WAS MORE THAN ENOUGH for me in that apartment and we began to search for a new place to live, or rather, I began to search as *Saba* was perfectly happy in that miniscule place. One rainy Friday morning, glancing at the newspaper, I saw an ad for an apartment in the Diskin area. The instructions to each Real Estate salesperson was that we wanted to live fifteen minutes walking time to The Great Synagogue – Diskin Street filled the bill. That same morning, when the door was opened, I saw MAGIC and *Saba* almost fainted!

To say that it was a "Fixer Upper" was the understatement of the century. The salon / dining room measured fifty-four meters, which was perfect for our future entertaining, but everything was broken. Many floor tiles had been removed so that the squatters could cook in the sand. There was no kitchen or bathrooms as they were destroyed. Had a bomb fallen on the apartment, there is no doubt that its appearance would have been improved. There had been a large dog whose leavings dotted the floor. The floor-to-ceiling mirrors were cracked. It was a disaster, but when I saw *Saba's* ashen face, I knew that it was perfect for us! This was exactly what I had been looking for ... a perfect location, a spacious duplex with its two stories. Sachar Park is our front yard with the *Knesset* and the Israel Museum our neighbors. What could be better?

The negotiations to purchase this *Churban* with a well-known Jerusalem builder could be the subject of another entire chapter. To be sure, the gentleman saw before him the ultimate *Frier;* a woman and an American *Olah.* I'm sure that he saw easy dollar signs before his eyes. Suffice it to say that after three months of negotiations, I left him actually sputtering in anger, not believing that this Anglo woman had actually purchased this apartment for many dollars less than his absolute LOWEST PRICE ... and I never raised my voice, which got him even angrier. Of course, I couldn't argue with him in Hebrew, at any rate, as my facility with Hebrew was non-existent.

My only problem was *Saba* ... he hardly spoke to me for the three months that it took to renovate the *Churban* into a luxury dwelling. It was a bit difficult as I shuttled back and forth from the "Hole" on Herzog Street to what would become a home featured in decorating magazines and the design section of The Jerusalem Post, as well as on European cable television.

Avi Kara, my partner, my *Kablan,* and the crew went into overdrive to finish the work. He was also a bit skeptical about the outcome and when Avi is not positive about my suggestions, I am no longer Ruby, but, "*Bossit.*" I got a lot of "*Bossit*" during that time. But, as they say, "The Proof Is In The Pudding." The apartment is lovely, practical, functional and I feel very blessed to live in it.

But what happened to *Saba*? On the very day that we moved,

with cartons everywhere and our new home in total disarray, we had to return the keys to the new owners of #9 Herzog. As we were waiting for the door to our old apartment to open, *Saba* looked at the dark, oppressive, hall and said, "How did we ever live here?" We hadn't even slept in the new apartment as yet. If I ever wanted to clobber him − that was the time!

Each Grandchild as they have reached Bar/Bat Mitzvah age have received a key to our home to be used at their discretion. One wonderful aspect of living in Jerusalem is that the grandchildren have used it as a hotel stop as each required a "flop-in joint" in place of their homes, which are all in distant places. So a bonus is that we have enjoyed the kids as they grew and matured. This was an aspect of living in Jerusalem that was unanticipated and it has turned out better than we ever expected. We have lived at 1 Diskin, Jerusalem, for over twenty-five years, and are truly enjoying the premises and the magnificent view, more with each passing year.

Our Russian Adventure

1987 was the time of *Perestroika* in the Soviet Union. The government of Israel signed an agreement that made it possible for Russian Jews to emigrate, providing they had an invitation from the Jewish Country. The puzzle was how to obtain the names so that the possible *Olim* would receive the desired exit visas and make *Aliyah*.

A plan was devised by the *Mossad* and carried out by the Foreign Office to send citizens of Israel in twos, in secrecy. This was not to embarrass Russia so that the world would not be aware that there were thousands of its citizens who wanted to emigrate and leave their Soviet "Paradise."

One day we received a phone call from Rabbi Aaron Rakefet, who along with his wife, Malka, had the honor of recruiting Israelis for a special mission. We all knew that it was very important and minimized the dangers entailed, but, in truth, they existed. In our minds, we kept thinking about it as an adventure, a lark, perhaps, but the perils were indeed real.

They laid out the details of the plan. *Saba* and I were to travel to Moscow, Leningrad (the name of the city was changed back to St. Petersburg in June 1991), Minsk and Vilna, and spend approximately three weeks there. Our task was to bring back as many names and addresses as possible for the precious invitations to be sent. We would do this by holding a meeting each night at which *Saba* would speak in English and an interpreter would translate into Russian. His topic was, "Love, Marriage and Sex", a topic of interest that would appeal to a large group of people. The meetings were moved to a different apartment each evening, as it was still illegal to gather, especially to speak about Zionism and *Aliyah* which we did constantly.

As each person entered a tiny, dark salon, they were inspected by the organizer to be certain that they were not spies of the KGB (The Russian Police). If someone was suspect, the meeting would be cancelled and held the next evening at a different location.

While *Saba* was speaking, I would pass out legal-size sheets of paper, and urge everyone to write their details in a readable fashion, collect them and hide the pages, carrying them with me at all times, as we knew that our hotel room and luggage was searched daily.

There was a great deal of preparation before our departure for Russia. Luckily, we had planned a trip back to America before our Russian foray, as we had to have clean passports WITHOUT ANY ISRAELI ENTRY OR EXIT STAMPS.

I purchased makeup and other items there, as no Hebrew letters could be marked on anything. I cut the Hebrew labels out of our clothing. Everything had to seem like we had never even visited Israel, much less be residents of Jerusalem.

We were traveling as RICH Americans. I wore my mink coat and matching hat and was swathed in jewelry. I could have sold everything I wore, including the coat and hat a dozen times over. People sidled up to me and asked if I wanted to sell this or that. It felt like we were actors in a "B" movie at times.

We were instructed to learn the rudiments of the Russian language, but we found it too difficult. Had we mastered it, trying to interpret the Underground transportation system would have been much simpler. However, we only learned a few letters and flew by the "seats of our pants" while there.

Saba devised what he thought was a foolproof system for an address book. All people and places regarding Minsk was under "B" for Burlesque. Why? Because a famous place in America for that type of entertainment was Minsky's Burlesque Theater. Similarly, all items connected to Vilna were tagged as *Gaon* for obvious reasons. Leningrad was "Lenny" and Moscow was connected to the *Parah Adumah* of the Bible. It worked for us. Would it have been successful if we were detained and the addresses and telephone numbers of the *Refusniks* as well as other information have been safe. It's anyone's guess.

We were given items such as pairs of blue jeans, Nike sports shoes, tape recorders, and other desirable products to distribute to some lucky Russians Jews, so that they could trade them on the black market, as once they declared their desire to emigrate, they lost their employment and were in dire needs of funds. We also brought a set of requested Rabbinic literature to Leonid Volvovsky, an ardent *Refusnik*, as well as pairs of *Tefilin*, *Talitot*, *Tzitzit*, and candle for *Shabbat*, *Havdalah* and *Chanukah*, and what item was so valued that people had tears in their eyes when they clutched them ... key chains with the symbol of Israel etched on them.

How did we ever expect to enter the country with four pairs of *Tefilin?* Should they ask, our answer was that *Saba* needs a pair for everyday prayer and one for the Sabbath. Similarly, I needed the same; that makes four pairs! We had an answer for everything. Of course, *Tefilin* are not worn on the Sabbath and women do not utilize any of the items brought.

Food was a huge problem. No Hebrew markings allowed. Luckily, cans of Starkist tuna were Hebrew letters free. I transferred everything into plastic bags; raisins, nuts, crackers, cookies, hard cheese, peanut butter, salami. and so on. There was no *Chabad* House to rely on for meals and fresh fruits and vegetables were scarce. What would I do with a potato, an onion or a turnip in any case? There was a type of very hard Pumpernickel Bread that we could buy. By the end of the trip, we were dunking the bread into Coke – we have not eaten Pumpernickel Bread since! The food disappeared more quickly than I had figured. I think that the surly women who manned each floor in the hotels, scrutinizing all comings and goings and whose job was to daily search our suitcases, enjoyed snacks at our expense. Meanwhile, our store of *Kosher* food was disappearing at an alarming rate. But to whom were we going to complain?

Secrecy was of the utmost importance. Our friends and family were not to be told that we were leaving, nor where, or any of the details. The only people who were told in confidence, were our children, who begged us not to go. It was all well and good for others, but not us. Of course we had to smile at the times that they were on the "leaving track" and totally ignored what we said. But that's par for the course! We also told my sister and brother-in-law, Roslyn and Howard Zuckerman of New York, as Howard is a doer and a man of some influence. Should we need some type of aid, we would be more confident of a hopeful ending if Howard were on our side and knew where we were. The only other person who was aware of our activities was Illinois Congressman Abner Mikva. The Foreign Ministry had reiterated over and over again that we should be careful, but that if we were caught … Israel never heard of us. We were on our own, but knowing that Abner Mikva was aware of where we were made us feel a bit better. Having him in our corner likened us to owning an insurance policy, however shaky it was!

Departure day finally arrived and we were as ready as we ever would be. Going through Passport Control at LOD Airport, we were quick to explain that the clerk must NOT stamp our passports, but insert a different slip of paper. Mine was done properly but as she listened to *Saba* explain once again, she unthinkingly stamped his NEW passport with an Israeli EXIT stamp. Disaster! How would he enter Russia? This was a problem that had not been covered. We were to fly to the USSR via Britain. We had a short few hours to decide what to do when we landed in London.

(L-R) Illinois Congressman Abner J. Mikva, Speaker of the House of Representatives, Congressman Tip O'Neil, Yours Truly, Jay Karzen – Washington, D.C., 1979

Saba decided to go to the US Embassy to obtain another new passport. As luck would have it, the consular officer on duty had been to Israel and had served his time at the American Consulate on Agron Street in Jerusalem. He didn't believe that only *Saba* lost his passport and that I had mine. He claimed that couples always keep them together. (He was right.) He quizzed *Saba* on various Jerusalem landmarks and finally said, "I don't believe you, and I don't know what game you are playing, but we'll give you another passport." When the new, clean with no Israeli stamps, passport was handed to him, we finally took some deep breaths. That was close and we hadn't even begun our Spy Adventure! So, we rushed back to the airport and caught the British Air airplane that would carry us into "enemy" territory.

Our first impression of Sheremetyevo Airport was disbelief.

It was gigantic, but dreary and empty. At 1:30 p.m., airports are normally hubs of frantic activity with passengers constantly entering and exiting, with shoppers excitedly buying Duty Free items and a sense of excitement. It was empty … no stores, no Duty Free, no people. It was dark as though the highest bulb wattage in use was 30 watts and even though it was December and Moscow is dark and gloomy much of the day, we were surprised to say the least. The airport was not only gloomy, but when one looked carefully, the floors were scuffed and dirty, the waiting room seats were torn, the windows were filthy and forget about the rest rooms … they were dirty and, wise advice would be to avoid using them at all cost!

We approached the counter where the personnel was to welcome the passengers and check the contents of the luggage. Surprise number two was that the airport workers were uniformed soldiers with weapons on their hips and they were young kids, probably eighteen years old. Some looked too young to shave. They acted surly, as though we were spies (did they guess?) visiting their country and glared at us. I went into an Ugly American mode and began to shout about their ineptitude in checking our luggage. I didn't want them to look too closely and tried to take their minds off the chore of going through the bags. I was so obnoxious; there is no other word for it. I began ordering them around and told them not to touch certain items, because they were clumsy and would soil or break the precious things that I had brought from America. We were at least twice their age and I treated them like germs that would infect the suitcases. They glared and I glared. Finally they closed the bags and then brought out the Jewelry and Money form that passengers are required to fill out. It was a small piece of paper with ten lines. I had more than ten pieces of jewelry just on my person at that time. What about the jewelry that I was carrying in my purse? I started yelling again that the paper was too small and I couldn't possibly list everything as well as our funds. Finally, in chicken scratches, I listed a few items, including between the lines and the list soon became illegible. Of course, these kids couldn't speak English,

Moscow, Soviet Union – Check Out the Obnoxious American Tourist!

much less, read what I had written. I think that they let us go much sooner than they would have regularly, because the lady in the furs, the "Ugly American," was acting so badly, they wanted to get rid of us as soon as possible.

The first hurdle was over. We were on our way in a very old taxi to a government-owned hotel. We had reservations at The National Hotel, a world class (Russian style) facility, where important tourists are housed. It was on Red Square and overlooked the Kremlin and the tomb where Lenin, an architect of New Russia, lay in an embalmed state, with a constant snaking line of visitors awaiting their turn to honor their hero. The view from our window (dirty) was spectacular, and with the *Moskva* River running nearby, it was charming. I love the elegant architecture of old world European cities, but like everything else in this country, the buildings were dirty and needed repair.

The National Hotel was built in the early 1900s. It was decorated in "Fading Elegance" style. A water-powered elevator with an audible wheeze hoisted us to one of the higher floors. As we emerged, a fierce looking, eagle-eyed woman showed us to the room. In every Intourist hotel there is a "Floor Guard" who all look identical (unkempt); dress identically (shabby) and are there to keep an eye on the guests' activity. She was also the person who daily searched our room and luggage. We used a tip from detective novels that we had read and put a thread in the opening of the suitcases and, behold, it was gone everyday when we returned. As I wrote previously, she helped herself to our food as well, and snooped into the drawers and luggage.

The room was large, with heavy, dark furniture, red velvet draperies and large floral-printed wallpaper. The bathroom looked like it was the latest in fashion, if the year was 1900, with stained facilities – not too inviting, but that's what was available. We were informed in the briefing that the rooms were bugged and that we should not discuss anything between us because the walls have ears! Thus, all important conversation between us was undertaken outside in the street. The other way to discuss important issues was to write it down and then destroy the note and flush it down the toilet. Every night, *Saba* would talk directly into the overhead lighting fixture (wattage of bulb ... probably 40) and say, "Well, it's time to go to sleep." I was waiting for someone to say, "Goodnight," but there was always silence. We would talk innocuously into the bed lamps about tourist places that we had visited, or the family, but of course never a word about Israel or our true mission.

The difference in standards of living between Russia and the West was light years apart. The city streets were clean; there was no sign of candy wrappers or trash on the streets. Of course, at all hours of the day and night there was a woman, a *Babushka*, who looked to be in her 80s, but was probably in her 50s, bent over a stub of a broom sweeping streets. This was Communism at its basic, as each person had to work and these women, their job, day after day, was leaning over a small broom cleaning up mostly non-existing trash.

We were amazed at the hugeness of the main streets; many

were four lanes in each direction. Crossing the eight lanes was an exercise in agility, as crossovers for pedestrian traffic was unknown. When we asked our Intourist Guide the reason for the extremely wide roads, she answered without missing a beat, that it was because of the army tanks which paraded quite regularly. It certainly wasn't because of the auto traffic – there was none. Unknown in Russia at that time was Rush Hour which plagues and continue to bring commuters' stress level to unheard of heights in every developed country. The few cars that trawled the streets were Soviet made; ugly and boxy, named the Lada.

But, the Moscow Metro, the Underground, was a work of art. Each station was decorated in a different style. Some had crystal chandeliers that were worthy enough to be hung in a palace. Others were built with costly woods and another even had semi-precious gems embedded in the walls. The subway was run efficiently and we spent much time there, even though the language was incomprehensible and English was an unknown entity among the population.

Walking down main streets in the dark, I couldn't understand why main shopping avenues were so gloomy. Then it hit me that there were no neon signs advertising anything. There were no signs; neon did not exist there. Only a few restaurants were open in the evening with poorly-lit windows.

Changing money in banks was an experience. Once again, dark, unfriendly places and, unbelieving to us, there were no systems of personal checks or credit cards. Checks were introduced in January 1988, and we spent some time explaining what a check was. The concept of signing a piece of paper, an IOU, was a foreign concept. Credit cards were unknown until later and in one store, we actually saw the clerk using an abacus! This was incredible to us, with the modern banking systems that we used regularly.

I kept picturing in my mind the scene which took place in the lofty halls of the United Nations, when former Soviet Statesman Nikita Khrushchev removed his shoe and was banging on the table shouting, "We will bury you. We will bury the United States!"

It was shocking and inconceivable that this was supposedly a modern country.

In an Art and Architecture trip to the Soviet Union in which I traveled in the middle 90s, drastic changes had taken place. Not only were there checks and credit cards, but there were kiosks in the cities who dealt in foreign currency and were Change Places. One afternoon, suddenly there was a flurry of activity as they hurriedly closed due to a drastic fall of the Ruble. They were shut for a few days until the Ruble reached an acceptable level. Big progress in a short few years had occurred.

Our hotel was located in Red Square which was the business and political center of Moscow, the capital, and thereby the focus of Soviet life. Not far from our hotel was the GUM Department store. This was the largest and only department store in Moscow. It sported an imposing black, metal-grilled façade and looked promising from the outside, but when we entered, we found a totally unique shopping experience. Shopping for anything, food or clothing, was a shock. Mostly empty shelves, no selection, and shoddy goods were the norm. The lighting was dim – no bright colors, no advertising, and amateur-looking carpentry work held the modest offerings.

In the streets, wherever one turned, there was a queue or line. People stood in line to buy anything. There were times that they didn't know what was being sold, but a line meant that there was an item available and you knew that you could most likely use it, so you joined the queue. We once joined a lengthy line only to discover that the prize was a tube of toothpaste. Not only did we see this, as it was a common everyday experience, but the hopeful émigrés that we met related the same story time after time. That was life in Russia, 1987.

In every Intourist Hotel in the larger cities, there was a special store for tourists which was very popular. It was off limits to Russian citizens. That is where the items for export were sold. The ethnic clothing, Russian shawls and "Mamushka" dolls were plentiful and you were able to purchase any quantity. The quality varied, but these items were handmade, and it was difficult to refrain from shopping. The desired currency in the country was dollars and the exchange rate made purchases bargains.

Every tourist was required to register with a government-licensed guide from the Intourist Board. They would spout the party line about the success of the Communist system and I would mentally roll my eyes and groan. We knew the answers in advance, but we asked each guide if they had ever traveled abroad. They had no understanding, having never seen London, Paris, New York, or even a smaller version of a modern society, as to how their country compared. They simply had no frame of reference.

However, as we were "tourists," we visited museums like The Armory, The Pushkin and other points of interest, as well as attended the Bolshoi Ballet and The Moscow Circus. It was fascinating, but these were a diversion to draw suspicion away from our true activities.

Each morning, we would need an excuse not to be accompanied by the Intourist Guide. We explained that we loved walking and visiting parks or the zoo and didn't require a guide. There was a big controversy at the time as the zoo had acquired two pandas from China and a pair of elephants from India, and could not provide for them properly. The zoo was one of the largest in Europe with over five-thousand creatures. She always wanted to accompany us and made a sour face if we rejected her offer. We understood from her that even the animals were living the high life, as were citizens of Moscow, but then why couldn't the pair of elephants and pandas be accepted? She didn't appreciate it when we asked questions.

On the days that we managed to escape from her, we would take the fabulously decorated Underground and spend the day going from one *Refusnik* family to another, bringing general items for them to sell or the gift items of Judaica that we were given. Our suitcases became lighter each day.

We relied heavily on taxis and would give them a different address, overshooting the correct address of the apartment, than we needed. It was dangerous for a family to be known that they had foreign visitors, and there were a few who simply would not open the door. When we did enter, we would find bare rooms with a few sticks of furniture. These people had sold or given away their belongings. The government would give the *Refusniks* a short time to leave, two days was lengthy; many had just hours. They were literally sitting on their suitcases or trunks just awaiting the word to leave. Even in such dire straits, we would be offered food and drink; people desired to be hospitable. We refused, knowing how difficult it was for them to acquire even staple items of food.

A daily excursion was to take a rucksack and spend a few hours finding food for the family's dinner. There were times that we were forced to take a bite of something and it would stick in our throats, for we knew that our portion was that much less for the family. Before we left, the little provisions that remained were given to some families. You would think that we had given them something really spectacular, not a few grams of raisins and nuts.

Among their many other problems, many of the women were distraught as to the meager pieces of jewelry that they owned and the fact that they were not allowed to take them along. One woman had her *Bubbe's* necklace, and another, a ring, and a third, a bracelet and so on. I listened to their situations and decided to take the pieces from them and return the items should they be fortunate enough to make *Aliyah*. And so I did. I collected these very old, gold pieces of treasured jewelry and wore them during the trip. At one time, around my neck was probably five necklaces, a few bracelets on my arms and rings went into my wallet for safekeeping. These were joined by my "Rich Lady" collection. The Jeweler, Stern, had nothing on me. Fortunately I never walked near a magnet!

One Friday evening, *Erev Shabbat*, *Saba* wanted to visit a certain Synagogue for prayers. He took just enough money for a taxi ride to the Synagogue. On the trip there, he watched carefully as the driver made various turns. After services, he began the walk home and turned the wrong way. After a while, he realized that he was utterly lost in this strange, totally dark city, with no knowledge of the language and no money. Sabbath had begun. He walked and walked and could not get directions as there wasn't an English speaker anywhere. It was a frigid December night, snow was falling and the situation was hopeless. Finally, an English-speaking gentleman stopped and tried to persuade him to take a taxi back to the hotel, and he would even pay for it. Even though *Saba* was kilometers away, he refused the offer. With the kind man's instructions, he finally stumbled into the hotel room. He had been walking for over five hours in the bitter cold – even his mustache had icicles on it!

And I, well, I was certain that the KGB had arrested *Saba* and he was interred in some Soviet jail. As the hours passed, had it not been the Sabbath, I would have called the American Consulate or Congressman Abner Mikva in Illinois. Even so, all offices were closed anyway as it was after nine in the evening when he appeared. That was the low point of the trip.

The next day, *Shabbat*, we went to the *Archipova* Synagogue. It was a large, beautiful edifice in the Old World style. However, as with all the other buildings in Moscow, it needed repair and cleaning. As we entered, elderly men and women would sidle up to us and whisper, "*Gut Shabbos*," and disappear into the gloomy interior. There were no young people, but present were KGB agents sprinkled among the worshipers. They were assigned there on a weekly basis and all the regulars knew exactly who they were.

Saba was asked to lead the *Musaf* service, and afterwards the Cantor requested that he tape record his chants when they return for the Afternoon prayers. When *Saba* refused to violate the Sabbath by using the tape recorder before the end of the Holy Day, the Cantor was puzzled. He didn't realize that he was dealing with such a religious person!

The Rabbi was an appointee of the State, and when he voiced the prayer for the health and safety of the government of the USSR and that the Almighty should bless them because of their benevolent attitude towards their people, I had a hard time stifling my laughter. Sitting next to me were four women judges from the United States on a Soviet-sponsored visit. The judge next to me appeared to be interested in Me, another American tourist, and we chatted. When she sensed why I was there she hurriedly moved to another seat. She appeared to be afraid that she would catch something from me. (Zionism, perhaps?)

Leningrad followed Moscow, Minsk and then Vilna. In each city we followed the same pattern, but found that we had more freedom of movement once we left Moscow. Except in Minsk, the agents' hats were visible whenever we looked around. I am reminded of the story that former *Refusnik* and hero, Natan Sharansky relates that one time he offered the KGB men that followed him to share his taxi so that they would all save money!

At the end of the three weeks, we had collected over 125 names and addresses. It was time to return home with this booty, but how to get it out of the country? We decided to put the dirty laundry in one suitcase with the Russian information on tiny pieces of paper, in spitball form, buried among the smelly clothing, hoping that if the bag was opened, the odor of the three-week collection would deter the soldier from searching the bag. That is exactly what happened.

We arrived at the airport with our four suitcases. They opened one after the other and probably wondered why we needed the four, as they were indeed light. We had also given away numerous articles of clothing that both of us had brought. Sweaters, scarfs, hose, socks and toiletries as well as other articles of clothing were left with the hopeful emigres. Everything was so scarce that the clothing was like *Manna* from heaven. The airport soldier finally came to the last suitcase. He opened it, took a whiff, blanched and quickly shut it. We casually walked away, boarded the British Airways airplane and were soon out of Russian airspace. I think that we took our first deep breath in weeks.

The Foreign Office was pleased with our success in bringing out the Russian details, but our debriefing came to an abrupt end when I mentioned that I would like to know when certain women reached Israel as I wished to return their jewelry. They were apoplectic at what I had done and would have thrown me out of the window, had there been one. They were shouting in Hebrew and I really didn't understand what they were saying, but I got the drift. I could have been charged with smuggling, sent to Siberia for life and perhaps even caused an international incident.

Nevertheless, our Russians did come and as we handed the precious articles of jewelry over to the grateful women, there were many tears and exclamations of thanks. I would never tell this to our handlers, but I think, no, I'm sure, that I would have done it again despite the risks.

There is the story of a Russian *Oleh* who gets off the plane and this reporter on the ground asks him how life was in Russia. He says, "I can't complain." The reporter then asks him how his apartment was in Russia. "I can't complain." The reporter then asks him about his job in Russia. "I can't complain." So, replied the reporter, "If things were so good in Russia, why did you come to Israel? To which he replied, "Here, I can complain!"

Epilogue To Our Russian Adventure

Years later after delivering our car to the garage repair shop, *Saba* tried, to no avail, to hail a taxicab. He had never hitchhiked before (or since) but, stuck out his thumb, when to his surprise a car stopped. The driver was a Russian *Oleh* from Moscow and when *Saba* explained that he had been on a trip lecturing, he inquired, "Are you Rabbi Karzen?" As *Saba* answered in the affirmative, the gentleman blurted out, "You saved my marriage!"

It seems that he and his wife were on the verge of a divorce, when he decided to come to one of the furtive *Aliyah* meetings. He was so impressed by *Saba's* presentation on Love, Marriage and Sex, that he urged his wife to attend the next evening. The result was that they made *Aliyah*, had a *Sabra* child and are living happily in Jerusalem! Unfortunately, *Saba* never learned the man's name, but here was an unbelievable direct result of our trip.

Note: As marriage was one of the few freedoms that the Russian citizens enjoyed, it was used freely. The divorce rate was astronomical. Also, as we were told, a family with one child was the norm, not only because life was hard and resources were meager, but that housing was scarce and apartments small, as well as parents were apt to live with a couple. Three generation with families living in small spaces was common.

The second incident occurred as I was being discharged after a stay in the hospital. The floor doctor was busy scribbling on my chart, when I noticed his name tag. It said "Volvovsky." I told him the story of our adventure in Russia, years before and that we had brought Leonid Volvovsky a set of books of Rabbinical literature that this famous *Refusnik* had requested. He slowly stopped writing, lowered the pen and uttered quietly. "You brought my family out! I was a youngster when my uncle told us that he had signed us up to receive an invitation from the State of Israel, from some visitors who had brought him some books that he was so eager to receive." His eyes were wet, the nurse was crying and came to the bedside to hug me, and of course, I was teary-eyed. Who knows how many other people were affected by our adventure to Russia? There were many others, both Israelis and Diaspora *"Chutzpadeers"* who made the same trip bringing *Chizuk* and items to our Jewish brethren. It was one of our finest hours, and I say this for all of us.

Saba and I were in *Ulpan,* on February 11, 1986, when Natan Sharansky took his famous stroll over the *Glienicke* Bridge, also known as The Bridge of Spies, and sauntered to freedom, his trousers held up by a length of twine, and shoes two sizes too large. He entered Israel, already an honorary citizen, and quickly won the hearts of its citizens and the world. He was hailed as a hero, one of the famous Prisoners of Zion who settled with his wife, Avital, in Jerusalem. It is still a wonder how our lives became intertwined.

A few days after his arrival, I was shopping at Mayan Shtub Department Store on Jaffa Street in Jerusalem. It was so old-fashioned in structure that purchases were still paid by a series of money cans whizzing over your head as cash flew from salesperson to cashier sitting somewhere out of view. As I stood at the counter awaiting a salesperson, I noticed a familiar face in the act of choosing clothing. It was Natan Sharansky having a friendly discussion over the price of the chosen articles. The storeowner wanted to make the clothing a gift and our hero would have none of it. It was hard to overlook their voices and Natan turned to me and said, "This happened to me in a taxi yesterday; the driver refused to take the fare." In the end, Natan left the store, with numerous bags of new clothing, but at a heavily discounted price.

Within a few short years, with much prodding from admirers, Natan decided to run for the Knesset as head of the party *Yisrael B'Aliyah*, which he founded. It was a party for *Olim*, mostly Russian, but we Anglos saw a leader whose interest was that of spotlighting the needs and concerns of immigrants, no matter from where they hailed. The Anglo arm of the party burst upon the political scene. I was the Jerusalem Chair of AACI and politically active in a number of past campaigns and important governmental issues, and was requested to be a part of his election committee.

Headed by Eli Kazhdan as Executive Director, Aryeh Green, Director, *Yisrael B'Aliyah*, Anglo Division, Shmuel Blitz, Sherwin Pomerantz, Shana Mauer, Michael Hirsch, Larry Roth, (*z'l*) and numerous others, we met, argued into the late night in the election offices located on Ben Yehudah Street, Jerusalem. It was a time of nail-biting tension when Natan seemed to rise and fall in the pre-election polls.

After that election, in 1996, the party won seven seats and he was appointed a Minister. In the election of 1999, the party captured six seats, and he was again appointed an official, this time as the Minister of Jerusalem Affairs. However, the election of 2003 saw the party with only two seats in the Knesset when he resigned as Chairman with MK Yuli Edelstein as the chair.

I sent the following e-mail to the group who had truly made every effort to win the election for the party in a big way.

Dear Y.A. Buddies, I have often said that Anglos and Bulgarian Goat-herders have the same influence on Israeli politics. However, now that the initial shock of only

*Natan Sharansky runs for
Knesset. Ruby – activist,
advisor and supporter*

capturing two seats has worn off, my perennial optimistic outlook has surfaced with the thought … What if the Anglos hadn't come through for Sharansky? Can one imagine a *Knesset* without him? That was our huge contribution and it was no small feat. To Eli, the sun came up today just as every other one and one day, you will be an integral part of that governing body. To Arye, your e-mail was a masterpiece; I can imagine how hard it was to pen. To the rest of us … *Kol Hakavod* for all of our work and hope to see you on Friday morning. With only encouraging words for all of us. Sincerely, Ruby

In the 16th Knesset, Arik Sharon was elected as the Prime Minister. He admired and liked Natan and offered him a spot in the cabinet of a newly created position of Minister of Jerusalem affairs. It was a marginal spot and Natan was truly bored with the lack of activity. His small office, with one secretary, was indicative of the position that his ministry and party, *Yisrael B'Aliyah*, which consisted of only six seats in the Knesset, held in the administration.

But as it is said, "Timing is Everything" and an international "Hot Potato" issue began to dominate the headlines. The old argument of the division of Jerusalem, once again reared its ugly head. As the City of Jerusalem was under the auspices of Natan's ministry, the core group of the party convened. After brainstorming and kicking around several ideas, I quietly said, "Let's have a rally!" No one heard or responded to my suggestion, as it was the norm that everyone speak at once, and it wasn't the quietest group, to begin with. I said it louder … again no response. Finally, I got up from my chair and stood right in front of Natan and said, "We need a rally; a big one. It's such an important issue that not only Anglos and Israelis would be interested, but internationally as well. Jerusalem is the heart and soul of the Jewish nation" or some such statement. Eli Kazhdan was sitting next to Natan and heard me and the rest is history.

The idea was presented to Ehud Olmert, the mayor of

Jerusalem and to Yechiel Leiter who headed a group called ONE JERUSALEM, which was dedicated to the opposition for the division of Jerusalem, as well as others who were against the plan. Malcolm Hoenlein and other Diaspora community activists were notified. The idea spread like wildfire ... It was Jerusalem, our Jerusalem, which was at risk.

After only thirteen days of planning the event, on January 11, 2001, the world witnessed one of the largest demonstrations ever held in this country. The estimates were between 300-400 thousand participants. I was asked to speak at the rally, representing the female population, but as I was the National President of AACI, which has always been non-political in nature, I asked my friend, Hindy Walfish, the chairman of *Amit* at that time, to speak on my behalf. Hindy is my friend-for-life, as she asserts that speaking at the rally was certainly one of the highlights of her life; she'll never forget it! We, as well, won't.

A number of years later, Rabbi Stewart and Susie Weiss of Raanana were having a Torah Scroll written in memory of their son, Avi, a *Tzahal* hero, who fell in battle. Natan was asked to complete a letter in the scroll and to be the guest speaker.

The Weiss's are long time Chicago friends, and we were in attendance at this moving, holy event. *Saba* and I were sitting in the front row, when Natan walked hurriedly past us on his way to the *Bima*. His glance fell on me and he stepped back a few steps. I stood up to shake his hand and he grabbed me around and hugged me very enthusiastically. I always joked that I must remind him of an old girlfriend of his youth. This happened in front of an overflowing, filled hall. To this day, I can't imagine what thoughts ran through the heads of that crowd.

Concerning Ethics

Howard Lark (named changed) died last week. Lark was an American citizen who, because of his crimes, was indicted in 1983 on charges of illegal trading with Iran, who was, even then, an enemy of the United States, tax evasion, racketeering, false statements and dealing in arms to countries that were anti-

American. This was following the time when the United States had been bogged down in a war in Vietnam (1961-1975), the longest period of war ever for the US. More than 58,000 army personnel perished in that seemingly never ending, terrible period whose casualties not only in body and mind shook the very underpinnings of the country. There were over eight million soldiers in arms, over one million American army injured; there were two million civilian casualties in Asia. The carnage was unbelievable.

I remember vividly watching the six o' clock news. At that time and never to be forgotten were the flag-draped caskets which emerged from the airplane, one following the other, evening after evening. It was a soul-wrenching period of time for America.

Lark, along with his associates, were exiled and he resided in Europe. They were unable to return to the United States for fear of arrest. The US President pardoned only Lark immediately prior to his leaving office. It has been reported that the President felt remorse at the pardon for Lark; who knows the wheeling and dealing that preceded that Presidential act.

So what does Lark have to do with this book? As is written previously, this work has two goals. The first is to leave our children an Ethical Will and the second is to relate the magnificent story of your families. We want you to know upon whose shoulders you are standing, so that your lives, through your thoughts and actions, will be worthy of the blessings that the Lord will bestow upon you. Also, that you will learn and understand what type of people you come from and will guide you all through your lives.

Again, why bring in Howard Lark? Because this is the section concerning ethics; what constitutes a person of honor ... how should one conduct their life ethically?

In Lark's honor, there were many obituaries in the newspaper placed by at least twenty of Israel's leading universities, museums and charities of every stripe. He was a magnanimous donor and benefactor; perhaps, even one of the most important benefactors that Israel has ever had. One columnist wrote: "The bitter irony is that without his bending the rules to the extent that he did, he might not have become affluent enough to support so many worthy causes."

Well, I'm not so sure. Yes, he did countless acts of charity but I, for one, will not judge him. The Lord will do that in his own way. But this is a very fine line and there are no easy solutions.

There was a period when I was President of AACI, that the state of finances were more abysmal than usual – we were even afraid that we would be forced to close the doors. Sleepless nights were followed by frantic phone calls from Evie Weidenbaum, the Executive Director, in the morning. The banks were considering canceling our credit line; creditors were beginning to get restless and rightfully requested their money ... in cash. The *Tzedakah* Fund was almost bare and one woman who desperately needed money to turn her electricity back on was helped by a number of us underwriting her need, as the AACI Fund simply couldn't accommodate her. It seemed that one problem after another arose before the previous difficulty was resolved.

A gentleman approached me with an offer of a donation of $15,000, with no strings attached. I was aware of his connection to an unsavory character and inquired whether the money came from him. He answered in the affirmative and I thanked him and turned him down flat. This was more than tainted money. I felt that it was blood money and couldn't accept it on behalf of the organization. We muddled through. The doors didn't close and our integrity was intact.

I was reading the magazine, The Jerusalem Report, and my eye caught the story of Jake Leibovitz. He was a young man, who with his wife Devorah, were trying to establish and build a new community near Beit Shemesh in the Ela Valley. Jake had been a successful builder in New York and his dream was to provide a new concept for Israel, that of an upscale area, with homes like those that thousands of *Olim* left behind in the Diaspora, transfer and create that style of living to the State of Israel. He felt that these people would become immigrants and be attracted to a place which would be familiar and comfortable for their families, thus bringing more people to live the Zionist dream. The Leibovitz's had spent twelve years and much of their funds on this endeavor and they had yet to put a shovel in the ground.

Reading further, I sensed that this was another case of an American pounding his head against the wall and getting nowhere, simply because he is a foreigner and an American yet, trying to buck the Israeli building system. I mentioned this article and showed *Saba* the picture of Jake and he said, "I know that man, we *daven* together!"

This situation smelled to high heaven and meeting with the Leibovitz's, I found them to be eminently sane and filled with a marvelous sense of entrepreneurship and Zionism in its purest sense – just what Israel needed. I didn't trust my own sole opinion, but as President of AACI, called a meeting to meet with him. A dozen community activists, whose opinions were widely regarded, grilled him for a lengthy period of time and with the exception of one naysayer, it was decided that he deserved whatever help we could offer.

The reputation of builders in Israel, deserved or not, probably ranks below used car salesmen, worldwide. Jake related incidents where he refused to "play ball" with the authorities, was shaken down for bribes, which he wouldn't pay and many nightmare stories. During his recitation, his ethics were very much on display, and we felt that we could trust him. However, because of his above-board beliefs, his actions had been thwarted time after time and the Eden Hills project was still a dream.

Natan Sharansky was the Minister of Housing and Construction at this time. Jake related to me that he needed his signature and then the final stamp of approval – that of Prime Minister Arik Sharon. Obtaining those would finally put Eden Hills on the building track and the infrastructure for the project could begin. Natan was in mourning after the death of his mother and was "sitting *Shiva*" in his home. *Saba* and I were planning to perform the *Mitzvah* of *Mnachem Avel*, and telephoned Jake to accompany us.

With a bit of luck, we were the only three visitors at the time, and Natan asked, "What's new?" and "How are things coming along?" Frankly, I wondered at the idea of approaching him at this time, but as long as he had asked, we just plunged in. Jake started with the background, all the way up to that day, and Natan, by nature, is a good listener and especially, most understanding of the plight of immigrants. He mentioned that he had a meeting scheduled with Sharon the day of the death of his mother and it had been postponed. He was to see the Prime Minister after he returned to the Knesset, at their bi-weekly meeting. He not only saw in the project, the value for the State of Israel, but an *Oleh* was being treated with disdain and dishonesty, and this he could not abide. The next week was most tense, but when Jake received the papers, signed by the Minister of Housing and Construction and the Prime Minister, both he and Devorah finally felt that maybe the project would become a reality after all.

Currently, a billboard advertising Eden Hills stands at the crossroad. A huge *Lag B'Omer* bonfire that could be seen for kilometers was one of the celebrations which *Saba* and I attended when the model home, offices and roads were completed. Many homes have been built and it should not be long before the playing of children is heard in the Ela Valley. *Kol Hakavod* to Jake and Devorah. They have the *Zechut* to not only build and settle *Eretz Yisrael*, but to bring others here. What could be finer?

Another example of ethics at work. The Finance Committee of the Knesset slipped into the proposed annual budget a line to the detriment of *Olim*. It affected not only Americans, Canadians, British, and Russians, but even the four *Olim* from Iceland. We contacted Natan and he called a meeting of the Immigrant Associations and the Finance Committee.

We, the *Olim* from AACI, were the most numerous as this was prior to the large waves of Russians that have been absorbed. As Natan entered the room, he gave me a hug (Remember his friend from Russia?) and sat opposite the glum, poker-faced representative of the Knesset Finance Committee. After forty minutes of hearing the sides of the *Olim* and the argument of the official of the Finance Committee, Natan arose, gritted his teeth, narrowed his eyes and turning to the official declared, "I can't listen anymore, but know that if you harm a hair of any *Oleh*, there will be dire consequences!" The proposed tax died that day and was never heard of again.

Ethics and integrity are the same sides of the coin. Nothing can replace that of a sterling reputation. As it is written, "A good name is better than fine oil" (wealth) (Ecclesiastes 7:1).

Ethics, honesty and integrity are not just descriptive of an individual's personal character, they are crucial social values. Integrity is the ability to say what you mean and to mean what you say. The saying, "My word is my bond", is not a bit of chit-chat to be said casually. It is real. By honoring one's word, you are revering the spark of The Lord that resides in each person.

Association of Americans and Canadians in Israel

There have been many references to AACI in this book and it is time to recount my lengthy association with The Association of Americans and Canadians in Israel.

Saba and I were busy with new *Olim* activities, not the least of, was receiving our lift, moving to a new home, dealing with the bureaucracy from attaining a drivers license to the purchasing of the new apartment and car. We were dizzy from the activity in a language that we really began to understand how much we did not understand! We spoke Biblical Hebrew and people were charmed by our old-fashioned speech, when they were not laughing out loud. Even when we attempted to make our most simple needs known in Hebrew, the person would size us up, and promptly answer in English. They wanted to practice their English and here were two "Greenhorns" trying to speak in a language they obviously were not adept. To this day, I have a hard time speaking fluent Hebrew in the morning. I have to slip into it gradually and by ten or eleven in the morning and I can then speak fluently. Both *Saba* and I have mastered the art of public speaking and can handle a presentation in Hebrew. It's not easy, but we can do it.

Our good friend, Sherwin Pomerantz, was the AACI Jerusalem Chairman at the time and persuaded us to take part in the activities. The irony is that except for a lecture now and then, during all the years that we have participated in being on the Boards and most of the committees, year after year, we have never used any of the counseling or information services. We have given, not taken from the organization. Of course, it's an enormous help to have Tammy, Morris, Uri and Shelli, all who have undertaken the task of interpreting and keeping us legal, as well as speaking on our behalves, with all types of business companies, government agencies, utility companies, etc. Being put on hold and having the other end babbling quickly in Hebrew, and asking question after question brings me to the brink of despair and then, it is a call to one of our children that settles my blood pressure. This is what AACI does as a matter of course. We are fortunate to be able to have the service "In House!"

Saba and I have been blessed with unusually wonderful and caring in-law children. Early on in the marriage of Tammy and Morris Rubin, on his birthday, we included a greeting card which read "To our Dear Son-in-Law." Morris was thrilled with the gift, but miffed at the card – he didn't like the "in-law" wording. We never made that error again. He is our son as well as Shelli is our daughter. Morris is our touchstone with any problem or task that involves a legal issue. He is an outstanding attorney and we know that we can depend on him.

Within a few years, I was elected Jerusalem Chair. It was most fulfilling as the motto of the organization is, "We Make A Difference." And it certainly does!

The Mission Statement of AACI is:

1) To facilitate the immigration process, accomplished most ably by staff, even to attending Fairs in North America.

2) To enable *Olim* to remain in Israel, acting as a "*Landsmanshaft*" and community center.

In the bi-monthly bulletin which every member receives, are listings of activities from Tots And Music to the weekly Retired Persons Group. I would stare at the plethora of activities offered and mentally agonize how the budget is going to handle these wonderful happenings. Today, there are even more offerings, with a thicker and classier bulletin.

Kol Hakavod to the devoted and tireless staff led by Executive Director, David London, who was hired on my watch and which I consider one of my best accomplishments.

Holding the office of the Jerusalem Chair has many privileges as well as enormous responsibility. Besides the efficient running of the organization, the dedicated staff labored tirelessly, and I do not use the word lightly. There was a time when as the major immigrant organization, we received the munificent sum of $960,000 per year from The Jewish Agency. However, that lasted for a limited time, when money was easily available. However, since 2008, when the financial world literally exploded, and donors to the Federations in North America were hit by financial catastrophes, not only from governments, but due to the nefarious actions of certain worldwide crooks, AACI and other Jewish Agency affiliates were downgraded financially, until within a few short years, we were on our own and expected to raise those funds by ourselves. It was impossible to do so and AACI was forced to close the National Office; for all intents and purposes, the Jerusalem Chair morphed into assuming the role of the National President of AACI.

Once a month, the National Board met in Tel Aviv. Barry Ernstoff and I would take the bus to this august body of AACI members such as Yitzchok Heimowitz, Judy Jochnowitz and Aaron Korzon, who had given years of their time in the effort to run a top quality organization. It was always an interesting and fun time, and I looked forward to spending some time with these quality people. At one memorable meeting, the storm broke quickly. After the initial camaraderie ended, the then National President heard the abysmal treasury report and literally stormed out of the room. He resigned on his way out, as the door slammed shut behind him.

The twenty of us stared at each other. We were truly in big trouble. Everyone was down on us; the banks, the businesses which with we dealt, the landlords of the five branches including Jerusalem, Beersheva, Netanya, Tel Aviv and Haifa, as well as 30,000 members who were depending on AACI. And now, we were leaderless, as well. At that moment, we were so stunned that it was utterly quiet in that room The joke was that no employed person could be at the helm, as the twenty-four hours that is allotted to all human beings would simply not be enough!

To this day, I cannot recall exactly what happened. All I can now remember, was that on the return trip, I kept preparing ways in which to tell *Saba* that I was now National President of AACI. It was an absurd situation. I had complained, on occasion, that being the Jerusalem Chair was too taxing for me as I was working full-time as an Interior Designer. What can I say now? The National President of an organization that was bankrupt on paper, and problems galore. *Saba* wished me *Mazal Tov* and that he was proud of me, but that was another night of lost sleep. What had I done and to myself, yet?

On the top of my "To Do" list was to assemble a committee to try to unravel the financial aspect with all its strands that led directly to our underlying problem. There was simply no way to raise the monies that were needed to run the organization. Three gentlemen stepped up to face that enormous challenge. The heroes were Marvin Silverman, Bernie Barnett and Don Edelstein. The hours that they spent together deliberating as to the best course for AACI to take and implementing it, deserves an entire book dedicated to them. How they succeeded, I cannot fathom, but AACI muddled through and came out of the tunnel, bruised and battered, but not beaten.

Much thanks goes to the staff, who persevered, even accepting a cut in salary for the good of the organization. Staff members, like Carol Kremer, and Josie Arbel, with David London in the lead, all who weathered those turbulent times, have much to be proud of, and I am personally grateful to them.

There were so many occasions that were happy and fulfilling, that when I recall those times, it is the rewarding ones that come to mind.

In celebrating AACI's Fiftieth Anniversary, our *Yovel*, there was a year's long expression of activities, such as:

The Cinematheque Theater, headed by Lia Van Leer, held benefit performances for the organization.

A medical / layman conference was held on the grounds of Schneider Medical Children's Hospital, under our auspices with Judy Itzkovitz Siegel, The Jerusalem Post medical columnist, being awarded a certificate of achievement for her bringing medical information to the public.

Caroline Glick, the noted Jerusalem Post columnist, was the guest speaker at the annual convention in Raanana and presented the "Golden Pen" award.

We wanted to have the year proclaimed, "The Year of The *Olim*", and who better to receive a scroll with thousands of names of *Olim* inscribed and who were an integral part of Israel, than the President, Moshe Katzav. As we entered his large, well appointed office, the four gentlemen who were part of the delegation took all of the available seats. The President realized that I didn't have a place to sit, arose from in back of his desk and brought a chair to the seating area of the room. He was impressed with the scroll and the amount of names. He thanked us effusively. We had a most pleasant meeting and the announcement was made that this was officially "The Year of The *Olim.*"

Jonathan Pollard had spent decades being jailed for aiding Israel by sharing secret documents. The fact that Israel is an ally and should have had access to this information in any case, is a salient fact, which is well known. At three conventions, the situation was brought up with the goal to make him an Honorary Member of AACI. Heated discussions arose on both sides, pro and con, whether it was the proper action. Finally, it was voted to do so, even before the government honored Pollard with Israeli citizenship, although we were limited in how we could aid him. It was a proud moment for all of us. His wife brought him the news of the honor with the hopes of all of us, that it brought him a bit of pleasure. An ailing Pollard has served over twenty-eight years of his personal Hell as of this writing.

On the political scene, being the President of AACI had its perks. Among the activities were meetings with the various heads of the American Consulate on Agron Street, Jerusalem. One, a woman, Counsel General Susan Veres gave AACI an open door to her office. She would invite us twice a year to a briefing and listened intently to our concerns. She was eager to be of service to her constituents, even though we were ex-pats.

However, following her, there was a man appointed who always seemed to be in Ramallah, meeting with his constituents, the Arab Americans. There was little communication between AACI and the Consulate when he was in charge. It was no surprise that following his stint in Jerusalem for The State Department, he became a special envoy to the Arabs, and disappeared from the Israeli / American political scene.

Holocaust Day brought an invitation to lay a wreath of flowers at the foot of the moving Memorial Statue to the six million victims of the *Shoah*. Arriving at the Yad Vashem Museum and clutching my invitation, I remembered that I needed some flowers and decided to pick a small bouquet from their well-kept gardens. My conscience told me that I wasn't taking them off the premises, just moving them to a different location on the same grounds! I must say that *Saba* didn't approve, but it was late and I simply didn't have time to buy anything else.

Every immigrant organization in Israel appeared to have received the same notice and was being given the honor of being part of this moving undertaking. As the lengthy line slowly edged forward, I noticed that every representative of the organizations had a wreath; it was only AACI which had not brought a lovely bouquet. When it was my turn, a woman official inquired what I thought I was doing with this bouquet. I explained what had happened and you could just about see the wheels turning in her head thinking, "Another *Meshugana* American!" She then sold me a traditional wreath and the honor of AACI was reaffirmed.

July 4th, American Independence Day, brought invitations to attend the festivities at the Consulate in Jerusalem, but also at the residence and manicured grounds of the American ambassador. The weather was unbearable. It was always hot and sticky, and there was no place to park, but the crowd consisted of "Everyone Who Is Anyone" i.e. diplomats and politicos, rubbing elbows with the wealthy, the journalists, theater folks and the "in" crowd. The program featured speeches by the Prime Minister and the President, but the favorite activity of the evening was rubbernecking to see which famous celebrity was entering the area. There were elaborate food stations. The munching continued throughout the evening. One problem was that until recent years, there was no *Kosher* food. When Martin Indyk assumed the post of Ambassador, there was finally a table with suitable food, but it happened to be a Fast Day, the Seventeenth Day of *Tammuz*, and waiting until it was dark enough to eat, found us with empty platters – the food had been all consumed!

Sachar Park, Jerusalem, was the venue for The July 4th / Canada Day Picnic for many years until security issues forced us to find another place. It was not unusual for fifteen hundred to two thousand people to enjoy celebrating The American Independence Day and Canada Day, together with their North-American compatriots. The traditional food of hot dogs, hamburgers and potato chips supplanted hummus and felafel for one day, and with a baseball game, a jazz band and other nostalgic happenings. It was a fun day for all.

Mayor Ehud Olmert of Jerusalem loved Anglos and we would have occasional meetings in his office to discuss subjects of mutual interest. He was always eager to appear before the AACI population and bring warm greetings to his Anglo friends. Each year at the picnic, he would bound up the stairs to the stage in his exuberant manner, TV cameras following. We were a great photo-op, and he knew it!

One day, my seven-year-old grandson telephoned me with an important question. He had been awake the previous night, watching the midnight local news program and couldn't understand why the Mayor was kissing his *Savta* on television! Of course, what had happened was that I was emceeing the program at the picnic and was videoed with Olmert. I also asked him a very important question – "What was he doing watching television at midnight?"

I realized that there was some clout in being the President of AACI and there were times that I used it. Of course, normally, that title and fourteen shekels will get you a cup of *"Café Hafuch"*... but sometimes it even works.

It was election time in the US. We feel that it is important to vote, not only for issues that affect America, but for the welfare of Israel. We appreciate being Israeli-Americans and will do whatever we can to be good citizens of both countries. Bill Clinton was a candidate for his second term as President. We waited for our ballots to arrive via "snail mail" and they finally did – one day before the deadline. Knowing that they would never arrive in America to be stamped and approved by the election committee in Illinois, our official voting address, I called my friend at the Consulate. After hearing my tale, she offered the following suggestion. We had one-half hour to get to the Consulate, which was at that time in East Jerusalem. We were to see a specific individual and he would send our ballots by Diplomatic Pouch, thereby assuring their validity. So we did. We raced to the already closed building, mentioned the name of the US Counsel General, the door magically opened and our ballots were on their way. As they say ... If you know the right people, you don't need "Protekzia" (pull!).

Seeing a small notice in the newspaper caught my attention

... a picture accompanying it depicted the proposed new central Jerusalem Bus Terminal, the *Tachana HaMerkazit*, which is central to the city and one of its most important buildings. I couldn't believe my eyes, as it looked like a Soviet-built factory of the 50s, with small windows and lacking totally in style. The architect was one of renown, having designed the Bible Lands Museum and other architectural jewels that enhanced the city. This simply wouldn't do!

I wrote a letter to the City of Jerusalem, Architecture Division, the Mayor, Egged, the bus cooperative and Letters to the Editor of The Jerusalem Post, as well as anyone who I felt could help avert this travesty. The letter reminded all of the recipients that the building is the most trafficked building in the capital city. It will be in use for probably fifty years. It will be admired for its beauty, or be the butt of jokes for its ugliness. After receiving a hearing from *Egged*, the Mayor and other involved parties, enough pressure was brought to bear, that the design was changed. A lovely, graceful edifice now stands on Jaffa Street. The windows are proportionate and a giant clock adorns the front. The pink stone cast a subtle glow light and adds to the loveliness of Jerusalem.

One summer we returned from Madrid, Spain, being enchanted by the beauty of the city with its colorful flowerbeds planted by the municipality along major parkways and roads. The city appears to be a huge flower market awash in lovely hues. Very impressive. Also were the numerous artistic fountains with water spouts that magnified the beauty of the fountains, which dotted the city and even appeared to make the city feel cooler and a welcome respite from the intense heat. Why couldn't Jerusalem borrow the idea of public flower gardens and unique fountains? We had similar climates and it could only improve with these additions.

At a meeting with Mayor Olmert, I placed this thought on the agenda, although it had technically nothing to do with the proposed AACI meeting. "A more beautiful city makes happier

Olim," I stated, while my colleagues stared at me wondering from where I got this idea. He was delighted with the suggestion and not too long after, the city began getting spruced up with a more sophisticated and artistic look.

Some time later, at a wedding, I spied the then Mayor Uri Lupiansky, standing alone in a corner. I approached him and complimented him on the city's renewed look, with its flowers along the roadways and new fountains. He smiled shyly and thanked me profusely. Always wanting to give credit where it is due ... *Todah* to Mayors Olmert, Lupiansky and Barkat. They have brought the city to a new level of loveliness and its enhancement continues to this day.

There was an economic crisis in the radio broadcasting system and it was decided to remove the English language news from the daily broadcast. While the majority of younger AACI members were fluent in Hebrew, the seniors have little hope to be able to ever communicate freely in the language.

It is documented that to truly use Hebrew on a daily basis, one of two situations must occur; one is to be employed and work in Hebrew or to marry an Israeli and learn it through "Pillow Talk." *Ulpan* simply doesn't cut it. We have many friends who attend class faithfully for a few years and then leave in frustration. The radio news programs and reading the daily Hebrew newspaper are difficult to master.

Besides our members, what of the consulates and other bodies that need English. What do they do? Well, we discovered that the Consulates have their own sources for translation, but that still leaves the thousands of Anglos who daily depend on the news from IBA (Israel Broadcasting Authority). This was before the entrance of Cable TV, and we had the choice of two channels, boring and worse.

We decided to petition the government agency who was responsible for the TV programming in the country – the petition was a runaway success. One day I received a call from committee head who said, "Call off your people, we get the message!" They were overrun as thousands of names poured into their office. We Had Won! However, over the years, there have been difficulties. If any airtime would be required for a special program, then it would always be the English language news that would be canceled. The system works on numbers and we need more Anglos in the country for that, and other reasons. *Aliyah* is the answer to many of Israel's problems and AACI's door is always open.

It is interesting that the Israeli-Russians never had this problem. From the beginning of the great immigration from the Soviet Union, there have been radio and television programs for and concerning their interests. There are more than a million Russians currently living here in Israel.

The French are beginning to make their mark and we see and read the media in that language, as well. As the Jewish French citizens are seeing the handwriting on the wall in France, their *Aliyah* numbers are rising steadily. We warmly welcome them all!

There were many times during my years as head of the organization when the problems seemed insurmountable. The endless meetings which covered both essential items as well as downright silly things. One woman complained to us that there were too many city street lights that were burned out and she thought that AACI should make it a project so that it would be a safer environment. She was right, but even AACI couldn't do everything, no matter how powerful we must have appeared.

Naomi Katz approached the Board of Directors with a project that turned out to be one of the most inspiring, and brought untold benefits to *Am Yisrael*. Naomi had a friend who wished to fund a Library for the Visually Impaired. What an idea for AACI, as this is what we do best – make a difference in the lives of our members. We searched high and low for a place to install this operation. AACI was then located on Mane Street, and because of lack of space, even the small partitioned rooms that we had created, had smaller portioned rooms. We had a severe space crises, but this was too important a project to turn down.

At the start, the entire operation was placed in two cabinets and one table. Today, at the new facility in Talpiyot, the project fills a large room with enthusiastic volunteers that mail "talking books" to every part of Israel.

Sometimes an event occurs which puts everything in perspective. Walking down the street, I happened upon an elderly gentleman, a friend of long standing, who evidentially was losing his vision, and being guided by a white cane. He told me that he was a recipient of the AACI Visually Impaired Library and how happy he was with it. He grabbed me in a bear hug and explained that the books that he received each week were, literally, life savers. His tears mixed with mine as he explained that this was a fairly recent condition; that he had been a reader all his life and blessed AACI for their sacred work. He passed away soon after, but the volunteers who sent him the books each week are truly unaware of the great *Mitzvah* that they performed for my friend and dozens like him.

The following occurred when Stanley Fischer was appointed to be the Governor of the Bank of Israel. His wife was frustrated in obtaining a driving license and didn't know where to turn. The counselor at the Tel Aviv office was contacted and Mrs. Fisher was soon the recipient of a valid license. The Fischers were so grateful to the organization that any request was fulfilled. He was the honored guest speaker on several occasions and a large turnout was a certainty. We could do no wrong in their eyes. Unfortunately there are times, it seems, that AACI is the best kept secret in Israel. However, this is another instance where AACI came through with flying colors.

It seemed that overnight, a new Immigrant Organization appeared on the horizon. *Nefesh B'Nefesh* was instituted by Rabbi Joshua Fass and Tony Gelbart. The idea was to gather hopeful immigrants from America together and bring them en masse to Israel in a program that became highly successful. Each year the

With Bank Of Israel Governor, Stanley Fischer, Jerusalem, 2007

organization is responsible for adding four to five thousand new Anglo citizens to Israel, with few returning to America for lack of experiencing a successful *Aliyah*.

AACI welcomed the new effort with open arms and we were excited to be present at the initial welcoming ceremonies. Meeting at a separate Terminal at Ben Gurion Airport in the crisp early morning air, we waited expectantly and finally saw the airplane circling above our head, land on the tarmac, door open and a few hundred people, shading their eyes against the blinding sun, appearing dazed after the lengthy flight, carefully make their way down the stairs. There were entire families with many children, babes in arms, toddlers, and children of all ages. All were dressed in their "*Nefesh B'Nefesh*" blue and white T-shirt tops. There were people who prostrated themselves, in order to kiss the earth of the Promised Land.

Watching this magical scene, waving the blue and white flags, singing and cheering, there wasn't a dry eye in the place. We gave out balloons, candy, and drinks. There was much hugging and kissing taking place. Prime Minister Netanyahu, along with other dignitaries, welcomed them and repeatedly called this gathering historic – and it was. It was also pandemonium, but a happy sort, as these people were amazed at finally being here and that they had actually taken the step to become *Olim* to Israel.

It is not a simple act to be an immigrant and to change the direction of one's life. It is hard enough to move to another state, another neighborhood, another street, another home; but to move half way across the world, adopt a new language, a different culture and a new set of values is not easy. I believe that "cream rises to the top."

Olim are the "cream" and have the guts to change their way of life and confront the challenges that are faced each day. Is it worth it? A resounding "Yes!" Is it difficult at times? That too is answered in the affirmative. And that is where AACI and *Nefesh B'Nefesh* enter the picture in order to endeavor to have each individual have a successful experience. Especially summertime, as the *Nefesh B'Nefesh* airplanes land, with their logo painted on the body of the El Al airplane, it is among the most thrilling activities that we have had the good fortune to attend. May they keep coming and coming and coming.

During the dark days of the Intifada, the morale of the citizenry, especially those who lived in the Jerusalem area was low. Suicide bombers were rampant in their cruelty. Busses were being blown up and there were times that we were physically close to tragic incidents – twice in one day.

Three women living in Efrat decided to institute a theater program. Thus, the "Raise Your Spirits" theater group was born. As of this writing, five full length productions have been brought to the public.

One of the songs entitled "The Return" is so powerful that it should be the anthem of the Jewish Agency's Immigrant Department. The words of the refrain are thus:

They'll come down from the mountains
They'll come from the skies

They'll come up from the valley with music and with sighs
They'll walk across the deserts,
With laughter and with prayer
Their sisters and their brothers will be waiting there.

Only immigrants (Anglos) could pen this song. The lyrics, written by Toby Klein Greenwald and music by Rivka Epstein, are extremely moving and captures the hopes and in truth the deeds of all *Olim*. We had all experienced this very act by actually coming down from the mountains, up from valleys and across the seas. The collaboration of Arlene Chertoff, Toby Klein Greenwald and Sharon Katz have been inordinately successful. They have captured the hearts of the theatergoers and deserve a *Kol Hakavod*. The performers, all local residents, are volunteers. *Yasher Koach* to the actresses, singers, dancers, musicians as well as the folks behind the stage. We look forward to more heartwarming and delightful performances.

Saba and I spent decades being a part of the AACI family and we remain so. *Saba* is the Cemetery / Bereavement Chairman, and aids members and others in difficult times. Being a successful pulpit Rabbi for most of his life, dealing with lifecycle events with sensitivity, and an innate sense for the situation is second nature to him. He also has sold over one thousand plots in area cemeteries, and is by far, the largest single fundraiser of AACI. The name Rabbi Karzen and bereavement are linked in people's minds, as he has a bottomless capacity for caring and kindness. He would so love to officiate at more weddings and *Bnai Mitzvah*, but, realistically, bereavement counseling is an all time, all season need.

Today, I am called upon to chair the occasional event, or pen my name on a check to a long existing, seldom used, bank account. My involvement in the move to the new Talpiyot center was extensive, both the securing of the site and the design aspect.

Every two weeks when we receive the weekly e-mail, I feel a sense of accomplishment. Remembering the start of the e-mail program brings a chuckle as I remembered when it was begun,

 Jerusalem

Dear Friends:

We thank you for your generous contribution to the newly established AACI

"Karzen Victim of Terror Aid Fund". To those who attended our Toast N' Roast

 *Dinner, we humbly appreciate your sharing*

this memorable evening with us. To those who

could not attend, know that you were missed!!

Ruby and **Jay**

Event Honorees – Victims of Terror Aid Fund established by AACI

it was a novelty. Our Seniors, especially, protested as there were few who could handle the newfangled machine ... most folks did not own a computer. But currently, of course, there is little communication except electronically. Those folks without a computer have the information placed in their mailbox by a helpful neighbor who is a member of AACI.

The Nefesh B' Nefesh organization has adopted and adapted many of our practices and services. As a mentor in Interior Design, both organizations have would-be designers contact me for possible business opportunities. Being associated with the organization has been a marvelous adventure and I wouldn't have missed a moment of it. (I think!)

THERE WERE CULTURAL SURPRISES that popped up constantly. Like the *Makolet* man with his disdain for us in wanting paper plates to the "summer and winter ice cream." The first few years we did a lot of eyeball rolling.

The informality of the Israeli society both charmed and sometimes repelled me. Informality in dress was rampant, however, it was more than that ... it was, at times, notoriously sloppy. The joke is that now the Knesset members can still dress without ties, but their drivers are suited respectfully.

Newscasters seemed to wear their not even best T-Shirt on national TV – it has gotten better, but not much. TV Weather forecasters are in the same league. One day, after reporting the weather, he appeared to be uncertain as to the exact forecast and he blurted out, "Oh, *Kach Sveder*!" (Take a sweater!) We couldn't stop laughing at that one – we still are.

Also, early on, we were amused to discover that April Fools Day was taken seriously. Listening to the 7 a.m. news, it was reported that Switzerland had passed a law and would report all monies deposited in their country to the Israeli government. Panic set in! (NOTE: 25 years later, this has become no April Fools joke, but reality!)

A second item reported was that first grade had been eliminated and students would go directly to the second grade upon completing Kindergarten. What?

In Bayit V'Gan, a Jerusalem neighborhood overwhelmingly religiously observant, a bank changed the entire personnel to Japanese folks overnight. It was one of the leading bank branches and no one spoke Hebrew. People entered the bank and saw only Orientals! As if banking in Israel isn't confusing enough!

Then the pranks went too far: The signs in a major traffic circle in Jerusalem were all changed and once a car entered the circle, it was forced to go round and round with no exit permitted. A prominent doctor on his way to the hospital was caught in this prank and complained vehemently in the media how dangerous that had been. April Fools Day was outlawed. So much of Israel is colored in black and white; we seem to have a hard time living with shades of gray.

Two soldiers came to our front door and asked if I would accompany them up to our roof as a matter of national security. As nothing surprises us anymore, I did so and also inquired why this was necessary. It seems that our roof is designated a security risk as it is kitty-corner from the Knesset. It would be easy for a sharp-shooter to harm a person standing in the plaza of the building. I was puzzled as the Wolfson buildings are directly across from the Knesset and we are farther away. The soldier showed me the official list and sure enough, Diskin #1 was listed.

Now, every Sunday morning, the Prime Minister has his weekly cabinet meeting. There are times when hearing the decisions passed, that I am inclined to throw ripe tomatoes at all of them. However, I dare not, not living in this designated security risk edifice.

There is a fascinating story of the period just after our building was built that Moshe Dayan, who was the Minister of Defense and Security, visited our roof to determine whether we were a security risk for the Knesset at that time. We passed the test then, and here we are again on that infamous list. This happened in the 60s. I guess it takes a while for the bureaucrats to remove the innocent from the Black List!

Another story that surrounds this building is that when the infrastructure was being built, there were bones that were uncovered. In Jerusalem, because of its ancient history, the law states that all finds are to be turned over to the Antiquities Division of the government. Finding bones in this city always makes for a hassle as perhaps they are Jewish bones and require special treatment. No problem for this builder; the bones were spirited away and never heard of again.

My Shelli, who is the mutual President of the Shelli / Ima Fan Club – I for her and her for me – called to invite me to an event featuring Moshe Feiglin. Moshe was a shadowy figure in my mind. I knew that he had, as head of the Zo Artzenu Organization, blocked many of the major arteries in the country as a protest one day. He and his partner, Shmuel Sackett, never had a second chance to repeat this type of action, as they landed in jail. Upon their release, they realized that civil action protesting was not the answer. They had to become involved in politics. Thus was created the Manhigut Yehudit Organization which became an arm of the Likud Political Party.

Moshe's philosophy spoke to my heart, soul and mind and after that initial introduction to his ideas, at a *Chanukah* rally at the Ramada Renaissance Hotel, 2008, I was hooked. Everything about him pleased me. He reminded me physically, of the former Prime Minister, Menachem Begin, with his slight figure, intelligence, forthright speaking ability, interspersed with self-deprecating humor. He was my guy! Begin had been considered a terrorist in his time. At that time, Moshe, with his right wing views was a persona non grata in the political world. He claimed that he was prime minister material and aimed to fulfill that dream. Except for a few thousand people, of whom I am proudly one, he was jeered and accused of having messianic tendencies. He is kind, generous in spirit and a true *Mensch.* Bibi Netanyahu, the Prime Minister, pulled every trick in the book to marginalize him.

Member of Knesset, Deputy Speaker Moshe Feiglin with Ruby, head of the Jerusalem English Speaker Election Campaign, and most ardent supporter, 2012

One of Moshe's wonderful traits is that of all the times that Netanyahu publicly humiliated him, Moshe never uttered a single criticism of the Prime Minister in speech or print. When Netanyahu shook the hand of the leader of the PLO, but refused to shake Moshe's hand, Moshe exclaimed, "You shake the hand of the head of Israel's enemies, but you refuse to shake the hand of a fellow Jew?" Even that public insult was not dwelled upon. One time, I overheard an acquaintance of mine declare that he was far worse than the Palestinians, and that he "should %*&#@% be jailed and the key thrown away." I wish that this had been a singular opinion. However, it was the overwhelming majority; at best, he was a pariah; at worst, use your imagination.

Moshe, with his Jewish and Democratic philosophy, with G-D's blessings and no pandering to anyone was just what Israel needed, but the average Israeli didn't understand it and couldn't see that he was right on the mark. He needed publicity and wasn't getting it, especially for the Anglo citizens. We had information nights conducted in our home. The room was filled to capacity with our friends and acquaintances. It was interesting to see their reaction at the time. His spoken English was faulty and he, of course, expressed his ideas best in his mother tongue. My conclusion to the results of those meetings was that there were attendees who thought he was crazy. Others could see the germ of his ideas, but were not activists and a very few became devotees. I became the official Feiglin *Meshugana* and tried to present him and his ideas to Sabbath tables, mostly unsuccessfully. There were so many hard feelings that *Saba* asked me not to bring up the subject of Feiglin as the subject was too difficult. Even so, I felt strongly that he was urgently needed on the Israeli scene and so became the English-speaking Jerusalem Chair.

The Manhigut Yehudit core committee arranged for information nights in the Israel Center, elegant dinners in hotels and other events to get the word out about Moshe and his platform. It was clear that he MUST be featured in The Jerusalem Post so that the Anglo community could understand for what he stood; no English language newspaper had as yet, even printed his name. The first time I approached The Jerusalem Post, they looked at me as though I was insane and I think that they felt sorry for me. I had always had good relations with some reporters and columnists, and here was Ruby Karzen requesting WHAT! My bizarre request was that they interview Moshe regarding his ideas so that their readers could hear a different voice.

The second time, they were a bit miffed. Who did I think that I was? Moshe Feiglin, of all people! No way, except for one columnist, who a few weeks later mentioned his name. That was the first time that his name was seen in the English language press. A year later, his first picture was printed, very somber. Now there are pictures of Moshe laughing and smiling, in the course of his Knesset duties. Today, he is the Deputy Speaker of the Knesset. Am I proud? You bet I am, and I won't even say "I told you so," to my many friends who thought that I should be given a rubber room in the nearest nut-house, along with Moshe, of course. Daughter Tammy is very impressed that a Member of Knesset appears on my automatic dialing telephone list. Moshe is fifty years young now. There may even be a Prime Minister on my cellphone some day. *Am Yisrael* should only be so lucky!

THERE HAVE BEEN SO MANY HUMOROUS happenings; many of whom could only occur in Israel.

Going to art auctions is one of my favorite pastimes. Twice a year an authentic, public auction, a most elegant affair is held at The King David Hotel in Jerusalem. Upon arrival, participants are offered a glass of wine. The room is set up for over two hundred people, with a bank of telephones connected to Paris, London and New York. It is an exciting evening with bids being received and the sharp bang of the gavel as the auctioneer says "Sold to number whatever."

Sitting next to me have been gallery owners who purchase in quantity as well as single offering purchasers who spend from modest amounts of one thousand dollars to hundreds of thousands of dollars. A work of Reuben-Reuben, the deceased Israeli artist, sold for almost four hundred thousand dollars to a couple from Tel Aviv. The bidding was brisk between them and the phone bids. The audience clapped as the auctioneer's gavel banged "Sold" to the folks from Tel Aviv; they were one of ours!

A few weeks ago *Saba* and I attended the summer auction at the hotel. After signing in and receiving our paddle number, we chanced to sit behind a couple who were being televised for the local TV station. We found out that it was a prominent philanthropist and his wife, who were auctioning off a painting by Mogdliani, a Jewish-Italian painter of great fame. In the catalogue, the painting was offered at seven million dollars. To their great delight, the painting sold on the telephone, from Paris, at eight million, six hundred thousand dollars, a record for the artist as well as Sotheby's. The hotel should have served champagne instead of wine!

During the evening, his wife, being very friendly, kept turning around with comments concerning the offerings; we were enjoying her casual banter. She exclaimed that she noticed that we hadn't bought anything as yet, and asked if there was nothing that suited us. I used that old line that decorators are unfortunately known for – that I saw nothing that would match my couch. (In truth, we had never bought anything, just enjoyed the show.) She then understood that I was an Interior Designer, told me that she needed some work and gave me her business card. She hasn't called yet and I won't hold my breath, but inspecting her card closer, I noticed that there is a logo depicting an organization and she is listed as president. Most probably, if she ever does call, it will be to request a donation!

However, one memorable evening, before the auctioneer took a sip from his glass, he uttered a blessing over the water. As he finished, the entire audience sang, AMEN. Where else in the entire world would this occur … only in *Yerushalayim!*

While I was growing up in Chicago, I, more than once, wondered if I would ever know any famous people. To my delight, living in Jerusalem, makes you part of the history of the city and names that are easily recognizable surround you.

The minute that I saw the *Churban* on Diskin Street that was to be transformed into a "Showplace Home" as a reporter dubbed it, I could see the opportunities that we would have for *Hachnasas Orchim* (welcoming guests). Our home has always been "open" for any worthy organization undertaking events, including Emunah and Amit Women's Organizations, Hadassah, Regavim (retaining our deserts), Likud Anglos, Aish HaTorah Yeshiva's Discovery Program and Herzog Hospital Silver Plate Luncheon.

I SHOULD HAVE KEPT A VISITORS ALBUM early in our marriage; it would have been priceless. Natan Sharansky, Rabbi Lord Emanuel Jakobovitz, Yuval Steinitz, Gidon Saar,

Moshe Feiglin, Author Hanoch Teller and numerous others graced our Speaker's Corner sharing information or raising funds. A very special affair, a Shower for a Gush Katif Bride, (after the Expulsion) where there were so many gifts brought for the celebrant that Yad Eliezer, the sponsoring organization returned three times to pick up the boxes. Author Yaffa Ganz had spoken movingly as her children were among the thousands of Israelis uprooted from Gush Katif.

A case in point is that of Dovid, the owner of the beauty shop whom I have patronized for the past twenty-five years. Sonia Peres was his client, as well as a prominent Supreme Court Judge of yesteryear, the wives of several Supreme Court judges, Israel Prize winners and other clients who he surreptitiously points out to me. He also thinks that I am noteworthy and it has come back to me that he tells folks that I have been his client for a long time, which gives me a chuckle. The shop is in the heart of Rechavia and is a fixture of our middle aged / older clientele; not trendy, by any means, but refined. The lingua-franca of the shop is Hebrew and French, but the most unique aspect of the shop is Dovid himself.

He was eleven years old when his Syrian parents sent him and his sixteen-year-old brother to "Walk" to Israel. Holding his brother's hand, they arrived safely and were taken in by the Youth *Aliyah* Organization in whose institution they were raised. When one enters the shop, it is quite usual to see Dovid engrossed in a volume of the Torah anthology called *Me'am Loez*. I rarely leave before picking up a new thought for the following week's Torah portion. There are famous people living and working all around us, and people like Dovid are not well known, except for his work with his "Golden Hands" for a well-executed coiffeur. He is a regular citizen of Jerusalem, modest and unassuming, but to me, he is hero.

The President's House is a few blocks away, as is the Prime Minister's Residence. The Knesset, and the Supreme Court are practically in my front yard. I guess that it is akin to living in

Washington D.C.; a far cry from Chicago. We also reside near the hotel area which attracts well know personalities from around the world. Political personalities, the stars of stage, film and music walk the same streets and drive the same roads that we Jerusalemites travel each day.

Practically next door to our home, a kindergarten is located. Bibi and Sarah Netanyahu have traditionally enrolled their sons there. One day, exiting from the supermarket located on the second floor of the Wolfson Medical Center, I chanced upon a lost child. In Israel, a child in distress becomes the child of everyone involved. By the end of five minutes, the other two women and I realized that this was Yair, the Netanyahus' four-year-old son. Within a short time, Mother Sarah had enveloped the child in her arms. She was teary-eyed and stressed, he wasn't. Perhaps it was because of the candy bar that he was so engrossed in chewing!

Another time, I was awaiting a ride from a client standing in front of my building. Just as a leg (Netanyahu's) emerged from the chauffeured car, my cellphone rang. I started to put my hand in my pocket to answer the ring, when two Secret Service men pulled their guns and pointed them at me. My contractor had a question concerning tiling a floor − and they thought that I was Al Capone in a dress! We all had a good laugh when he emerged from the car. But, believe me, there is nothing funny about being at the receiving end of two pistols!

Crossing Jaffa Street one morning, a young fellow began to hit on me. He appeared to be approximately twenty years old. (Maybe!) He was following me and using his favorite pick up lines. Little did he know that my knowledge of Hebrew did not include his type of phrases. I didn't even understand much of what he said. I soon grew tired of his attentions and said to him, "Son, I have dresses older than you are!" Note: this inclusion is dedicated to my friend, Dr. Shelly Abramson, who never let me forget this incident, "Shelly, you're right … It's still funny after twenty-seven years!"

Tammy requested that *Saba* and I pick up Racheli from Kindergarten. Approaching the school, we saw her standing with her little friends outside waiting for us. Approaching them, I said in my newly acquired *Ulpan* Hebrew, that I was glad to meet them all – we were happy to know Racheli's friends. Racheli turned to them and said in her perfect *Sabra* Hebrew, "My *Savta* just arrived from America. Her Hebrew isn't good." My darling four-year-old granddaughter was apologizing for her Greenhorn *Savta's* lack of Hebrew knowledge. I thought that I was doing pretty well, but my Racheli really brought me down a peg or two – a Kindergartner yet, how humiliating!

Tammy and Morris went on vacation and *Saba* and I were the babysitters. One of the tasks was to retrieve Racheli, aged four, from her ballet lessons. We arrived early and the teacher requested that we take seats in the back of the room until class finished.

The scenario was thus: There were twenty tiny dolls dressed in pastel-colored tutu's and ballet slippers. At the teacher's order they would all leap up and down, crossing the room from one end to the other. They were so cute with their little legs and tummies protruding from the miniature ballet outfits, that I began to giggle and couldn't stop. Then, I was laughing so hard that tears were running down my face and I really tried to stop, but I couldn't. The teacher requested that I quieten down as my hysterical laughing was disturbing the ballet "stars." Finally, she asked me to leave. She banished me from the class and requested that we meet Racheli at the car. We were banned from the ballet school and it was doubly problematical as the teacher was a close friend of Tammy. How embarrassing!

Grandson Elichai, Tammy's eldest, was in *Kita Aleph*. The teacher assigned the class to draw a farm vegetable garden. Elichai drew a plot of earth with cans of corn, peas and carrots seemingly growing out of the ground. He thought that vegetables grew in cans! His teacher was another of Tammy's friends and she received a lot of teasing about Elichai's vegetable garden.

Well, to be fair, in Efrat where Elichai lived, farmland was not a part of the landscape. As a matter of fact, it wasn't in Chicago either, where his mother grew up. Currently, Elichai is quite the chef and uses fresh vegetables constantly. This story has become one of the funny incidents in Efrat history; even Tammy laughs at it now!

Another Racheli story involves my activities as a *Shadchan* (Marriage Broker). Racheli grew to be an accomplished person, a granddaughter of which to be extremely proud. Whatever she put her mind to, she excelled. In the army, she was promoted to Officer Status, had myriad of friends and thrown into the mix were her scholarly achievements, natural talent and unending energy and love of life. She was employed, shared a home with three friends and attending college ... the world was her *Blintze,* (Oysters not being *Kosher!*) However, with all these wonderful happenings, I felt that it was time for her to marry. She and her future spouse were exactly the type of individuals that Israel needed and the more Jewish babies, the merrier!

Speaking with her, she assured me that her life was filled with all of her activities. She also loves folk dancing and was even a Substance Abuse Counselor in her non-existent free time. It's all wonderful, but it is time to marry, I stated. She was not happy with me, but how angry can you become with a loving *Savta?* She reluctantly agreed to date men that I found and suggested to her, but, with the disclaimer that before I give anyone her telephone number, I MUST ... MUST check with her first. I agreed.

The first two potential dates telephoned her, but did not pan out and I knew that she was a trifle angry with me. Then, *Saba* and I joined a group of educators for a *Shabbat Shira Shabbaton* in Eilat. *Shabbat* morning, I entered the elevator where there were four people discussing the fact that young people today do not want to commit to marriage and how it will affect the future of the State of Israel along with other crucial issues. One man spoke of his nephew, another his son, and it went on that way for *fifteen floors* in a Sabbath elevator, which certainly took ten to fifteen minutes.

The *Shabbaton* was a success. At breakfast the next morning, a woman approached and requested Racheli's cellphone number. She was impressed by my remarks in the elevator, during that long descent to the Synagogue and thought that she would be a possible match for her son. I was in a dilemma, what to do? On the one hand, she looked like a lovely woman, had enjoyed the program and five lectures by the marvelous speaker, Rabbi Bennie Lau. That was a plus for the background of her family, but I had promised Racheli to call her first. On the other hand, Racheli was in Jerusalem, probably in class and she was miffed at me, anyway. I handed over the number with a bit of trepidation, thinking ... *no pain, no gain*. The happy ending is that Racheli and Nir have been married a year and a half ... a cuter couple you couldn't find. P.S. I think that she has forgiven me!

Over the years, we have become part of the history of the State. It was soon after the Oslo Accords and the Intifada was raging, seemingly, nonstop. The women of the Hadassah Organization, of which I am a Life Member since 1960, when *Saba* purchased it as a birthday gift, were holding their annual convention in Jerusalem at the Binyanei Haumah Convention Center. Always happy to have such an influx of tourists, our spirits were high, until it was announced that Shimon Peres was to be honored at the gathering. Peres had been one of the main architects in the creation of the accords and it was a tragedy on all counts.

The Women in Green (Hats) was a protest movement led by Ruth and Nadia Matar. We stood in front of hotels, the Knesset and other government buildings, the Prime Minister's and President's Residences. We, men also, held up signs in English and Hebrew and passed out leaflets, wherever we thought it would do the most good. Pictures in the newspaper of the group sitting on the ground, in an anti-violent stance were common. The police used horses to disperse and control the crowds at times. *Saba* was kicked by one of the huge beasts and felt it for days. Our Green

Hats and the Blue and White flag were the symbol of right wing protests.

It was the last night of the convention and time for the concluding dinner; the participants were awaiting the guest of honor. Outside along the path to the entrance, we, The Women In Green, were also awaiting Peres. As he approached the entrance, there was heckling from the large crowd carrying signs negative to Peres and his deadly actions on the political scene. Ruth Matar and I were standing together and as he passed, she yelled something like, "Peres is bad for Israel." He looked at her and said, "Why don't you go home to America!" She retorted, "Why don't you go home to Poland?" A newspaper reporter overheard this exchange and it became one of the well-known phrases that characterized the relations between Peres and the Anglo community.

The Hadassah Organization was the loser this time. Not only were there members who asked him "impolite" questions, but there were anti-Peres signs displayed in the hall. Unhappy members of the organization returned their membership cards. It was an unfortunate choice on the part of the committee. There have been numerous meetings and conventions since that time. Perhaps the committee is more circumspect concerning the speakers that are engaged, as it has been quiet. The only reports that are heard now is the wonderful accomplishments of this marvelous organization; and that is as it should be.

Interior Design

Of all professions, how did a nice Jewish girl choose to be an Interior Designer? As already noted, when the 1955 class graduated high school, religiously observant young ladies had few choices of job opportunity. One either chose education or nursing because of Sabbath restraints. Even the career to be secretaries was problematic, as how are short winter Friday afternoons handled? To a person, education, teaching in some form, or perhaps, psychology, where one could establish their own hours were the desired choices.

In the Chicago Jewish Academy yearbook, next to the name of Ruby Ray is written as profession of choice: millinery designer. With no idea as to how to attain this goal, I also chose education as my field. The economic strata of my crowd was middle class at best, and only two friends whose parents with means were fortunate to attend the newly established Stern College for Women. Everyone else remained, living at home. To this day, when I hear that contemporaries attended Smith or Barnard College, I am amazed. In our crowd, had you said that you're attending these colleges or one on the moon, it would have been the same thing. For us, they were all unattainable.

Planning our *Aliyah*, I truly didn't know at what I wanted to do. I knew that I would be employed, but at what, I couldn't hazard a guess. A few weeks after we arrived, I was contacted by a Yeshiva for the position of Executive Director. For certain, that I wasn't interested in at all.

As with so many situations in life, I kind of fell into the career; and it was a fortuitous fall! We arrived in December, bought an apartment and I was off and running. As it needed a total remodeling which took eight months, much planning, shopping and work was needed.

Saba and I spent months driving from one hole-in-the-wall to another; there were even workshops located in caves. I am not joking! Jerusalem was in a pre-growth stage and coming from Chicago where everything is available, I was in shock. Slowly, I gathered service workmen, carpenters, plumbers, painters, upholsterers and refinishers. We located furniture, appliance and mirror stores, one Do-It-Yourself store, as well as art galleries. These held me in good stead, when they were required for future clientele. Jerusalem was in a primitive state vis-a-vis shopping resources. Shopping malls did not exist and even food shopping was at the local corner grocery store, being that the only two supermarkets were *Shufer Sol* on Agron and one on Pierre Koenig in Talpiyot. For American products such as corn flakes or peanut butter, shopping in Bet Lechem (Bethlehem) was an option. No Israeli company, as yet, manufactured these common products to which we were accustomed and wanted.

A few months after we moved to our first apartment, a friend from Chicago called and requested that I come over immediately. I had done a bit of decorating for her lovely, large home in Peterson Park, a neighborhood in Chicago and she owned one in Jerusalem, and wished to remodel it. I tried to decline as I didn't feel that I knew enough suppliers and trades people to do a fair job and I explained that to her. Besides, my lack of Hebrew language skills was a definite detriment, but she was undeterred.

Entering the apartment, I felt that I walked into a place that surely a cyclone had hit! My friend's daughter and her three companions, who also were attending seminaries, had been living there, following her son and his friends using the place as a dormitory for a number of years. It was a "Gap Year," apartment and looked and smelled like one. It was an unbelievable mess; just my meat! This occurred on Thursday afternoon. She was flying back to Chicago after the Sabbath. With instructions to "Make It Nice," she handed me a set of keys and blank checks, and made her farewells. Three months later, she returned to a place that was my first inclusion in the design section of The Jerusalem Post. I was on my way and haven't stopped since then!

Fortune smiled when I was involved in that project. I was awaiting a carpenter who didn't show for his appointment, outside the building. Noting the concern on my face, a *Kablan*, who was also working in that area, struck up a conversation. He, in his atrocious English, and I, in my terrible Hebrew, connected. Twenty-seven years later, his English hasn't terribly improved, as much as he has tried. He simply has no aptitude for languages, but, my level has reached that of public speaking in Hebrew (if I must!). The rest is history – Avi Kara is my friend and partner since that day. He has a heart of gold and truly tries to do the best job that he can. Notwithstanding the disreputable reputations of the run-of-the-mill *Kablan*, he is honest and I trust him implicitly. We keep each other balanced. When he is not totally happy with my design, I know it immediately, as he calls me "*Bossit!*" But, our partnership is based on mutual respect. I am aware of what I can do and he complements my work. There are times that when we are working on a complicated project, we see more of each other than of our spouses! *C'est La Vie!*

The neighborhood of Har Nof was being built and work was abundant. There were many projects and Avi and I went from one apartment to another creating beauty, where at the moment, there was sand as far as one could see. The problem was that the area was empty, save that of workers, mostly of who were Arabs, and supervisors who were generally Jews. The quiet was broken by the bang of hammers, but I often felt very conspicuous, being the only woman around. My children hounded me, reiterating the instances that Jews were being stabbed, some killed, by their own workers. The feeling was one of disquiet and I decided that perhaps, I should invest in personal protection. But what? A gun was out, there was no way that I would carry one. Mace was illegal, so that was not viable. A hat pin, one had to be close to the attacker, forget it! Oven cleaner was my weapon of choice. So, along with my attaché case filled with papers, a measuring tape, samples of paint and other paraphernalia, I added a can of oven spray; never had to use it, but I guess that I felt safer. Har Nof was not the only area which I felt that I required some protection. Walking through David's Village near the Old City walls, where the only sound is your own footsteps, my trusty can of oven cleaner is in my hand!

Our crew consists of a number of workers including those who do the backbreaking tasks of carrying heavy tiles and other grunt work. These workers are generally Arabs and have been with us for many years. Shaker has been an employee for over twenty years. He was a teenager when he began and is now the father of four children. He is not the only one who have become adults while working with us. The plumbing, electrical and specialty work is the work of both Jews and Arabs. Before the two Intifadas and Gulf Wars, we went to their houses of mourning as Muslims sit *Shiva* for three days. However, we never attended a wedding, as we would have been so conspicuous that we would have been uncomfortable.

There was an excellent carpenter in Bethlehem and we would frequently go there to plan projects with George, a Christian Arab. His shop was far off the beaten track, but we had no fear of traveling there and were always welcomed by a tall, handsome, smiling college-educated gentleman who would buy *Kosher* cookies to serve us when a meeting was planned. The period of using George, an excellent craftsman, ended when we were approaching the center of the city and saw the newly formed Palestinian Police marching in front of us. They were a sight, smart looking, outfitted in new black uniforms, bright red belts, berets and boots. The group, looking fierce, struck fear in our hearts and we never again traveled to Bethlehem. George called me a few times, but circumstances never permitted us to use his services again. I must add at this time, that when one of our employees works in our home, they never leave without asking if there is something else with which they can help. We treat our workers with respect and they reciprocate.

Before the Gulf War, one of our work supervisors just disappeared. We heard nothing of him or his whereabouts. He was away for over three months. We thought that it might have something to do with his army service, but we knew better than to inquire about it when he returned. A while later, he asked if he was missed while he was gone and the answer was, "You Bet!" He related that he had been in a special unit formed for the purpose of assassinating Sadam Hussein, the dictator of Iraq. The mission was called off due to the exhortations of the United States President, George Bush.

Having had over ten grandchildren in *Tzahal* or *Sherut Leumi*, we have gotten used to bizarre happenings and reports of their activities. Because a soldier is not to talk about where he is or what he is doing, if asked he or she will say, "I would love to tell you, but then I'd have to kill you!" HA! HA! One never gets used to hearing such things, but we're living in dangerous times and we are so proud to have had soldiers and officers, both men and women, among the ranks of the IDF.

In the meantime, a wondrous revolution has occurred during

the past fifteen years. Everything is available and can be bought right here in the city. (Except for a brass bed headboard, but that's another story!) Our economy has become so sophisticated. We either create or import items that are unique; truly to marvel at. The slick design Israeli magazine, *Binyan V Diur* pictures houses and items that are international in scope. Homes that I have created have been pictured in the design section of The Jerusalem Post. A few months ago, I was interviewed and featured in The Jerusalem Post's, My Working Week column. A number of years ago, a cable show in Europe, which featured Interior Designers in different countries, used my website as the Israeli contribution.

Everyone is interested in Interior Design. I would like to have a shekel for every person who has told me that they should have been / would have been / tried to be, (or in every possible combination) an Interior Designer. Presently there are, but at that time, there was no English language course for the subject and I decided to open a school with various design subjects taught. The classes ran for two hours each for a period of eight weeks; Interior Design 101; and due to request, the course Interior Design 102 quickly followed.

The school was in existence for three years and as I was the only instructor, when my business became more time consuming, I hung up my instructor's hat. I stated at the beginning that I didn't bestow degrees on the students who completed the two classes and that there were no diplomas involved. The instruction was for women and men who had talent in that direction and who enjoyed working on their own homes, beautifying them to their own satisfaction. Although I didn't envision any of the students actually becoming my friendly competition, there were those who did exactly that. In Israel there is no license for designers, and I have yet to meet one that has any qualified certificates.

From time to time, I receive calls inquiring when the next semester will open. I keep their names in a special file and I treasure this vote of confidence, as one never knows what the future will bring!

For a number of years I wrote articles on Interior Design for

my working week

■By YOCHEVED MIRIAM RUSSO

Ruby Ray Karzen
Interior designer

www.rubydesigns.net

Age: 70 plus

Marital status: Married to Rabbi Jay Karzen

Job description: I'm a designer and contractor, both of which require being a bit of psychologist, too. I work to enhance the beauty of Jerusalem by creating elegant and functional living, office and community spaces for my clients. I do everything from just enhancing a room with new wallpaper or draperies, up to full-scale makeovers, including a full-service home set-up for people coming to Israel who want their new home to be completely ready when they arrive.

Education: A degree in educational psychology and a master's in Jewish thought, plus a degree from Parsons School of Interior Design in New York.

Aliya: From Chicago, on December 15, 1985.

How did you get started? In Chicago, I'd furnished and decorated a couple of model homes for a friend, making them look like, well, model homes. Then we made aliya, and after I'd redone our own home here, a friend called and asked me to decorate her apartment. I tried to decline – I didn't know anyone here, I didn't speak Hebrew well, I had no resources, I didn't know where to find things. But she insisted I come to her home, and when I got there, she gave me the keys and a stack of signed checks. "I'm leaving," she said. "Are you insane?" I said. In the process of doing that first home, I met my building partner, Avi Kara, who was working in the same building. We've worked together ever since.

How did you begin? Jerusalem was a totally differ-ent place back then. My husband and I started by just looking for all kinds of craftsmen. We'd find little corner stalls, really just little holes in the wall where someone was making something interesting. Some were so small, you could hardly stand up – all mom and pop places. We found ironworkers, drapery makers, upholsterers, everything, just by going from place to place, seeing what was available. Even today, I get 95 percent of the furnishings in Jerusalem.

First job? At age nine, I was the little girl in the white apron at my father's grocery store.

Worst job? Wow. I administered a very large Hebrew day school in the Chicago suburb Skokie. I've been a real-estate agent. I've done a lot of things, but I don't think any of them qualify as "worst." If I did it, I didn't hate it.

As a kid, what did you want to do? In my high-school yearbook, I said I wanted to be a millinery designer.

Who hires you? It started with people moving here from Chicago and New York who'd heard about me from someone else. I used to accept work outside Jerusalem, but not anymore. Right now I'm doing a lot of "refreshments" – updating older apartments where people have lived for many years. They don't want to move, but they want a fresher look. The best client is one who knows what they want but still has an open mind.

How do you charge? Usually by a percentage of the cost of the job. I don't like to charge by the hour, even though I'd earn more that way.

Unusual request? Many years ago, before online shopping, a lady called me saying she wanted a Japanese rose-wood living room. Wow! Where would I find that? But I found a place in Rishon Lezion that specialized in it. The room was beautiful.

High moment? Just recently I was redesigning a house. There were workers everywhere – plumbers, carpenters, carpet layers – total chaos. I was sitting in the living room, and the thought just came to me, "I am really happy!" Some people would have a heart attack with all that noise and dust, but for me it was lovely.

Low moment? It is more of an anxious moment: When I bring clients into their finished house for the first time. Especially before we came to e-mail photos back and forth, I'd be waiting for the people to arrive. I wanted to walk them in and hear them say they really loved it, so it was always a little tense.

Controversial? No. I get very close to my clients, involving them as much as I can. Even if it's just finding two chairs, I want to reflect what they want, so no, there's not much controversy.

If not this? Probably an art historian. On Fridays I go to an art appreciation class at the Israel Museum. I love it.

Biggest accomplishment? My family, including four great-grandchildren, especially the fact that we're all here in Israel.

Dream? I suppose I sound like a beauty pageant contestant, but if we had peace and God's blessing in Jerusalem, it would be wonderful for the entire world. ■

Ruby Ray Karzen – Interior Designer – Featured in The Jerusalem Post

The Jerusalem Post. They were called "INSIDE STORY" By Ruby Ray Karzen and ran the gamut from designing storage units for salons to terrace gardening. The introduction of unique elements such as wallpaper and fabrics, as well as how to have the maximum impact in featuring antiques in home décor, was unique to the Jerusalem public. I received many questions and comments, but nary a client. However, it was an enjoyable undertaking and the column seemed to fulfill a niche in the English-speaking community.

The Jerusalem Post prints a special Purim section and one issue contained a spoof of my column. This was a time of Intifada and the question reflected the tense mood of the country in a tongue-in-cheek manner. The column was titled "INSIDE MOVES" by Rube Raybeam and the following questions were asked. "What kind of draperies go best with bullet-proof glass?" And "How can the security guards who stand outside the doors be attired in the most aesthetic pleasing way possible? The answers were in the same vein and it was written in black humor style – one of the strengths of Israeli society to find a humorous angle to every situation. P.S. The answer to the drapery problem was Khaki-Fatigue or camouflage green; it was funny at the time.

Feng Shui (No, it's not a type of Chinese food!) is an aspect of interior design that I have studied and it is an integral part of my design philosophy. There are clients that request that I utilize the principles of this interesting set of ideas and I am happy to do so. However, as with many things in this world, one must pick and choose what is suitable. Taken to the extreme, Feng Shui can become religion-like and there is no room in my life or yours for those ideas.

Once I received a call and the caller confirmed that a government agency in the country of Jordan was interested in using my services. However, as an almost afterthought, he mentioned that I would be required to enter his country by using my American passport. I told him in no uncertain terms that I would cross Allenby Bridge only using my Israeli passport – the conversation abruptly ended at that point.

One morning I entered the only store that supplied quality closets in Jerusalem at the time. A young man was deliberating which closet would suit his needs. The proprietor, who I had prior dealings with, turned to me and said, "Why don't you help the young man out?" After aiding him with his decision, he inquired if I would be interested in working with him, it was a large commission, but I turned him down. The venue was the Village of Abu Ghosh and he, an altruistic citizen had returned from Illinois after winning the Power Ball Lotto. It was the largest win thus far in the game's history and he was interested in upgrading sections of his native village. Following this story in the newspaper, I learned that he, indeed, invested huge amounts of funds and the citizenry of Abu Ghosh benefited greatly, but the firm of Ruby Ray Karzen Interiors wasn't part of it. I am aware that this community is the most Israeli friendly of all the Arab communities anywhere, but I didn't feel right to undertake this work.

At an AACI Memorial service, where IDF Soldiers and Victims of Terror are honored by affixing the names on plaques in the Rabin Memorial Forest, I found myself sitting next to a minister of a notable church located in the Old City. A Christian tourist who had attended his church was murdered in a terrorist attack and in her memory, he was attending as a representative of the Christian community. When he learned of my profession, he immediately requested that I visit his community, as he needed advice on architectural planning and other items. I wasn't eager to accept his invitation and he sensed my reluctance to work in a church setting. He quickly described the community center that he was interested in remodeling. It wasn't the first time that I had dealt with the Christian community and I shortly found myself on the designated property.

Entering the Old City through The Jaffa Gate not more than 100 meters into the city, is a decorated iron gate and walking through that gate brings you to the enclave that was built for the British Lord High Commissioner in the late 1800s. The elegant stone buildings are connected by flower-bordered paths, which house a hostel, said community center, the minister's home and the church. In that park-like setting, closing your eyes transports you to a rural area. The quiet was broken only by the songs of birds. It was magical and utterly unbelievable that the hustle and bustle of the Old City with its commerce and constant flow of tourists was so close.

The minister was an affable fellow and I enjoyed working with him and his wife, who run the church like, *L'Havdil*, a *Chabad* Center. They had come as students to study at The Hebrew University in the 60s and never left. Ultra Zionist in their beliefs, right wing in their politics, we had a meeting of the minds on many subjects. Oh, they were very pleased with the outcome of their Center; all in a day's work!

The City of Hebron, the Jewish section, required extensive renovation. The Avraham Avinu Synagogue, part of the Gutnik Center and the City Council offices, badly needed attention. The creation of a hotel including a dining room that would double as a *Simcha* hall was also on the docket. Although this was during an Intifada, the work proceeded on schedule with a few unusual twists. There were days that the Army deemed it too dangerous to travel on the road and we were forced to cancel work. Normally, the protected bus with bulletproof windows was my transportation. Alighting from the Jerusalem bus, there would be a car awaiting me at the bus stop with an armed driver. He would accompany me as I made my way from site to site. A bonus was that each afternoon, praying the Afternoon prayers at the *Maarah Hamachpayla*, became part of our regime. It was an unusual venue, but it was inspiring to work at such a holy and renowned site.

A request was made that on the corner of *Esrog* and *Lulav* Streets there was a large home that needed in-depth design work. Even though the area was a longer distance than I ordinarily accommodate, how could I turn down a home with that address? Whether it's Talpiyot, where the streets are named for the Heroes of the State, Rechavia and Shaarei Chesed where famous Rabbinic personalities are featured and *Mercaz Ha'Ir* (Downtown for former Chicagoans!) where Biblical personalities are the stars, tickle the imagination. I still get a kick out of going to Shlom Tzion Hamalka Street, a Queenly one, for sure! Only in Israel … Street names are definitely one of its charms.

There are suppliers that I have dealt with for over twenty-five years; I am considered a *Bat Bayit* and more than one of my shop owner friends quotes *Megilat Esther* when they say "Until half of my Kingdom is yours." It makes for good relationships and assures my clients of quality merchandise and excellent service. One of the owners hired me to redo his store, which is one of the largest furniture shops in Jerusalem.

After the project was finished, the owner decided to have a Grand Opening Gala and he invited as the special guest of honor, Rav Kaduri, the renowned *Mekubal* (mystic). This gentleman was very attached to the Rabbi, and wished that he bless his establishment. It was to be a special treat for his friends. He invited me by saying that I must come and be introduced and receive a blessing. My friend is a Kurdi, *Sefardi* in practice and *Mekubalim* are part and parcel of his belief. We are of *Ashkenazi* descent and *Mekubalim* are not traditionally accepted. However, I went, so as not to hurt his feelings. The event was in full swing as the doors to the store opened and four men shouldering a pallet on which a throne-like chair entered – Rav Kaduri had arrived. Dozens of men quickly queued up in front of him and he blessed each one in turn and they kissed his hand. My friend hurried over to me and began to pull me toward the *Rav*. I tried to hold back, but he was much stronger than I, and I suddenly found myself facing the great Rabbi, with my friend explaining who I was. I uttered not one word, but heard the wonderful blessing that the holy man bestowed upon me. However, I mumbled *Todah*, but didn't kiss his hand. I was the only woman who received this wonderful gift; it was indeed special!

Another time we were enjoying the holidays in a local hotel. An important Rabbi, also renown as a *Mekubal,* was giving a Bible lesson to the guests. We enjoyed it and when he ended, dozens of men and boys gathered around him requesting blessings and he complied. After his presentation, walking down the stairs to the dining room, I was surprised to see him next to me. I asked him if he could bless me, as I had noticed that no women had been among the people that received one. He smiled and said, "Why not?" and proceeded with a blessing that covered every base; it was truly a magnificent one. When he concluded, he said, "Now, you bless me." I was dumbfounded, I never expected to reciprocate and this exchange was in Hebrew! The only reply that came to mind was, "May the wonderful blessing that you showered upon me, be bestowed upon you, as well! Or, in shortened form, "Ditto!" He appeared most grateful and beamed a wide smile at my response.

A while ago, I was sitting on an overturned box in a home in which extensive remodeling was in progress. All around me, the workmen were each doing their jobs. The dust swarmed around the room as the carpenter was banging his hammer, the plumber was in the kitchen *hocking* on the pipes, the electrician was drilling into the ceiling in order to hang the light fittings. There were some materials that were being carried down to the storeroom and everyone added to the cacophony of noise as they called instructions to each other in loud voices, so that they could be heard over the almost deafening noise. As I watched this *Balagan* through the cloud of dust, I suddenly thought to myself, "As crazy as it might seem, I am having a good time. I love this mess, which to someone else would be intolerable, but I am happy." I was happy because to me it was an orderly mess, as after they all leave today, in a short time, a beautiful creation will emerge – a home which will be a delight to the eye. I truly believe that in a way, this is Holy work, especially when Jerusalem is the site. To make

Jerusalem more beautiful is a privilege that I take very seriously.

So, to answer the question that is asked constantly, "Yes, I do love being an Interior Designer!" Museums, Synagogues, schools, hotels, hospitals, clinics, villas, apartments, both large and small, offices for every type of need, community centers, stores and restaurants in cities, large and small as well as projects in *Moshavim* and *Kibbutzim* have been my turf. The only venues that I haven't as yet explored, is an airplane or a yacht, but there is always tomorrow!

Life in Israel is always interesting, as the Chinese folks have a saying, "May you live in interesting times!" I think that they penned it especially for us, the Israelis! One *Motzai Shabbat*, turning on the radio, we learned that hundreds of Ethiopian Jews had arrived in Israel and were being housed in Jerusalem at a local hotel. Hurriedly, people packed their cars with every type of clothing, food, diapers, toiletries and whatever was thought necessary. These new *Olim* had come with nothing and they required every item one could think of − we thought.

The Zohar Hotel in Talpiyot was overrun with generous Jerusalemites who brought everyday, useful items. There was only one problem, the Ethiopians were totally ignorant of what they were, and how to use them. These lovely people had made *Aliyah* from a primitive society and they had no knowledge of elevators, stairs, Western-style toilets, toothbrushes and other everyday items.

The plants in the hotel were denuded after a few days as their guests used them for toothbrushes. Lessons in the proper usage of toilets, bathtubs, showers and the like were held. Now, we are not to think that all Ethiopians were as primitive, however, as these particular people had come from a rural area and that was their cultural level.

A joke was told that there was an Ethiopian gentleman who was watching the elevator and he saw an elderly woman enter and the doors closed. A few minutes later, the doors opened again and a beautiful woman emerged. Whereupon, he ran to get his wife and pushed her into the elevator!

Physically, the Ethiopian men are handsome and the woman are truly lovely. There are times that I have openly stared at a woman, as it appears that Queen Nefrititi is alongside me walking the streets of Jerusalem. As they emerged from the airplane seemingly floating in their native dress, only a colorful swarm of butterflies could match their beauty and gracefulness.

So what happened? Within twenty-four hours in Sachar Park, out of our window, we saw piles of clothing; the women were being outfitted – in Blue Jeans! Gone were the butterflies; they wanted to be 100% Sabras. Personally, I felt like crying. Thus, Operation Solomon became part of history.

The ads for the Jewish Genealogical Society to be held at the Ramada Hotel in Jerusalem were fascinating. As *Saba* and I are most interested in history, we decided to attend and to spend the three days of the convention hopefully, learning additional information about our families and the world from which they came.

Upon arrival, the registration was on two tracks; there was one for Russia and one for Poland. The bulletin boards were packed with notes from participants hoping to connect with friends and family. *Saba* chose the Russian track and I, the Polish, never dreaming what the outcome would be.

In a large ballroom 300-400 participants were assembled. There was a screen which welcomed the participants, and the speaker was a woman with a doctorate in Genealogy. Her name was Dr. Judith Frazin which didn't mean anything to me at the time. I glanced down, admiring the new carpeting that had been laid recently and then looking up, I noticed that the slide had been changed and the speaker was reading out names and explaining how to interpret the Polish legal document. For a moment, I just stared, as the names written on the document as they sounded so familiar … By gosh, they were my family! The Polish name Raja was the forerunner of Ray and there listed were my great-grandparents and their children. Baruch Raja (Ray), the third son was my grandfather. Interestingly enough, the names of my sisters and cousins were noted there and my great-grandmother, Chaya Rivka indicated my own name. I was in shock! On the table there was a pile of fifty pages of microfiche and the speaker had chosen my family!

When the session ended, I rushed up to the speaker and told her of my excitement at seeing my family's documents reviewed. She then said, "Don't you remember me? I am your fourth cousin and live in Northbrook, Illinois. The study of our family was the original research for my doctorate."

Well, *Saba* and I took "Cuz" out to dinner and we had a marvelous evening. Two things stand out in my mind as regards to her presentation. The first is that when her survey was undertaken, the aunts and uncles were still alive so that she could obtain the correct information. The second is that although our children's generation are named after these ancestors, they will never recognize for whom they were named, as the names have been altered. Today, the custom is not to bestow both a Hebrew and secular name; the modern Hebrew name has emerged the victor.

Daughter Tamar Minda is named after my mother, Chana Mindel, and Uri David is named after *Saba's* grandfather, Shraga Feivel. Yiddish names wouldn't have cut it in 1960s America. However, in truth, their given Hebrew names stuck out in Iowa also. One never knows where life will take you, but even then we knew that the children should carry only Hebrew names – and so it was.

It fascinates me that even after twenty-seven years of being a citizen of Israel, perhaps the biggest success story of the twentieth and twenty-first century and living in Jerusalem, the most storied city in history, the question is asked too frequently: "How do you like living in Israel?" It's amazing, as no one ever questioned whether I enjoyed living in Chicago or the United States. It is a given. America is a great country and as Jews we owe a tremendous debt to her, for our People as well as personally.

Israel is neither better or worse a society than that of America in everyday life; but Israel is different. As a Jew, it is the place that they take you in because you are family and Jews help family.

There is a supposedly true exchange between a revered Anglo-Saxon politician and a Jewish journalist. Discussing the fact that the USA has been and continues to be a haven for immigrants since its inception, the politician replied thoughtfully. He mentioned the huge immigrations of the Irish, Italians, Jews and Puerto Ricans that have been citizens for several generations and helped to make America what it is, and then added, "But, of course, you are all visitors to this country."

Israel is home! We are not visitors, never have been and never will be! Do I have feelings of homesickness for America ... No, but for family and dear friends, Yes. The only drawback to *Aliyah* is not being able to share happy and sad occasions with loved ones, and that is a real issue. But, one cannot have everything and that is definitely the downside.

During the Gulf War, it was the only time that I couldn't fathom that I, Ruby Ray Karzen, could be involved personally in a war. War was for books and movies and happened to someone else, not me, a citizen of America. The country has been blessed in not having wars fought on her soil since the Civil War, and I missed that one!

It was eerie to be a part of the scenario. Daily, the newspapers reported the saber rattling of the countries surrounding us. Israel called up the Reserves, now by SMS on telephones, then by code names on the radio. All citizens were issued gas masks and explained how to use them. There were even some ads in the newspapers from the medical community warning that patients who did not bring their gas masks would not be admitted to the office. AACI put out a booklet explaining the orders of making a safe room and other announcements in English. On the radio, a special channel was the designated station on which the Red Alert siren would be heard. We were instructed to keep the radio on, tuned to that station, even on the Sabbath. There was a run on plastic sheeting, tape, bottled water and other necessities in order to create a "Safe Room." The Israel Museum lowered the exhibit of The Dead Sea Scrolls into its specially built war bunker. The country was on a war footing. All airlines except El Al refused to fly to Israel. That was a new low at the time and since then, besides the fact that El Al is probably the safest airline, we try to fly with them. *Hakarat Hatov* and our gratitude to them should never be forgotten. It was getting lonelier with each passing day. But, I never once heard anyone say that they were afraid.

Then it grew quiet. The streets were emptier and the traffic was light. Every night we expected a missile through our salon window, as we are so close to the Knesset. Thank the Good Lord, Jerusalem never experienced any hits throughout any of the conflagrations. We seemed to be protected by a heavenly shield. When the first missile hit the country in the early hours of the morning, my friend Charlotte Gogek (*z'l*), called and asked what we were doing. Her husband had gotten up, dressed, shaved and was sitting on the couch in their salon! Never having experienced a war, people did not know what to do. Sitting in the "Safe Room," wearing a gas mask, watching TV, became boring after awhile, so the telephone was busy. Israelis love their telephones and it was a distraction.

There were comical aspects to this period, also. Once the war began, the hotels were booked with folks from Tel Aviv, as Jerusalem was to be a safer bet. The TA girls would walk down Ben Yehudah Street with their drab, brown gas mask boxes decorated with paints or covered in bright, colored paper, some to match their outfits. The cafes and restaurants were filled by day, as it appeared to be a nighttime war. I was in the midst of a large decorating job. At the time, Avi and I put in regular hours and days of work, hanging pictures, as I recall, with gas masks at our sides. It was a strange feeling. I felt that we were characters in a real life movie.

Not long ago, I was traveling with a client in a taxicab with a typical Israeli driver at the wheel. This gentleman was giving us a non-stop narration of every possible subject, as well as what the

Prime Minister should do in the next few days. Of course, the subject of origins was raised and he related that his ancestors had lived in Morocco for generations. I casually inquired whether relations had been peaceful between the Jews and their neighbors. He waxed poetic about the neighborhood and how life was good and peaceful, except for a pogrom against the Jewish population every now and then. Then he added, "Just like America!" When we explained to him that there had never been pogroms against the Jews there, he stared at us in amazement. He simply didn't believe us and as we exited the cab, he was shaking his head and we're sure that to this day, he is certain that we were not exactly truthful. He couldn't believe his ears that there was a place on earth that never attacked Jews because of their religion.

Our Travels

The story is told of a *Rebbe* who was diligent in his attendance in teaching and never missed a day of class. One day, he announced that he was taking a trip around the United States and would be absent for three weeks. The students were astonished and inquired how can he travel and be *Bitul Zman* (waste time) in the study of the Holy texts. The Rabbi explained, "The Lord created this world for his people. I want to see His handiwork and say the blessing of *Oseh Maasei B'reishit* on appreciating the beauty that he fashioned!"

Travel has always been a priority on our life agenda. Prior to living in Israel, we would visit Israel frequently and tack on another country or two to explore. However, since moving here, the world has been our playground and we have recited the same blessing as the Rabbi expressed above, many times.

By actual count, we have visited over thirty-five countries, and seen the sights of over seventy cities. There is a passage in the Talmud which states that "The Lord sent ten measures of beauty to the world; nine of them were bestowed upon Jerusalem." Perhaps that is so, but there are breathtaking areas that cover the globe in every direction.

THERE WAS A TIME THAT DEVELOPERS had built an area in Mombasa, Kenya in which they were marketing vacation homes to Israelis. For a nominal price which covered the airfare, lodging, touring and all expenses, the public was invited to visit the country and hopefully, purchase an apartment. We quickly took advantage of this opportunity. The plane left every Tuesday morning, packed with holiday revelers bent on seeing this unknown country, with a culture different than anything that we had ever experienced.

We traveled with friends that we had become acquainted with in the absorption center, Ruth and Sid Feibus. As Ruthie tells it, "One bright and early morning, the telephone rings and its Ruby asking if we would like to go to Kenya. Who ever thought of Kenya, but it sounded like fun, and we unhesitatingly said, "Sure, why not?" And I'm so glad that we did.

The country was lush with fauna and flora and green as far as the eye could see. We looked forward to meeting the natives in their own villages, and as there was a safari on the itinerary, exotic animals in their own habitats.

Our hotel was simple, individual units, cottage style with thatch roofs. Each morning, the patio doors opened to the sight of a hundred plus monkeys assembled there with mothers grooming their babies and others playing and jumping from branch to branch. The chattering of the monkeys was accompanied by the large variety of colorful birds, singing and screeching in the same trees. Only in the National Geographic Magazine had we ever taken in a scene like this – it was a far cry from Chicago, or Jerusalem, for that matter.

Each day, a group of six persons would enter into a van with a hatch at the top. While the bus traveled, we would stand and look at the amazing sights of the countryside. There were elephants walking trunk to tail in parade like fashions; huge beasts accompanied by their little ones. Behind a curtain of trees we spied a family of lions, father and mother looking on, as the two cubs frolicked in the tall grass. Once, there was an ostrich which was meandering down the trail and wouldn't move to the side, so the van was forced to creep slowly along following the bird. Antelopes, deer and all types of animals were constantly in view and we craned our necks and turned them from side to side to glimpse this fascinating world.

We visited a Kenyan village complete with teepees, a chief and villagers in colorful, authentic native dress. In the village was the school where the children sang welcome songs while we distributed gifts of paper, pencils, small toys, and puzzles. I wanted to bring pairs of socks, underwear and hair ribbons, but the travel office reminded us that my ideas were indicative of our culture and not theirs. They convinced me that these items would not be welcome, so we brought picture books and school supplies. When the children were performing, I felt like a representative of an occupying power bestowing largess to the poor natives; it was not a pleasant feeling. Women were selling beaded bracelets, necklaces and other trinkets. Everyone purchased something to add some monies to the village economy that they so desperately needed.

One memorable day, we sailed on four types of water transportation in the course of twelve hours. As there were no piers, one had to walk into the water and meet the canoe, raft or small boat. You were then pulled into the vehicle and paddled away. First, we were to travel by canoe. We were each lifted up out of the water, and deposited in the canoe. They paddled to an island where we again were put into the water and made our way to an island. After an hour of exploring, seeing hippopotami, which appeared to be large rocks and huge turtles, we were to meet the rafts. The same process took place, walk into the water, be lifted out and placed on a raft. This time we paddled to an island where there were fish being broiled on outside spits. All the meals were *pareve* or dairy, but it was like dining in the fanciest restaurant with canopies of trees sheltering us from the brilliant sun. After eating, we reversed the process; canoe to raft, raft back to canoe with small boats sandwiched in between. We were in the water and out and then in and out. It was hilarious and upon arriving back to the hotel for dinner, Ruthie and I had laughed so hard and so long, that eating dinner wasn't an option as our stomachs actually hurt from all the hilarity that entire day.

Saba was a bit uncomfortable as he is in the habit of wearing a necktie for all occasions. Had I known of all this water activity, I would have bought him a plastic tie so that he would feel comfortable even being hauled out of the water so many times. As it is, he has a plastic tie for showering. He always wants to be well dressed, being the dapper gentleman that he is!

The Safari Park was the location for an unforgettable adventure. It was located in a jungle, with hanging vines from huge trees, streams of which there was one behind our thatched roof hut, and birds, animals and reptiles were everywhere surrounding us. It was incredible and I was speechless as we absorbed this wonderland. When we were shown to our room, I was sure that we stepped into a movie set. The beds were draped in flowing mosquito netting and a huge fireplace covered one entire wall; in front of it was an animal skin rug with teeth! I kept looking for Lauren Bacall and Humphrey Bogart behind every corner. I was certain that we had seen these interiors in movies; it was incredible!

We were awoken at 4 a.m. and led to a lagoon where animals and birds stood side by side drinking their fill of water and then trundled away. I kept thinking of the UN in New York. Here were natural enemies, minding their own business, just standing at the waters end slurping away. We were warned to keep very still, but we would have, in any case. Our eyes were wide open in disbelief and so astonished at this view that we had no inclination to speak. By the time the sun rose, all of the animals had vanished into the countryside. The birds with colorful parrots among them, also disappeared and the lagoon remained utterly still, awaiting the next morning's drinking session.

Each morning, we would enter a bus with guides that delighted in teaching us a bit of their language and showing off their Hebrew language skills. They had learned not only words and phrases in Hebrew, but had visited Israel and our guide knew the streets of our Jerusalem neighborhood of Rechavia. It was a fantastic trip, one of the best, and we still speak of it. The Kenya adventure for Israelis ended abruptly as a terrorist blew himself up in front of the hotel. It is well known that the good stuff in life doesn't last forever, Kenya vacations included.

FROM THE FJORDS AND WATERFALLs in Norway, Montenegro with its stunning views, from mountaintops to the breathtaking Greek Islands, notably Santorini, the world is indeed breathtaking in its beauty.

Historical venues like Corsica where Napolean was born, Scotland whose every street breathes life into all the historical

novels that I have ever read, Japan and China, whose cultures differ markedly from ours, we found the trips educational, expanding our horizons greatly and worthwhile.

Norway, Fjords, Waterfalls, incredibly beautiful!

Meandering through the old city market of Corfu, we entered a linen shop. To our shock, there was a familiar suit of clothes being displayed. It was that of an inmate in a Concentration Camp, with its black and white stripes, tattered and dirty. The proprietor approached us and explained that it was the clothing that he had worn when he returned to his home after the war. He had put it on display as a memorial to the millions of victims, so that society would never forget the horrors of the Holocaust. It was a display so unexpected that we were in shock.

He then noticed *Saba's Kippa* and inquired if he, by chance, is a Rabbi. Upon his affirmative answer, the storeowner explained that a granddaughter had recently been born, and that as she was the first Jewish addition to Corfu in decades, he would be grateful if *Saba* would name her. Within a few hours the entire Jewish community assembled in the local Synagogue where the child received her Hebrew name in the traditional manner and blessings that she grow to be a true daughter of the People of Israel. This emotional ceremony concluded with the group dancing and the words of *Am Yisrael Chai* filled the small Synagogue. There wasn't a dry eye in the place. Who would believe that a Rabbi who inadvertently arrived on a cruise ship could bring such happiness to a congregation, but he did!

When in London, we take the walking tours that are offered. One of our favorites is the Author and Book route. When the homes of Sherlock Holmes and other notables are pointed out, we gawk along with the other tourists. We find it fascinating.

One Sunday morning, meandering in the posh area of Belgravia, we were following a guide that was outfitted in authentic Elizabethan dress. Approaching us was a dapper gentleman walking two large, well groomed, shaggy dogs. (In truth, it was hard to tell if the man was walking the dogs, or the dogs were walking the man!) As we passed the gentleman, the guide paused, tipped his hat and wished him a hearty "Good Morning." He then introduced us to this elegant person as Andrew Lloyd Weber, the famous composer. He is the composer of such notable musicals as Phantom of The Opera, Evita, Cats and others. At that time, he had seven productions on London's West End Theatre District running simultaneously. Sir Weber was most gracious. What a thrill! Now that's a way to spend a glorious morning in London!

The MSC Cruise line was sailing to Singapore and *Saba* was the Rabbi aboard this magnificent vessel. The ship was a floating, elegant hotel lacking nothing. An art gallery was aboard, which held showings each day and auctions every other day. I spent hours browsing among the artistic pieces. It was such a rare treat! An Oceanographer and a Professor of Astronomy, who lectured on these interesting topics, were part of the rich Scholar-in-Residence Program. We flew to San Diego, California to board the vessel and for the seventeen days at sea, each day brought a new adventure.

December 8th, the day after Pearl Harbor Day, we found ourselves on the island visiting the moving memorial. Standing and inching forward in the long queue, we began conversations

Hearst Castle, Getty Museum, Long Beach, California (A Decorator's Dream Palace!)

with the travelers around us. The usual questions were asked starting with, "Where are you from?" I always proudly answer, Jerusalem, Israel. Now when asked this question abroad, one never knows of the reaction of the answer to it. The couple with whom we were speaking were most obviously not Jewish, as she was wearing a gold cross around her neck. The man was over 6 ft. tall. I came barely up to his chest, beefy, with a large head and red face. When he heard that we were from Israel, he drew me to him in a tight bear hug, making it almost impossible to breathe! Then he exclaimed, "Israel, I love Israel." He was a retired Marine officer who had spent years teaching at the United States War College in Pennsylvania.

Over the years he had many Israeli soldiers in his classes and claims that they were the best; that the others couldn't compare with them. He still communicated with his former students and couldn't stop praising them. He fascinated us describing how his students learned the art of war and battle tactics. I then inquired as to how he teaches about our Six Day War. He grew pensive and answered, "We don't teach The Six Day War as we cannot explain it."

Bora Bora Island, even the name evokes a unique beauty and serenity. Approaching the island is accomplished by small boats as there is no deep water harbor to accommodate a huge cruise ship. As we stepped on land, it began to rain. I correct that, it began to pour "cats and dogs" and it continued for fifteen minutes or so, during the half hour that we were touring. The island is indescribably beautiful, lush with vegetation, a virtual *Gan Eden* and I couldn't help but burst out into song as I am certain that this place was the inspiration for the play "Brigadoon" and the renowned song, "Bali High" from the musical production "South Pacific." It was magical! It was also wet, because of the constant rain and we were soaked through and through. Why the ship's personnel hadn't warned us to bring umbrellas, I can't say, but they didn't.

Transportation to see the sights was provided by taxi service; the driver filled up the car with passengers from the ship and took off. He would follow a dirt road in circular fashion around the island, meanwhile pointing out the various communal facilities, which were few and primitive. There was no school, library, community center or any normal services; all had to be obtained on the mainland. He related to us that there was a very sticky situation with the teenage girls, as the teen pregnancy rate at 65%

Hawaiian Cruise, (Served as Rabbinic Couple, Some Work, Lots of Fun!)

was BECOMING ALARMING! Since there were no facilities for children or youth activities, he thought that perhaps was the problem. We saw one children's playground where the slide and swings were rusty (from all the rain, DUH!) and appeared deserted.

I inquired why he didn't store umbrellas in his trunk for tourists. At the cost of $5 per unit, he would have earned more money on sales than on that short, bumpy ride around the island. He shrugged his shoulders, appeared bored at the prospect; definitely did not possess a head for business. To this day, he is probably still ferrying soaking wet cruise tourists on that rutted road in "Fairyland." But, it was, indeed a wondrous setting!

Micronesia, a tiny North Pacific island, was on the route that our cruise ship was to visit. We were very curious to tour this tiny speck on the map. Why? Because Micronesia is an ally of Israel and constantly votes for us at the United Nations General

Assembly. The old story is that Israel, since its inception, has helped emerging countries all over the globe with agricultural, technical and health care training. All this aid has been forgotten in the other places, but, not Micronesia. The reason appears on their website. It states: "Israel has assisted the Federated States of Micronesia in its early development. We need Israeli expertise, so I don't see a change in our policy anytime soon." It is well known that countries do not have friends, they have interests. Since their and our interests converge, they are now our allies. Needless to say, regardless of the reason, we need all the friends that we can muster.

At any rate, we approached the beach by small boats again due to the lack of a deep water port. From the vessels, all that was visible were a dozen "shops" delineated by vertical poles, no solid walls, canvas roofs, with "floors" of sand. They were "chachka shops." (A chachka shop is an establishment that sells no item that is needed by humans, but trinkets that people love to own!)

Once ashore, we realized that we had not erred. The only building was a small hut, which was a postal office, but unfortunately, they were out of stamps and had nothing for sale. But, no matter, we all searched for something to buy because of their loyalty to our country. We bought seashell bowls that we didn't need and jewelry that we would never wear, just to help the store owners see a bit of profit that day.

Their dress was interesting. Unlike the natives in other locales that we had seen who were attired sparsely, these woman wore cotton dresses with trousers underneath. The men were mostly dressed in pants or Bermuda shorts and shirts; everyone went barefoot. Even though it was beastly hot, modesty in dress appeared to be a value. Were these people religiously observant and their attire an expression of that modesty? We never found out the reason for their uniqueness; it remains an open question.

We thought to explore the land a bit, but beyond the "Shopping Center" there was sand as far as the eye could see. It must have been at best a kilometer until one reached the villages, but after a short while, we turned back to avoid the searing rays of the sun. We climbed aboard the ship, happy to return to civilization, air conditioning and the world as we know it. But, we did wave as we left these folks, our United Nations "Buddies." May they continue to support us for many years to come.

AACI sponsored a series of lectures on the Works of Shakespeare; it was a great success. Pamela Peled, the instructor, suggested that we form a study travel group and visit Stratford-upon-Avon, which is situated among the rolling green hills of England. The group was bivouacked in private Bed and Breakfast homes and except for the *Kashrut* aspect, as I was the lone observant participant, the trip was a learning experience, par excellence, and fun, fun and fun!

The entire area is devoted to The Bard, from the ridiculous to the sublime. Trinkets with his iconic pictures, as well as costly paintings, antique furniture, both authentic and fake, can be purchased in the shops which retain their 15th century atmosphere. There are at least ten stores that are named Ye Olde something or other. The village was charming with cobblestone streets under one's feet, and thatched roofs under the clear blue skies. Costumed guides are found in the various important sites such as the Shakespeare family home or that of Ann Hathaway's cottage. The stream, the Avon, that meanders alongside the city center has a small waterfall and wildlife, such as swans, ducks and geese in large numbers. The loud chorus of "fowl talk", both quacking and honking, fills the air constantly.

Among the surrounding green rolling hills, not far from the Cottswald area, stands Warrick Castle. It is a "working" royal home with its magnificently furnished suites and a cellar that was used as a torture chamber and prison. As I was raised on this lore and always was interested in history as it is portrayed in novels and movies of this era, I was in heaven. A smile was permanently affixed on my face; I had a wonderful time.

There are three entertainment venues nearby each other. Every evening as well as afternoon matinees, there are performances of the The Royal Shakespeare Company who present the entire gamut of his works, in such famous venues as The Swan Theatre. We had indulged in theatergoing each day, but the last production that we saw was memorable. Henry VIII was the work being presented. In the last act, the stage is magnificent as his daughter, Elizabeth I, newly born, is being presented to the court. The set is a riot of royal colors; red, purple and gold. There is even a live horse on stage with brass face armor.

The King is relating how he wishes that this child will grow in a world of peace between neighbors and he waxed eloquently with high hopes for a place where kindness and goodness is the ultimate value. At the ending of this speech, the audience sat immobile and completely quiet, then tumultuous applause rang out. As we were standing, applauding and shouting "Bravo," a rain of small, metallic, gold-colored four leaf clovers wafted down from above. The world became golden, matching the golden stage; it was magical. I collected a few of these bits of gold and carried them in my wallet for years. Whenever I saw them, they reminded me of happy times, a very special trip, indeed!

One day a small ad appeared in the local newspaper. A well known Israeli educator and tour guide was planning to lead a group from London on a Holocaust Tour. She had taken students from Carmel College of London, England on this tour and now, the parents wished to have the same experience. *Saba* had been urging me in that direction and I agreed to join with these Britishers.

As we were the only participants coming from Israel, we had an opportunity to spend three days in Poland before the group arrived. We decided to visit Stashov, the town where the Ray family had lived for over two hundred years. The guide greeted us at Chopin Airport in Warsaw. Josef was a most interesting individual. His hometown was Auschwitz where he was born and bred. When we first heard that, a chill ran up my spine; What were we in for? He soon related that his grandmother was interned and perished there as a political prisoner. As are most guides in every country, he was personable, charming and an excellent guide, helpful in every way. As the Polish language was unrecognizable to us, we were dependant upon him for everything; and he certainly came through.

Stashov is a six to eight hour drive from Warsaw and we arrived there in the late evening. We had explained to Josef my family's involvement in Stashov and when we entered the hotel, he was excited to explain the Raja family situation prior to the war. The hotelkeeper immediately showed me a book which told the history of the town's Jewish population. It was written in Polish, I bought a copy and weeks later, my neighbor, Sol Meyersdorf (*z'l*), did confirm that the slim volume was dedicated to the Jews of Stashov and translated various articles to me.

When we were shown to our large suite, Josef explained that it was the most luxurious set of rooms in the hotel. The owner wanted us to have the best that was available. I was pleasantly surprised at his attitude. The room resembled that of the movie sets in the 1930s, with wallpaper that sported huge red and orange roses, mahogany furniture, burgundy-colored, heavy, velvet draperies and lamps with fringed shades. Of course the lamps were illuminated by at least 20 watt bulbs, making seeing the room most difficult. On the bright side, we had never occupied the best rooms in any hotel!

The next morning we set out to explore the city. The hotel was in a prominent spot on the central square. The square also housed the City Hall, the Courts and other public buildings. On one end of the square stands the train station and half of that building, houses the public library. No matter where we are, I try to find literary places; bookshops and libraries, and assess the number of newspapers published and sold. I find that it is a "Rule of Thumb" to the degree of culture that thrives in the various places. The fact that the library was in so prominent a place, boded well for Stashov; and it stood up to its promise. There were actual bookstores, as well as newsagents with numerous magazines and newspapers for sale. Perhaps, as their Jewish population had been interested in a culture of literacy, by osmosis, it had rubbed off on the general population. Whatever the reason, Stashov was head and shoulders above many places that I have investigated.

In the area where the Jews had lived, we visited one of the residential sites. There was a dilapidated wooden gate with a broken latch. Entering the courtyard we could see depressions on the doorposts of the houses where, at one time *Mezuzot* had been prominently displayed. The homes were built around what could have been the ovens for communal cooking. As we stepped inside the enclosure, an old hag opened her door and yelled at us and spat curse words at us. Josef told us that she was probably afraid that we would want to reclaim "our" property. Frankly, that was the one incident of pure outward hatred towards us, visible during our three-week trip.

City Hall was the next on the itinerary. They had computers, but just a few and Josef recommended that we wait while he navigated the search for birth certificates for the family. After a short wait, Josef bounded into the room with the news that the clerks had found some information, but that it was very expensive to print them out from the computer. I asked him what was the charge and he replied, "Five American cents for each one!" We ecstatically left the building with certificates for four of my cousins who were, most likely murdered in the Holocaust, but the proof was in my hands – the Raja family had lived in Stashov.

Our next stop was the place where the main Synagogue had stood. It had been destroyed and in its place stands a handsome municipal building with an etched stone plaque prominently displayed. On it are carved the words, "On this site stood the Synagogue where six thousand Jews prayed." The words were bordered with a *Magen David* in all four corners.

From the road, The Jewish Cemetery appeared to be located in an overgrown field desolate and forgotten. However, a surprise awaited us when we discovered that a gentleman from London had restored parts of it and had created a touching, large monument by cementing hundreds of tombstone pieces together. We stood in awe of this work. We searched for family graves, reading tombstones, one after the other, but did not find any relating to the Raja family.

A plaque in the Stashov cemetery memorializes the Jews of Stashov who perished in the Holocaust.

Josef read the Stashov book and pointed out many things that we would have missed on our own. Among them were city sidewalks as well as paths leading to private homes that were paved with Jewish tombstones – the Hebrew letters and Jewish symbols still visible on them. We stood at the corner of two streets from which the Jewish population was forced to march, first to the Nazi trains and then, in terror, transported to Treblinka where the majority of them were murdered.

It was finally time to meet up with the group. We took with us plastic bags filled with earth from Israel and an Israeli flag. At the beginning, we would proudly carry and wave the flag by ourselves. Some of the other participants appeared to be embarrassed by this act. However by the end, they were bickering over whose turn it was to have the honor of carrying and being responsible for the Israeli flag.

Our memories of that visit are indelible, powered by the

earth that we brought and spread over the many mass graves
that we visited, and as we cried copious tears hearing the *El
Malay Rachamim* prayer recited. More than a generation of our
oppressors have come and gone, but the seminal hatred of the
Jew lingers on.

It was unlike any other trip that we had undertaken. Arriving in
Auschwitz-Birkeneau Concentration Camp early Friday morning,
the members of the group decided to pray the Morning Prayer
there. The upper room in the famous landmark of Auschwitz
where the trains entered, became a Synagogue and the feeling
upon seeing the men in *Talit* and *Tefilin* in this graveyard was
one of unbearable sorrow, not feelings of satisfaction. Later, the
rooms filled with hair, shoes, suitcases, gold teeth and other items
stolen from the inmates was but a foretaste of the horrors yet to
be seen. The barracks, the yard where the victims stood for hours
in the sweltering heat and unbearable cold with gallows in the
background, all lead to the oven buildings that belched fire and
smoke twenty-four hours a day. Those flames that never slowed,
bringing death to one-third of our People, are halted now, but
anti-Semitism, which was frowned upon by the world for fifty
years, has once again appeared in polite society worldwide. More
than a generation of our oppressors has come and gone.

Perhaps we cannot hold them directly responsible, but we
cannot forget – never can we forget!

In those two weeks we prayed and jubilantly danced at the
memorial place of Rebbe Elimelech of Lisensk. We stared
intently at the Kitchenware factory owned by Oscar Schindler, the
reluctant hero, who saved Jews from extermination by employing
them, claiming that they were needed for the war effort. A
Chicago woman broadcaster is the result of the union of the
couple who were married in this factory, as depicted in the movie
"Schindler's List." We visited mass graves of children, partisans
and Jewish *Korbonot* in forests, fields and rivers. We spread Israeli
earth on every one of these Holy places, while the Israeli flag
stood sentinel over this unbelievable horror.

There were teenagers in the group and more than once we

had to answer their question of "Where was Israel? Where was *Tzahal?*" It was unimaginable to them that the Jews were helpless in the jaws of the Nazi beasts. It was a lesson in reality, World War II style.

We must remain diligent in our resolve to combat discrimination in every place and at every time, but as observantly religious Jews, we also pray to *Hashem* that this never, never again will happen.

The youngsters of Israel, with their schoolmates, go to Poland and observe first hand what happened. It is a very important undertaking, as the survivors are as per nature, dying off and in ten years there will be no living witness to this horrendous era. Our grandson, Benzion, was photographed standing next to the memorial stone which reads Stashov, holding as Israeli flag. That is our triumph, the fact that an Israeli teenager realized the importance of the connection from his past and his future. Israel is the land of the Jewish future ... period.

When we were parting from the group, one of the women, hugged me and said, "Thank you for being my Mum on this trip!" So much for feeling like one of the gang!

When a person returns from a Holocaust experience and tells me that the trip was "Wonderful," I can only stare at them in amazement at that description. The trip was educational, moving, and emotional as well as other words of that kind, all of which are appropriate, but "wonderful" is not anywhere near the mark. Returning to Israel, putting the trip in perspective, reminds us that there is still much *Tikun Olam* that must be done, but, also one must remember to look beyond and see how far we have come!

In the whirlwind of time, Stashov has not been forgotten. There is an active Stashov Research Organization. At one of the meetings, I was excited to meet a gentleman who remembered my grandfather quite well. He was a child at the time and admired the teenage Baruch Raja for his qualities as a leader in that small town. He has since passed away, but I was grateful to him for opening a window to another aspect of the Ray family.

A major achievement of the group has been the procuring of a donation from the Stashov Municipal Government of $200,000 in 1998, which was donated to the Schneider Children Hospital in Petach Tikvah, where a plaque in memory of the once flourishing Jewish population of the city is affixed. The money was given to the group as payment for the site where the main Synagogue once stood. On the building, which is now a newly rebuilt Community Center, a plaque remembers the *Kehilah* that once was.

AACI runs one two-week cruise each year. Mano, an Israeli Cruise Line, is the carrier. Visiting the Bridge, the Captain pointed out the various instruments that are used. Prominently displayed was a framed copy of the Traveler's Prayer – now that's

In China, resting luxuriously!

a ship to depend on!

Saba is known as the "Cruiser *Rebbe*." When he is standing outside the bar, he is known as the "Boozer *Rebbe*" and when he is near the casino, he is the "Loser *Rebbe*!"

As the Ship Rabbi, *Saba* organizes the daily prayer services and is the head of the *Kashrut* Supervisors. I am the *Shlep*-Along. I help the AACI staff and give presentations and lectures on various subjects from Interior Design to Unknown Biblical Heroines. But, my most valuable addition to the cruise does not appear on the program. On deck, trying to read or relax for awhile, I will hear hesitant footsteps approaching and a soft, "*Rebbetzin*, have you a minute?" I think to myself, "Yes, Mam, I'm on this ship with you for two weeks, I think that I have time." I don my virtual *Rebbetzin* Coat and settle myself comfortably to listen to what is always a tale of woe. People need someone to speak with and they pour out their sad story, many times accompanied with tears. I listen attentively and rarely utter a word. On the whole, they don't want advice, neither am I qualified, but they desperately need a willing ear. That I can provide and I'm free! The session usually elicits a comment such as, "Thank you so much, I feel so much better now!" This is one *Mitzvah* that I can do and if a person feels so much better and will enjoy the cruise that much more, I have created one more friend for AACI.

Wisdom To Be A Good Person

This narrative has a double purpose, firstly to hand over to our beloved families, their life-stories that have hopefully brought to life our ancestors. Because of the background information that has been recorded here, we can better comprehend their actions and the milieu in which they lived, that have caused us, their descendants, to arrive at this point in time.

The second purpose is to leave an Ethical Will for our children, grandchildren and great-grandchildren. A document of this kind is a uniquely Jewish idea; a custom which has largely been disregarded in our day. This missive is not a challenge to Death, but a legacy to Life.

Having lost my parents and grandparents at an early age, it is a pleasant surprise to me, as each birthday passes, that I have now reached my seventh decade of life. I have been truly blessed; especially as the sages say, "Who is rich? He who is satisfied with what he possesses." I can honestly say that I have what I require, the rest is just commentary. No doubt, it would be nice to have somewhat better health, additional funds, a bit more intelligence and I could probably think of a few more items, but to reiterate, being *Sameach B'Chelko* is a good place to be.

This book is dedicated to serving as a guide to living a Jewish, moral life both towards *Am Yisrael* and the Good Lord. I distinctly placed *Am Yisrael* first in the list, as we tend to forget that the Ten Commandments list five Commandments to perform towards the Lord and five dealing with people. They are side by side, on purpose.

What comes forth from your mouth, *Lashon Hara* is just as important as what you put into your mouth by observing the laws of *Kashrut.* Being *Sameach B'Chelko* is no mean feat in these times. The outside world is obsessed with materialism. From the pen of an interior designer these words sound out of place. However, there is a place for a comfortable, tasteful home, attractive clothing, jewelry, cars and other luxury items, but the watchword is "Moderation."

Be charitable with not only your money, but your time, talent and heart. One morning, upon entering into one of the largest furniture shops in Jerusalem, that of the Rabbi Kaduri story, I arrived as the owner was speaking on the telephone. By the one-sided conversation, I understood that he was donating the carpeting for an organization. When he finished, I remarked how charitable he was for helping the struggling group.

He looked at me intently and held out his hand in a fist. He explained, "When I hold my hand in a tight fist, *Hashem* cannot keep filling it up with funds, but when I have my hand open, He can keep refilling it. Then I can be generous with the funds with which He constantly showers me."

What a beautiful parable; he taught me a valuable lesson.

We must learn from everyone we meet, from taxicab drivers who discuss the Bible, to grandchildren who are technology oriented and who are happy to instruct their "Tech-Dummy" grandparents.

The society that I grew up in, according to today's world, would be considered monetarily poor, but it was rich in spirituality and morality. A poem, as edited, entitled, "All We Have is Words," by Rabbi Jack Reimer, is a reminder of this philosophy.

> When I was young and fancy free
> My folks had no fine clothes for me,
> All I got was words.
>
> When I was wont to travel far
> They couldn't provide me with a car
> All I got was words.
>
> I wanted to increase my knowledge
> But they couldn't afford to send me to college.
> All I got was words.
>
> The years have flown, the world has turned.
>
> Things I've forgotten,
> Things I've learned,
> Yet I still remember –
>
> Zog dem emes
> Gib Tzedakah
> Hob Rachmanus
> Zy a MENTSH
>
> All I got was words – Yet, I am truly rich.

Mark and Eva Levy (names changed) are extremely generous and charitable. When they built a new house, a novel idea was included. On the lower level, there is a paneled and carpeted room, complete with expressive artwork hanging on the walls, but no furniture. The room is for community events, such as organizational and parlor meetings and such.

When an event is scheduled, Eva orders the amount of tables and chairs required and the rental company picks them up after the affair. Many events have been successfully held in that venue, and the Levys rightly hold the title of "The Hosts with the Most!"

On occasion, I would find myself in Mark's business office. He has a deep feeling of responsibility for *Am Yisrael*. Over the years there have been community situations which required attention; I'm proud to say that, to my knowledge, he never faltered.

I must share with you one of my favorite Mark stories. One time I was visiting with Mark on one of my trips to America. I was there to ask him for a not insignificant amount of money for a mutual friend who lived in Israel. She was ill and her soon-to-be-ex-husband had sued for divorce. She needed the money to pay for the divorce attorney; it was not a pretty story. But she was a friend and Mark readily consented. While there, the phone rang and hearing just one side of the conversation, I believed that I knew what the call concerned. That week, there was a young man who was undergoing a difficult operation. Mark committed himself to another large sum. When the call was finished, I asked Mark if that donation that he just pledged was to cover this person's expenses. He said that it was. "Do you know him?" I inquired. "Not personally," he said, "But he is a deserving person and he needs the community's support." End of story … that's my friend Mark!

Eva and Mark have taken parenthood seriously, and especially as noted, the *Mitzvah* of *Tzedakah* runs deep, as illustrated in this next anecdote. Their children are all phenomenal and have made deep impacts on their community. Son, Dovid, (name changed) was in the eighth grade at a Day School and became chairman of the graduating class *Chesed* Fund. The students were charged with finding creative ways to raise funds for charity. One day, Dovid called the office of his uncle's friend, who was a renowned benefactor of every good cause. He gave his name as Mr. Levy and asked the secretary for an appointment. At the appointed time, the Benefactor looked up from his desk, expecting to see an adult Mr. Levy, when Dovid entered the room. When told of the project, being a person who could always be counted upon to help, he reached for his wallet. "No, No, said Dovid, "Cash won't do ... a check will be fine!" Needless to say, the class never raised as much money for charity before or since. With Dovid at the helm, can one be surprised?

This document records many acts of charity and if you are fortunate in acquiring large sums of money, remember that you are but the caretakers of it. Having met many wealthy people who are truly charitable and realize that the funds allotted to them is to make the world a better place and alleviate suffering, as well as to underwrite projects for the future, which is the correct outlook. But being arrogant because one is wealthy, debasing others not so blessed is ugly. I always joke that I would love to be a philanthropist for the numberless projects in need, as well as to help individuals, when all it would take is money. But the good Lord in his infinite wisdom fears that it would have an adverse effect on me and I would become arrogant because of it. So, He has decreed that I never fall into the wealthy category, so that being arrogant due to having money is one less personality defect that I must worry about!

However, I cannot overemphasize the importance of giving *Tzedakah*. It is one of Judaism's cardinal principles. To be a *Baal Tzedakah* is performing an ideal Jewish act. It need not be a large amount of money (ideally tradition speaks of ten percent or *Maaser*) but getting into the habit of always extending your hand to help the poor and needy is a great holy act. Even a few shekels in the charity box daily gets one in the habit of giving and sharing our resources.

One Thursday afternoon meeting with a client, we were interrupted by Ilana, (name changed) her housekeeper, who had completed her work for the week and was awaiting her pay. The client dismissed her, saying that she would pay her on Sunday. Ilana's face fell as she had intended to shop for *Shabbat* and seemingly would use her salary to purchase food, and now she would not be able to accomplish this. The Torah states that a worker must be paid on time, to avoid this particular situation. I whispered this to my client who quickly found the cash and settled with her loyal housekeeper. Be conscientious in this matter; pay your debts on time!

Being a serious volunteer is charity of the heart. There are hundreds of organizations, medical and social that cover all aspects of life. It would be hard to imagine the low quality of life in Jerusalem without the input of the volunteer. This is a special gift of the Anglo immigrants to Israel. The "How To Do" and "What To Do" has been transferred here and is the envy of many places in the world. Charity and volunteerism must have a special place in every life.

Be generous in spirit. This is harder than it sounds, but again, a MUST quality in the development of a healthy personality. Envy of another's success can be likened to a parasite of the soul – it festers and can destroy you. It happens to everyone – a friend attains success in their work; wins a prestigious award; publishes a book; becomes wealthy; perhaps even wins the lottery or any manner of fortunate circumstances. Be sincere in your happiness for them and don't keep it to yourself. Mark the situation by expressing out loud, telling them how proud you are of them. Be truly pleased that they have attained that level. At times, to be sincere is difficult and this is one of those achievements that can take a lifetime to bring to fruition. Don't think about it – Do it!

The other side of being generous and graceful in the giving of charity of any kind is the expectation of gratitude. Don't expect gratitude. We do good things because we are good people and it is the right thing to do at the time. If you want to see gratitude, look it up under the letter "G" in the dictionary!

Our 25th year of *Aliyah* was approaching, *Saba* and I wanted to mark it in a special way. We decided that donating a Torah Scroll to the IDF would be a fitting tribute to the occasion. Young Israel was the vehicle from which we obtained the Scroll; it was a Holocaust Torah and had been found in a warehouse in Czechoslovakia with others. Hitler, (May his name be blotted out) wanted to assemble scrolls and items of Judaica and display them as artifacts of an extinct People. Our Torah Scroll, after being scrutinized by a Scribe, and repaired to its original holy status, was to be the guest of honor at the ceremony.

However, we had a problem with providing the funds to cover the donation to the Young Israel Organization and repairs. Our experience of years of fundraising for organizations came to the fore. We decided to explain the situation in a letter to friends, old and new, as well as family and former congregants.

It was a Win-Win situation – $14,000 was collected and gave the participants an unusual opportunity to perform a charitable act. Daniel (Mush) Meyers, the Executive Director, who organized the event, was happy; *Tzahal* owned another scroll and we were ecstatic. *Rosh Chodesh Nisan*, 5772, saw four buses wend their way towards the army base in Gush Etzion, near Efrat and Alon Shvut. There was music and dancing accompanying the Scroll to its new home and to be lovingly placed in the Ark of the Synagogue on the base.

When the doors were opened, the two hundred plus guests were faced with something that they had never seen – a totally empty Ark! Immediately, however, our Torah with its new, elegant blue velvet cover came to rest there, comfortable in its new home. I had expected a few refreshments, such as the usual stale cookies and Gatorade, but a surprise was in order for us. With the efforts and prodding of Mush, the Army catered a "Hotel" breakfast. I was astonished. I don't think that I ate even a morsel.

The speeches were brief, but meaningful. However, our guests couldn't stop praising the base commander, who was a young, handsome, Ethiopian *Oleh*. The gist of his words were that we

Torah Dedication, Gush Etzion Tzahal Base, Jay and Grandson, Officer Bentzi Rubin, 2011

were all immigrants, fortunate to live in the State of Israel. Many of the soldiers that joined with us, including him, the guests and even the Torah was now privileged to live in this promised land. Shmuel Katz, a cousin who is a publisher, featured the event in his newsletter. We received comments and congratulations from as far away as Maine in the United States. It was an occasion to remember.

Our Synagogue in Des Plaines, Illinois, closed its doors due to the changing patterns of Jewish neighborhoods, as well as other reasons. Years before, we had requested that the Synagogue Board send one of the Torahs to Israel as they possessed no less than eight and both youth groups and the Army were in desperate need of them. The Board voted to send one, but what to do? We had just presented one, with the ceremony and all the trappings. Eventually, this Torah was given to the IDF, also. But the reception was at the Spy Museum in Tel Aviv and after the ceremonies, it was ferried away to a secret base. No one could say where it was going, but, we know that it will be of use, just as is the first one.

Recently, a friend, who had attended our ceremony, gave a lift to a soldier on his way to his base where our Torah rests. He was enthusiastic about the base having their very own Scroll and he related how it is used for everyday services as well as the Sabbath and Holidays. Sometimes, just sometimes, one does the right thing!

Education is an ongoing process that lasts a lifetime. It doesn't end with a degree from a university.

A man who seeks true wisdom learns from everyone and sees everyday challenges and personal experiences as informal learning.

Saba and I are each other's *Chevruta*, (study partner). It is a wonderful marriage togetherness opportunity and I frequently share this with couples who are engaged to be wed. These people are busy-busy with the details of the wedding bash, which will be a an extravaganza for six hours, but give little thought to what will be going on in their lives for the next fifty years. Everyday, for many years, time is made in our busy lives, to study sacred texts. The Bible, with the chapter of the week, is a favorite, as new observations lead to various explanations, no matter how many years one devotes to it.

We have gone through The Five Books of The Torah with its history, geography and poetry. Whether it has gone through us is another story!

The first time that we completed the entire cadenza, we hosted a dinner for the children and grandchildren. Even those that were in army uniform attended, receiving special permission to attend as their officers had never heard of this type of celebration. The kids tested us and we didn't get more than 75-80% correct – of course, they knew the right answers as they were still studying those passages. We had studied them five years before that night.

It just proves that studying should never end.

One of the best opportunities for learning the Bible is by osmosis and by simply residing here. While we are studying the various texts, we try to make it an actual living experience by visiting the site mentioned in the text. Dan, one of the twelve sons of Isaac, our forefather, is buried not far from Jerusalem, near Bet Shemesh. With text in hand, we walk the site and the Bible actually comes alive.

The legend concerning Dan is one of my favorites. When the Children of Israel were wandering in the desert for forty years, his tribe marched last. They were the original Lost and Found Department. Their task was to pick up the lost items like pots or any item that had been dropped and lost by the Israelites as they journeyed. The tribe of Dan collected these items and kept them safe until they were returned to the owner.

How human is this idea. Having lost so many things during my lifetime, I could have used a couple of "Danites" just for my personal use! I'm certain that somewhere in the stratosphere there is a whole room with my name on the door where the jewelry, scarves, etc. that I have lost can be found!

The tombs of Samuel the Prophet and Shimon the Righteous One, as well as the Little *Sanhedrin* are all within the Jerusalem area, as are the archeological digs currently being uncovered in the *Kotel* area. One fascinating site leads to another and the list is extensive.

The tomb of Rachel, Our Mother, is mere kilometers from our home and we have often visited the site and prayed there – they are all unbelievably inspiring. The Ela Valley where Samson dallied with Delilah is forty minutes by car and the tomb of Absalom is literally a few minutes walk from our front door.

One of these days, we would love to travel to Iran and see the tomb of Esther, the central figure in the Scroll of Esther. Until that is possible, there are the resting places of Prophets, Kings and Judges, as well as important sites from our history to keep us occupied. Day trips to explore the country is a favorite Israeli activity.

A trip to the city of Shechem (Nablus) in the Shomron area, which features prominently in the Bible, was an eye opening, though disturbing, outing. We traveled in a protected bus, i.e. bulletproof windows and army accompaniment. Before the procession of the three buses entered the city, the Israeli flags were removed and we noticed that the soldiers, both within the buses and in the Jeeps that followed, donned plaid and striped sport shirts over their uniforms. At first, we were puzzled, then remembered that the Arabs controlled the city. This was the only way that Israelis could visit the ancient tomb of Joseph the Righteous, who was a son to Jacob, and grandson of Abraham of Biblical fame. It was an embarrassing act to us and we felt humiliated, but we made our way to the ancient tomb, marveled at its history, prayed the Afternoon prayers and let out a sigh of relief as our entourage left the city limits of Shechem. The guards were not happy that we had entered "their" territory and the hate in their eyes was palpable. This was the singular incident that I felt totally unwanted in all of my dealings with our "cousins."

There is another tradition that *Saba* and I have instituted which brings us much pleasure and we would like to share it with you. Between the holidays of *Rosh Hashanah* and *Yom Kippur*, it is traditional to go to a body of water, say prayers and "throw" your sins into the water. *Tashlich* is a colorful practice and most enjoyable. In the nearby neighborhood of Shaarei Chesed there is a well that has been closed and topped by heavy stones for many years. Literally, thousands of worshippers gather each *Rosh Hashanah* to perform this ceremony. They surround this dry well and say the appropriate prayers, but there isn't a drop of water to be seen! *Saba* jokes that they should at least put a jar of gefilte fish on top, as a reminder that there should be water and fish! This practice just didn't seem correct to us and we had to find a meaningful way in which to fulfill this obligation.

The nearby Botanical Gardens is the answer. After the holiday, we go to this beautiful area where, among the thousands of flora and fauna, there is a pond with fish, ducks, turtles and swans gracefully swimming. We say the prayers overlooking this peaceful scene, which includes a Japanese-style bridge and water lily plants. It is not only a scene fit for an artist to record, but spiritual, as well. Nearby is a restaurant which feeds the stomach while the eyes are nourished by this peaceful scene. Each year we have a *Tashlich* Date and we look forward to it as a time to spend with each other – a quality time date, if you will!

There are times in life that one is called upon to bear an uncommon burden, or *Mesirat Nefesh*, i.e. a spiritual burden of the soul. By living outside of a Jewish environment and by the Rabbi and Rabbanit having to be the spiritual rock for congregations, without any spiritual support for their own souls, is difficult. I didn't realize how much twenty-four hour effort it took until we were fortunate to live in Israel and our neighborhood of Rechavia. Praying with an all-observant congregation daily, having the Jewish calendar dictate holidays and Fast Days, and not having to fight outside influences every day, is a totally different situation than when we lived in the States.

I recall that before Cable Television was introduced, there were years that the non-Jewish holiday of XMAS would quietly pass and on December 28th, we would realize that it had come and gone. That would have been impossible in the States. Before the Chabad Organization and all the *Kiruv* efforts which are common today, the pulpit Rabbinical couples were shouldering that burden by themselves. They were raising families constantly going against the norm and by and large successfully.

I still marvel when, before any of the major Jewish holidays here in Israel, an ad in the newspaper appears from the electric company or any public concern, reminding readers that there are special hours due to the upcoming holiday. Or before the Sabbath, everyone, from the supermarket check-out person, to the telephone operator or a taxi driver, wishes one and all A *Shabbat Shalom*. It's a privilege and a pleasure to be the majority and we don't take it for granted for one minute.

Living abroad, you feel Jewishly comfortable when you enter

your home and close the door. Only then do you feel at home. In Israel, you are at home everywhere.

BY AN ACCIDENT OF BIRTH, you were born Jewish, but it was the most fortunate of accidents. Following the Torah, with its ethics and principles, can give you the basis for a meaningful life. It offers one faith in both the Creator as well as his / her fellowman. In the book, "Ethical Wills," Sam Levenson, a very funny man and a successful comedian, offers the following advice. He leaves his children, some four-letter for all occasion words, like "help," "give," "care," "feel" and "love". He describes a successful attitude towards life – the best word description of this approach is "Be a *Mentsh!*" A *Mentsh* utilizes all of the above attributes that Levenson admonished. It is an apt description of a successful human being possessing all of the above qualities.

A optimistic outlook is most desirable. "The Half Glass Full" versus "The Half Glass Empty" philosophy will hold you in good stead every time. A cheerful countenance with a smile on your face will win half the battle before it even begins. For instance, approaching a desk worker, a bank teller or the supermarket check-out person, put a smile on your face – their attitude changes immediately. The overworked, tired, underpaid employee will respond to friendliness and you have made a buddy who will help with whatever is required and return your caring attitude towards them.

One can always tell his troubles to whomever is met, but the truth is that, except for family and close friends, no one cares and you'll be known as an overburdened, sad individual whose company is not desirable. How one reacts everyday to whomever one meets can color the person's day. If in the morning, one greets another in a grouchy manner, both you and the other start your day cheerless. Even worse, if you ignore the person and create the feeling that he or she is not worth your attention – gray is the prevailing color. But if you greet your neighbor with "You look nice today!" or "That color dress truly suits you!" then their day is made, and there is a noticeable lightness to their step and mood. Now the warmth of the color yellow prevails.

However, it goes without saying that sincerity is the watchword. A fake smile or sneer is not what is meant. Even if you initially don't feel really cheerful, turn your lips up and try it; you'll be amazed how much better the world looks to you. As they say, "If you see someone without a smile, give him one of yours!" This motto was emblazoned on a T-Shirt; what a great thought!

A friend relates his experience of moving to Rechavia upon his *Aliyah*. Each morning, going to the Synagogue, he would pass a gentleman walking his dog and wish him a *Boker Tov*. The man would not reply, much less reciprocate the greeting. This went on for a while, with my friend's greeting met with silence. Finally, one morning, the dog said, "Woof." "Now, we're getting somewhere!" he quipped.

Ann Landers, the long time personal problem solving columnist for The Chicago Sun Times newspaper, once conducted an experiment. At a wedding party, she moved along the reception line and at each inquiry of how she was doing, she replied, "My dog just died!" Not a single person heard what she said. They gushed, "That's marvelous and congratulations to you, also." Nobody listened and while this episode could be explained as an exaggerated situation, the truth is that most folks are thinking of their next statement. Empathy or caring and listening is a much needed quality in a person's makeup.

Prayer is important and fortunate is he / she who can benefit from it. When Elimelech, the infant, who made us members in good standing of the Grandparents Club, entered the army, I decided to recite *Tehilim* every day, probably at first, as a lucky charm for his safety. I find it emotionally satisfying. It is as though a cone of spirituality covers me. Each day, I am seated with a list of those who need special blessings from The Lord Above, whether because they are sick or in a place where His blessings with special attention are required, and in quiet contemplation,

I speak to my G-D. I find it meaningful as it is personal, while intoning the regular prayers for morning, afternoon and evening are strictly regulated with little room for personal devotion. By now, we have had eleven precious grandchildren (spouses included) complete either the Army or National Service; five are currently on active duty. We have had the good fortune and *Nachas* of a number of officers among them.

Grandson Benzion is an officer in Intelligence and he is currently on the Syrian border, which has been increasingly active due to the war raging in that country. I asked him recently if it is quiet there. His answer could have been given by any number of our Israeli soldiers who are serving with dedication and distinction. He replied, "No, Savta, it isn't exactly quiet, but we, *Tzahal*, are there and we know what to do, so that you can go about your life and sleep well in Jerusalem. I just hugged and kissed him and tried to hide my tears of admiration. There is no reply to that statement.

I was scheduled to have a medical procedure at Bikur Cholim Hospital early one morning, but when I arrived the nurse announced that due to an emergency the doctor would be late. There were a few prayer books visible and I thought that it was a good opportunity to pray the Morning service. However, it was summer and with no scarf handy to cover my head, what to do? I needed something. I couldn't pray bareheaded. I spied a newspaper and fashioned a paper pirate's hat. Had I a sword I could have fought off every pirate ship sailing up Strauss Street, all by myself! Sitting in a corner, topped with my pirate's hat, I could feel the other patient's eyes boring into this strange looking person. Who cares? I had enough time to finish the Morning prayers and should I have needed to recite the additional prayers, I could have finished those as well! I must have been the main topic at many dinner tables that evening. The main thing is that valuable time was not wasted, but spent in a significant way.

Praying and requesting blessings is most natural and fine, but don't forget to say "Thank You" as well. A cartoon appeared which depicted Heaven with two structures; one a large mansion with a sign that read PRAYERS. There was a large crowd waiting at the entrance and it was a bustling place. The other building was a small shack with a sign reading THANKS. Other than one person waiting to enter, the place was deserted. Let the words "*Todah*," "Thank you," "Thanks" and other similar phrases be an integral part of your vocabulary.

Just remember to count your blessings and don't make mistakes in the arithmetic!

CARING FOR OTHERS IS A TRAIT which cannot be overestimated. Whether for the feelings of others, their health, or welfare, it is one of the cornerstones of humanity.

One of our grandfather friends related this meaningful and charming incident to us. Barry Rosen, a widower, was at the Sabbath table surrounded by his family, his children and grandchildren and had just concluded blessing each child in turn, as is the traditional practice. His four-year-old granddaughter raised her hand and wanted to speak. She said, "*Saba*, can I bless you. You blessed everybody and nobody blessed you." "Of course," answered her grandfather, who was sincerely touched by her request. She got down from her chair, walked over to him, put her hands on his head as he had done earlier and said, "*Hamotzee Lechem Min Haaretz!*" (It was the blessing over bread, not people, but it was done from the heart!)

One of *Saba's Rabaim* (teachers) at the *Yeshiva* was Herzl Kaplan (*z'l*). He was a modest, soft spoken, excellent *Rebbe* and his students loved him. Just a few years before our move to Israel, his wife was a patient at Lutheran General Hospital, which was a few blocks from our home. Prior to Passover, Rabbi Kaplan telephoned to request that he spend the *Seder* nights of the holiday with us. By doing that, he could visit his wife on the holiday, as his home was too far away. Of course, he was most welcome. However we were surprised at the request as the rules for Passover food preparation are very stringent and at that time, people generally celebrated the holiday within the confines of their home.

The *Seder* with the *Rebbe* was a unique experience. Besides his erudite commentary on the *Haggadah* and his general fine demeanor, he was concerned about my welfare. After each course, he would help me return the dishes and platters to the kitchen. When I insisted that he needn't help with the serving, he smiled and said to please allow him to do it, as for years he helped his wife in the same manner. He cared about her and now me, that we shouldn't overwork from the holiday's strenuous efforts. He was a wonderful, caring individual and an example for all to emulate.

THERE ARE TIMES IN THE YEAR where feelings of spirituality is palpable, especially in Jerusalem. *Tisha B'Av* is one such example. The "Three Weeks" leading up to this twenty-six-hour Fast Day has rules that make this a quiet time in the social calendar. There are no weddings or musical public events scheduled. Places of entertainment, such as movies and theater, are avoided. New clothing is not worn and "low key" is the watchword. The "Nine Days" preceding the Fast are even more stringent with the prohibition of eating meat or drinking wine except on the Sabbath. The Fast Day itself, besides not eating or drinking, also prohibits the wearing of leather shoes and is also marked by the reciting of the *Kinot* prayers.

Every year, the Three Weeks, followed by this important Fast, comes and goes and is marked by its place in the calendar, and then it passes. But, not this year. The sad *Tisha B'Av* atmosphere lingered overtime, because of events that occurred. The newspaper that we read each morning became impossible to comprehend, as it carried one sad column after another, day after day, reporting the local happenings.

An explanation is in order. The First and Second Temples that stood in Jerusalem over two thousand years ago were destroyed on *Tisha B'Av* by our enemies, mostly because of the baseless hatred of fellow Jews. This year, the election of the Chief Rabbis took place. Each day saw uglier verbal assaults being thrown at the candidates and their followers. One of the most important axioms of the Jewish religion is that if one embarrasses another person in public, it is as though one has killed him. The venom, the cruel words, sickened me as well as many other readers. To top off this sad situation was the fact that five tots were inadvertently left in cars and were broiled to death. The public atmosphere was one of tragedy; people spoke of little else.

One day as *Saba* returned from the Synagogue after reciting the Morning prayers, he found me reading the paper and tears were rolling down my cheeks. The name calling, the vitriolic attacks and the deaths had finally taken its toll. Have we learned nothing? Does anyone really think that the eating of dairy foods, wearing non-leather shoes, not listening to music and all of the other rules and regulations of this sad period in our history absolve them of acting decently toward their fellow man? I think not. This *Tisha B'Av* season, with all of its sad happenings that has finally passed, took six weeks instead of three. I only pray that these abominable happenings never occur again, but I wouldn't bet on it. Baseless Hatred is as common as mosquitoes in summer and one must be eternally on guard.

THE STATEMENT, "NEVER GO TO BED ANGRY" (at your spouse) is well known, but, I would take it even farther. The word Anger is just short one letter from Danger. Yes, someone hurt your feelings by (pick one or maybe all three): 1) insulting / belittling you; 2) ignoring you; 3) treating you in an unfair manner. It happens sometimes even inadvertently, much less, on purpose.

How do you handle the situation? 1) be a bigger person and take the high road and try to dissipate the situation or 2) hold a grudge and never speak to that person, his / her children and even his pets forever? This can be a lifelong repair job to one's personality.

There is a passage in the Talmud which states that you can tell the character of a person by three avenues: 1) his way of dealing with the idea of charity – his pocket; 2) his way in dealing with his anger – his temper and 3) the matter of drinking sensibly and responsibly – his cup.

There was a misunderstanding with one of the members of our community and she ceased being the friendly person that we had known for years. We realized that she must be unhappy about something and approached her to try to understand the situation. In truth, we had done nothing untoward, but she was hurt and we apologized. It was inconceivable to me that a person whom we see regularly should hold a grudge. Take the high road by putting your ego aside – apologize sincerely and go on with your lives. Life is too short to cross a friend off one's list for angry words.

There is a story of the father who finds out that his son has badly embarrassed a friend and rightly deserves punishment. The father takes the boy out to the barn and with a hammer bangs in a large nail in the barn door. After scolding him and explaining the wrong that the boy had committed against his friend, he extracted the nail from the wood and showed his son that although the nail was removed, the hole remained.

So it is after a confrontation with another person; one may sincerely apologize, but the hole, i.e. the hurt, will remain. "Think Before You Speak" or as it is said, not only in jest, "Place brain in gear before use!"

Friendship

Throughout these pages, names of friends crop up from time to time. These references belie the importance that I have always placed on friendships that we have enjoyed from childhood up to the present day. Besides the practical aspects of having friends who are concerned about you and whom you sincerely love, the emotional benefits of having true friends is invaluable.

Friends are hidden treasures, as they say, "A close neighbor is better than a far brother."

Diskin Street is "Angloville" and on any given *Shabbat*, at festive meals, we enjoy sharing it with wonderful people that we have come to regard as family. It is impossible to list all whom we regard as indispensable to our lives, but my buddy, Vivien

Auerbach, must be singled out. Each *Shabbat,* a soft knock is heard as Vivien comes to visit and we share our lives. Suffice it to say when her husband returns from Evening prayers with *Saba,* world problems, as well as those of friends and families, have been sorted out between us. We comprise a think tank of two and cover the world of books, art, politics and any additional area that pops up and interests us. We challenge each other's thinking. Every woman needs a confidant and a pal such as Vivien; without it there is a hole in one's life experience.

Find friends and treasure them. As one matures, one finds that it is more pleasurable to give than to receive – that's the important aspect of friendship.

There are so many lovely memories and countless occasions, both happy and sad, that we have spent with our friends over the years, wherever we have lived. The axiom, "To have a friend, You must be a friend" is a truism without an expiration date, and I sincerely believe that to be so. On my calendar are the birthdays of Beverly Serlin and Chaya Reiss, of the Betsy, Tacy and Tib triumvirate; and they receive birthday cards from "Tib" every year.

There have been an inordinate amount of deaths, especially due to Cancer, among my childhood friends. I have seriously given thought to the fact that perhaps there was a large amount of asbestos in the walls of the schools which we attended. With my personal history of losses, it is, no doubt, a part of my psyche and plays a part in my psychological makeup. It would be hard to think otherwise.

When Barbara (*z'l*), Sherwin's first wife, passed away, I was inconsolable. Even though it was expected, her death left me reeling. Barbara was the type of friend who truly cared about you. She once gave me a birthday gift of a Ruby Red zippered notebook to mark not only my important day, but the official launching of Ruby Ray Karzen Interiors. In those days, in Israel, it was difficult to find any product that was stylish or colorful. People were still wearing "*Dubonim*" (drab Israeli military style jackets) for winter coats, as fashionable outerwear was considered being "spoiled" by luxury. That was a lingering mindset in the 80s. I appreciated the fact that Barb had spent much time running from store to store to find my beautiful gift; I loved it. But, that was her nature. She was a good friend and wanted to make me happy.

One morning we decided to meet in a Ben Yehudah Street Café for breakfast. She drove from Ramot and I walked from home. Finishing the meal, we decided to walk to the La Romme Hotel (Inbal) where she had parked her car. It was a beautiful day and walking past the Plaza Hotel where they were having a Strawberry Festival, we decided to partake of their special offering. We both loved the special fruit dish served in a Sundae glass. We joked, laughed and enjoyed the time together. We left the Plaza and continued meandering to the La Romme Hotel. By the time we arrived there, we took note that since it was February (strawberry season in Israel) they were also featuring a Strawberry festival. We couldn't pass it by and enjoyed their special, too! What an unforgettable day! That was our buddy, Barbara. Myrna (still living in the USA), the third leg of the triumvirate and I had wonderful adventures together, never to be experienced again. Very Special Friends!

For three days after the news came that our Barb had passed, I was in deep mourning. I couldn't shake or lessen the sadness. The third evening as I lay in bed with tears still falling, I felt the spirit of Barbara telling me that I should not be sad and I felt as if she was tucking me in … and strangely I did feel comforted. I have no explanation for this, but it happened and I still miss her

Rachel (Babad) Bruckenstein, whom I met in second grade, was another dear friend who died too young. She also succumbed to Cancer at an age when she should have been enjoying her "*Savtahood.*"

It was September and looking to buy an outfit for the Holidays, we came across a Tartan plaid pleated skirt decorated in the front with a very large gold colored safety pin, in the blue-grey plaid that we had worn in high school. It had been all the rage at that time and each fashionably dressed girl had to have one. We each bought a skirt and decided that we would wear it on a special occasion. As we both had birthdays in May and according to the Social Security rules of the US, we had to register at the Consulate three months before, to begin receiving Social Security checks. We concocted a great plan. In February, we would go to the SS office, sign up and then have a festive lunch with our husbands to celebrate the occasion. We were going to be rich, collecting those checks! And the kicker was that we were going to both wear our "twin" skirts.

Well, the Yiddish expression that *"Men Tracht, un G-ott Lacht,"* loosely translated as, "Man proposes and G-D disposes" was carried out. The scenario never happened as Rachel died in November. However, I carried out the plan solo. I went to the Consulate, signed up, and went to a somber lunch wearing my "Rachel" skirt with *Saba*.

Pictures of both these special people hang on my kitchen cabinet. Their smiling faces remind me of happy times and friendships that will always be dear to me.

YOU ONLY RECEIVE ONE BODY per person. Take care of it. Don't neglect your health and don't take it for granted. The great Sage, Maimonides, writes that moderation in all matters physical is the best preventive to insure good health. Don't take good health for granted, it is the greatest of blessings.

Leisure time is not a luxury. The mind and body desperately need a break from the daily routine from time to time. We are all aware of individuals who are workaholics; who even if they are on vacation have their cellphones glued to their ears. One can be certain that no epitaph on a tombstone has ever been engraved that states, "I should have spent more time at the office!"

Stress can harm the body as well as shorten one's life. If a longer vacation is untenable, try this … for even an hour or two, take a stroll in a park or a quiet place; remove yourself from the four familiar walls and clear your head. You will return from it with your spark plugs renewed with vim and vigor and don't be surprised that additional creative thoughts will pop up in all that renewed energy!

Find meaningful work. I can think of few other situations as sad as waking up each morning and dreading facing the day. Not so long ago, people would spend their lives in one job and receive the ubiquitous gold watch after twenty-five years of service. It was a mind set and offered security for one's entire working life. Today, the work place has changed dramatically. There are opportunities for new employment that did not even exist yesterday.

Ruby's Treasures (children, grandchildren) as depicted on a memento of her 70th birthday

Don't be afraid to explore and change direction. Waking up each morning, feeling excitement at the schedule for the day and falling asleep with the satisfaction of a job well done is a blessing. Make a difference for good in whatever endeavor you choose. A life with purpose is a life of blessing and joy.

I heard a report the other day that the many deep problems that America is facing can be placed on the doorstep of the breakup of the family unit. Whether it is fatherless families, divorce, drugs, alcoholism or other evils in society, the expert traced them, one by one, to the family and its decline in society's structure.

Caring about others should have a high priority spot on your To-Do list. Nothing worthwhile comes by chance; relationships are hard work – husbands and wives, in-laws and family members.

Remember the maxim … "To have a friend, You must be a friend."

When daughter Tammy was once speaking about her *Ima*, she mentioned that everyone knew that according to her *Ima*, the family comes first – not sometimes, not often, but always, and she was right. At occasions, when we are all, almost thirty souls, (*Ken Yirbu!*) sitting together, *Saba* and I will look at each other and say, "Is this possible? Are all these beautiful (inside and out) people, because of that Sabbath in Camp *Moshava*? What blessings has the Lord showered upon us!" These are our treasures, our jewels, incomparable with any physical possessions.

From time to time, we learn of folks that have seemingly fulfilled their heart's desire. They have managed to obtain a 40" TV or a diamond bracelet (for a paltry $18,000, no joke!) or a luxury car such as a Jaguar, and they truly enjoy these luxuries. Truthfully, I am happy for them, but that's not my and hopefully not your style.

This refers to siblings, also. Sisters and brothers are the only humans on earth who share your history, who knew you "when"

The Karzen Klan at our Purim Celebration, 2012

and who love you no matter what happens. I hope that you will not only love, but like each other as well.

Over the years, thoughtless acts have been committed against us, by brothers and sisters. However, no matter what our siblings say or do, we will NEVER, NEVER stop talking to them.

When my Father suddenly died, he was not on speaking terms

with his brother and sister-in-law – a stupid quarrel about nothing was their last exchange; how impossibly sad. That was the Ray side of the family. The Karzens were just as bad in this type of situation, as noted in these writings concerning the wedding of Uri and Shelli.

At one time, my first cousins numbered thirty-six; presently there are seventeen living, and with whom we are in contact. Each one has high regard for family members. We have especially enjoyed the company of many of their children who have spent time in the Yeshivot and Seminaries of Jerusalem.

Daughter Tammy was overseeing the writing of a will on behalf of a couple who were our friends. The couple began to argue about which child would inherit what object, as they were concerned that they had to be fair to each child and didn't want any disagreements between their children as to the disbursements of the document. Tammy told them straight out that her mother had told her and her brother in a "Don't argue with me!" statement that if they fought over their parents Will, that her mother would come back to haunt them and she believes this! (Note: "Yes, I Will!")

Our Sages tell us that 30 days before a child is born, the future mate is announced; our announcement rang out loud and clear. Incredibly, *Saba* and I have spent almost sixty years together, loving, caring and sharing. If anyone ever tells you that they are involved in a relationship and have never had an argument, they are either telling a fib or have a poor memory!

Compromise is not a dirty word. In any relationship it is essential. However, taking one's spouse for granted is the death knell for a marriage. As is indicated by the statistics of 50% divorce rate, there is apparently too much "taking spouses for granted" and boredom rules in too many instances. Don't let it happen to you! Even a mundane activity can be labeled an adventure; enjoy each other and try to live in the moment.

As this homily states: "The *past* is history; the *future* is mystery. But *now* is a gift; that's why it's called the *present*!"

Take the initiative and make a date with each other. Spend time with each other alone, if only for an hour by taking a walk or having coffee together, away from the house, without children or friends. This break is just for the two of you and it's especially pleasant if the main topic of conversation is not the leaky kitchen faucet!

Be verbal in your declaration of love. I understand that it may not be your style, but the following story best illustrates the point. After the funeral, the husband refused to leave his wife's grave. The Rabbi urged the new widower to accompany him back to the car, as the sky was quickly darkening. "Rabbi, I loved my wife," the man exclaimed. "I'm sure you did. You were a wonderful couple!" But, Rabbi, you don't understand. I loved my wife and once I almost told her so." The wife never heard those three magic words, "I love you" or "You are special to me!" This is the saddest story I know.

Saba is my friend, my confident, my moral compass, my teacher and one of the best inspirational public speakers that I have ever had the good luck to hear and follow.

There was a marvelous public speaker named Leo Buscaglia. He inspired hundreds of thousands to lead happier and fulfilling lives by being moral, simply "good people," who cared for the guy next to him. That is *Saba*, with his good nature and wonderful qualities, we have overcome many shoals of life. I love this man and I tell him by word and deed every day … may it continue.

The "A" Team!

This Ethical Will and history book is at its end. An inheritance of possessions can be a wonderful thing, but it is not enough. I wish to gift you with another idea – this work is meant to leave to you values and a way of life that will give it true and substantial meaning.

With laughter and a few tears, I hope that I brought to you the past, that it is life-affirming and teaches about our illustrious family as well as vanished communities and times that will never return. We always look to the future, but only by knowing the past can you traverse it well.

Your Loving Ima, Savta and Savta Raba
Ruby Ray Karzen

Erev Rosh Hashanah 5773 (2013)

Bibliography

Cutler, Irving, Images of America – Chicago's Jewish West Side, Canada: Arcadia Publishing, 2009

Cutler, Irving, The Jews of Chicago – From Shtetl to Suburb, Illinois: University of Illinois Press, 1996

Rubens, Bernice, *Brothers*, London: Hamish Hamilton London, 1983

Reimer, Jack and Stampfer, Nathaniel, Ethical Wills / A Modern Jewish Treasury, New York: Schocken Books, 1983

Schor, Bayla, This Song (Hashira Hazot), Israel: Tzionim Hotzaah L'Or, 2011

Chicago Jewish Academy Senior Class – Memoirs, Chicago: Sovereign – Marmel Press, 1955

Cyberspace: Professor Google-Sites – Iowa, Buffet, Micronesia, Ancestors.com

Jerusalem Post Article: My Working Week, 2012

Michael Lando, Ellis Island – It's where we got our start.

Poem: All We Have Is Words, Excerpt from Sermon material of Rabbi Jack Reimer.

Song: The Return, Excerpt from the musical Esther and the Secrets of the King's Court, Arlene Chertoff, Toby Klein Greenwald, Sharon Katz, 2002 Bible Arts Production

Glossary

BELOW ARE EXPLANATIONS of the many words from Hebrew (H) and Yiddish (Y) used in this book.

Abba (H) – Father
Agunah (H) – A "chained" wife unable to obtain a Jewish divorce
Alav HaShalom (H) – May he rest in peace
Aliyah (H) – One who emigrates to Israel
Amit (H) – Women's Zionist organization
Am Yisrael (H) – The People of Israel
Am Yisrael Chai (H) – The People of Israel Live!
Aron HaKodesh (H) – The Holy Ark containing the Torah Scrolls
Asher Bara Sason V'Simcha (H) – From the marriage ceremony
Asimon (H) – Slug used for payphones in the early days of State
Ashkenaz (H) – Jews who descend from European stock

Baal Tefilah (pl. *Baalay Tefilah*) (H) – One who
     chants the Synagogue service
Baal Tzedekah – (H) A contributor to charity
Balabusta (Y) – Jewish homemaker
Balagan (H) – Slang for chaos
Bar Mitzvah (H) – Ceremony for 13-year-old boy to adulthood
Baruch Hashem (H) Expression for Thank God (or Blessed be God)
Bat Mitzvah (H) – A Girl at age 12 assumes adult status
Bashert (Y) – Concept that life is predestined – fate
Bayit Neeman B'Yisrael (H) – Privilege to build an ideal Jewish home
Ben Bayit (H) – "Adopted" person for Shabbat
     / Yom Tov at a caring home
Ben Torah (H) – A "Son of Torah" – a serious Torah scholar

Ben Yehudah (H) – Popular street in the center of Jerusalem
Bet Shimush (H) – Archaic for toilet
Bimah (H) – Platform or stage
Bituach Leumi (H) – Israeli Social Security
Bitul Zman (H) – Wasting time
Blatt Gemorah (H/Y) – Page of the Talmud
Bnai Brith (H) – Popular Jewish men's organization
Bnei Akiva (H) – Religious Zionist youth organization
Bogrim (H) – Senior students of Zionist organization
Boker Tov (H) – Good morning
Brit Milah (Bris) (H) – Ritual circumcision
Brustdeckel (Y) – Inexpensive cut of meat
Bubbe (Y) – Grandmother / *Savta* (H)

Cafe Hafuch (H) – Latte / Coffee
Chabad (H) – Lubavitch movement
Chag (pl. *Chagim*) (H) – Holiday(s)
Chag Samayach (H) – Happy Holiday
Challah (pl. *Challot*) (H) – Braided loaf of bread for the Sabbath
Chanukah (H) – Holiday celebrating rededication
    of the Temple in 165 BCE
Chap A Mincha (Y) – "Catch'" a Mincha Service
Charedi – (H) Ultra Orthodox in practice
Chashuv (H) – Prestigious
Chassid (pl. *Chassidim*) (H) – Pious people who follow a *Rebbe*
Chatan (H) – Bridegroom
Chazan (H) – Cantor
Cheder (H) – Classroom for religious instruction
Cheder Ochel (H) – Dining room
Chesed (H) – Act of kindness
Chevruta (H) – Torah study partner
Chizuk (H) – To give strength
Cholent (Y) – Sabbath food (casserole)
Chupah (H) – The Wedding canopy
Churban (H) – Destruction (of the Temple)
Chut Hameshulash (H) – 3-fold cord – Expression
    found in Biblical writings

Chutzpah (H) – Impudence / NERVE!

Daven (Y) – To pray
Drasha (H) – The Rabbi's sermon or Dvar Torah

Ehrlich Yid (Y) – A respectable / honorable Jew
El Al (H) – The official Israeli airline
El Malay Rachamim (H) – "God is full of compassion" – Memorial prayer
Eretz Yisrael (H) – The Land of Israel
Erev (H) – Sabbath and Holiday Eve
Eruv (H) – Enclosed area which permits carrying on the Sabbath

Farfel (Y) – Food / Grain delicacy
Felafel (H) – Israel signature food; Chickpeas
Frier (H / Y) – To be a sucker!

Galitzianer (Y) – Family roots stem from Galitzia
Gan (H) – Garden, Kindergarten
Gan Eden (H) – Heaven / Paradise
Gaon (H) – Genius
Geknipt Un Gebinden (Y) – Intertwined
Gemach (H) – Free Loan Society
Gett (H) – Jewish religious divorce document
Gib Tzedakah (Y) – Give charity
Goldena Medina (Y) – Reference to America as the "Golden Country"
Gut Shabbos (Y) – Have a joyous Sabbath

Hachshara (H) – Program preparing candidates for *Aliyah* to Israel
Hadassah (H) – Women's organization supporting Hadassah Hospital
Haftorah (H) – Section from the Prophets read on the Sabbath
Haggadah (H) – Prayer booklet used for the Passover Seder
Hakafot (H) – Dancing with the Torahs on Simchat Torah
Hakarat Hatov (H) – Acknowledging / Applauding positive actions
Halacha (H) – Body of law governing the Jewish way of life
Halleluyah (H) – "Praise Be To G-d"
Hamantaschen (H) – Purim holiday delicacy

Harei At Mekudeshet Li (H) – "Behold you are consecrated
    to me" – from the wedding ceremony
Hashem (H) – Almighty God (literally "The Name")
Havdalah (H) – Ceremony ending the Sabbath
    using wine, spices and candle
Hatikvah (H) – Israeli national anthem
Hatzlacha (H) – Be successful!
Hob Rachmanus (Y) – Have compassion
Hocking (Y) – Verbal Disturbance

Ima (H) – Mother

Kabbalat Shabbat (H) – Friday evening service
    ushering in the Sabbath
Kablan (H) – Building contractor
Kaddish (H) – Mourners prayer recited at Synagogue services
Kapota (Y) – Black Chassidic coat
Kashering (H / Y) – Making food / utensils permissible
Kashrut (H) – Kosher, The Jewish dietary laws
Kavod (H) – Honor
Kayn Yirbu (H) – May they increase
Kedoshim (H) – Holy martyrs
Kehilah (H) – Organized Jewish community
Ketubah (H) – Jewish marriage document
Ketzeleh (Y) – A "Cat"; Term of endearment for a child
Kibbitzing (Y) – Joking around
Kibbutz (H) – Israeli collective farm (*Kibbutznik* – Person)
Kiddush (H) – Sanctification of the Sabbath
    / Holiday with a cup of wine
Kichel (Y) – Sugar cookies
Kippa (pl. *Kippot*) (H) – Skullcap / Yarmulka (Y)
Kinot (H) – Dirges recited on Tisha B'Av
Kita Aleph (H) – First grade
Klay Kodesh (H) – Clergy
Knesset (H) – Israeli Parliament
Kochalein (Y) – Vacation bungalows

Kol Bo (H) – A Multi-talented Jew (Rituals)
Kollel (H) – Advanced Torah study for married students
Kol Hakavod (H) – Expression of appreciation
Korbonot (H) – Those who perished in Holocaust
Kosher (H) – Literally "Fit and Proper" food or rituals objects
Kotel (H) – Jerusalem's Western Wall of the ancient Temple
Kugel / Kneidlach / Kreplach (Y) – Jewish "K" rations
Kumzitz (Y) – Gathering around the bonfire

Lag B'Omer – (H) – Minor holiday
Landsmanshaft (Y) – Association from the same geographic area
Lashon Hara (H) – Sin of gossip
L'Chaim (H) – A toast to "Life" with cup of wine
L'Havdil (H) – To differentiate between
Lishka (H) – Office
Litvak (Y) – Family roots from Lithuania
Lulav (H) – Palm branch used on the festival of Sukkot

Maaser (H) – Tithing to charity
Mabul (H) – Flood
Machane Yehudah (H) – Jerusalem outdoor market
Machatanim (H / Y) – Parents of in-law spouse
Magen David (H) – Star of David
Mah? (H) – WHAT?
Makolet (H) – Corner grocery store
Matzah (pl. *Matzot)* (H) – Unleavened bread used during Passover
Mazal Tov (H) – Good luck / congratulations!
Megilat Esther (H) – Book of Esther
Melamed (H) – Teacher
Melucha (H) – Kingdom
Mentsh (*Mentshlichkeit*) (Y) – Quality human being who
     acts with proper conduct / behavior / morality
Merkaz Klitah (H) – Absorption center for *Olim*
Meshulach (pl. *M'shulachim*) (H) – Emissary to collect charity
Meshuga / Meshugana / Meshugas (H) – Crazy! / Nuts! / Craziness
Mesirat Nefesh (H) – Spiritual self-sacrifice

Mezuzah (H) – Scroll affixed to the doorposts of a Jewish home
Midrash (H) – Rabbinic commentaries on the scriptures
Mikvah (H) – Ritual Bath
Mincha (H) – The Daily Afternoon Prayer Service
Minyan (H) – Prayer quorum (Ten males)
Miklat (H) – Bomb Shelter
Misrad HaChutz (H) – Office of Foreign Affairs Ministry
Mitzvah (pl. *Mitzvot*) (H) – Commandment of Torah
Mnachem Avel (H) – Condolence call
Moshava (H) – As in Camp Moshava
Mohel (H) – Circumcision specialist for Brit Milah
Montag un Donorshtag (Y) Expression for Monday and Thursday
Mosad (H) – Israeli Secret Service
Motzai Shabbat (H) – Saturday evening
Musaf (H) – "Additional" prayers for the Sabbath

Nachas (H) – Pleasure and joy from children
Neshey Chayil (H) – Women of Valor
Nosh (Y) – Snack

Oleh (f. *Olah* and pl. *Olim*) (H) – One who makes *Aliyah* to Israel
Ois Reden Di Hartz (Y) – Share your problems
Oy Vey (Y) – Oh my goodness!

Pareve (H) – Not meat or dairy – Neutral
Pesach (H) – The holiday of Passover
Parah Adumah (H) – Refers to the Biblical Red Heifer
Purim (H) – Holiday celebrating victory over enemies in Persia

Rav (H) – Rabbi, teacher, spiritual leader
Rabbanit (H) – Wife of a Rabbi (*Rebbetzin*)
Rebbe (H) – Loving term, refers to a Rabbi
Rosh Chodesh (H) – First day of the Hebrew month
Rosh Hashanah (H) – Holiday celebrating the Jewish new year
Rosh Yeshiva (H) – Head / chief Rabbi of a Rabbinical seminary

Saba (H) – Grandfather (*Zayda*) (Y)

Sabra (H) – Native Israeli

Sameach (H) – Happy!

Sanhedrin (H) – Ancient Supreme Rabbinic Court

Savta (H) – Grandmother (Bubbe) (Y)

Savta Raba (H) – Great-grandmother

Sameach B'Chelko (H) – One satisfied with his / her lot in life

S'chach (H) – Foliage to cover sukkah

Sefard (pl. *Sefardim*) (H) – Jews whose roots stem
    from Mediterranean / Mideast areas

Seder (pl. *Sedorim*) (H) – Family home celebration on Passover eve

Sefer Torah (H) – Scroll of The Torah

Seforim (H) – Books

Selicha (H) – A Penitential Prayer

Selichot (H) – High Holiday seasonal penitential prayers

Semicha (H) – Rabbinic ordination

Shabbat (Shabbos) (H / Y) – The Sabbath

Shabbat Shalom (H) – Sabbath Greeting

Shabbat Shira (H) – The Sabbath before *Yom Kippur*

Shabbaton (H) – Sabbath group experience

Shalom (H) – Greeting: Hello, Goodbye, Peace

Shalom Bayit (H) – Tranquility in the home

Shavua Tov (H) – A "Good Week" blessing

Sherut Leumi (H) – National Service by religious females

Sheva Brachot (H) – Week of celebrating following a wedding

Shlichim (H) – Instructors sent from Israel to teach abroad

Shlinging (Y) – Swallowing (Aspirins)

Shtiebel (pl. *Shtieblach*) (Y) – Small Synagogues, private homes

Shavuot (H) – Major holiday of receiving the Torah

Shidach (H) – Arranging a match for marriage

Shiva (H) – The 7-day mourning period following a death

Shlep (Y) – Carry; drag along

Shoah (H) – Holocaust

Shochet (pl. *Shochtim*) (H) – Ritual slaughterer of animals

Shofar (pl. *Shofrot*) (H) – Ram's horn – sounded on *Rosh Hashanah*

Shovav (H) – Mischievous (youngster)

Shmoozing (Y) – Friends chatting
Shul (Y) – Synagogue (*Bet Knesset*) (H)
Shliach Mitzvah (H) – Emissary to perform a good deed
Sinat Chinum (H) – Baseless hatred
Simcha (pl. *Smachot*) (H) – Any joyous occasion
Simchat Torah (H) – Festival upon completing Torah-reading cycle
Sponga (H) – Mop the floor – Israel style!
Sukkah (H) – Hut used for meals and sleeping
    during the festival of Sukkot

Taharat HaMishpacha (H) – Family Purity
Talit (pl. *Talitot*) (H) – Prayer Shawl
Talmud (H) – Encyclopedia explaining the
    Oral Laws of the Torah
Tashlich (H) – Ceremony of casting away sins
Tateh (Y) – Father – *Abba* (H)
Tchiyat HaMeitim (H) – Resurrection of the Dead
Tehilim (H) – Book of Psalms of King David
Teudat Zehut (H) – Identity card for Israeli citizens
Tefilin (H) – Phylacteries containing chapters of Torah
Tikun Olam (H) – Repairing the world
Tisha B'Av (H) – 9th of Av – Fast Day to commemorate
    the destruction of the Temples
Torah (H) – The Bible / The Five Books of Moses
Todah (H) – Thank You
Treif (H) – Non-Kosher
Tzadik (pl. *Tzadikim*) (H) – Holy / Righteous person
Tzahal (H) – Israeli Defense Forces
Tzaarat – (H) – Type of Biblical disease
Tzedakah (H) – Charity
Tzena (H) – Scarcity of food
Tzitzit (H) – The fringes affixed to four corners of a Talit

Ufruf (Y) – Ceremony for a Bridegroom before his wedding

Verein (Y) – Immigrant Society

Yahrzeit (Y) – Anniversary of death of family member

Yarmulka (Y) – Skullcap (*Kippa*) (H)

Yasher Koach (H) – Congratulations on a job well done!

Yeshiva (H) – Rabbinical Seminary; *Gedolah* – Graduate School

Yom Hashoah (H) – Holocaust Memorial Day

Yom Hazikaron (H) – Memorial Day for Israel's fallen soldiers

Yom Kippur (H) – Judaism's holiest holiday / fast day

Yom Tov (H) – Holiday

Z'L – Zichrono Livracha (H) – May his / her
    memory be for a blessing

Zayda (Y) – Grandfather (*Saba*) (H)

Zechut (H) – In merit of …

Zchor Brit (H) – Remember the Covenant –
    Prayer – Erev *Rosh Hashanah Selichot*

Zog Dem Emes (Y) – Speak the truth